THESE
HONORED
DEAD

THESE
HONORED
DEAD

"Reflections on the 20th Anniversary of 9/11"

BY
CHAPLAIN (COLONEL) JOEL P. JENKINS
U.S. ARMY (RETIRED)

XULON PRESS

Xulon Press
2301 Lucien Way #415
Maitland, FL 32751
407.339.4217
www.xulonpress.com

Paperback ISBN-13: 978-1-6628-2564-4
eBook ISBN-13: 978-1-6628-2565-1

A Tribute to America's Military Heroes,
Past, Present, and Future

From the chaplain who conducted the first
memorial service of the "Global War on Terror"
at the Pentagon on September 25, 2001

For Donna,

The absolute best wife, mother,
"nana," life partner, and friend!

Your support has always made the difference!

TABLE OF CONTENTS

. . . .

THESE HONORED DEAD

"No group of Americans has a greater claim to the love, appreciation and respect of fellow citizens than the warriors of the nation."-GEN Colin Powell[1]

T WO UH-60 BLACK HAWKS LIFTED FROM PHOENIX Base, Baghdad at 0900 11 November 2006 and headed out toward an Iraqi Air Base in the town of Habbaniyah, fifty-five miles to the west for an 1100 rendezvous. I was in the second Black Hawk, and seeing the AH-64 Apache attack helicopter pulling in behind us reminded me that we headed into a dangerous place at a dangerous time. Habbaniyah lay almost equal distance between Fallujah and Ramadi. Both deserved their reputations as "killing fields."

At his request, a number of others and I accompanied British Brigadier Hugh Monroe on this special mission. Though there were risks, we were determined on this day to pay our respects to a group of fallen soldiers and airmen.

Five years earlier...

It was September 25, 2001, and I was standing in front of an audience in the Pentagon auditorium officiating at the memorial service for Lieutenant Colonel Jerry Dickerson and Staff Sergeant Maudlyn White, two of the Pentagon personnel killed on that infamous day of 9/11. For personnel who died in the attack, this was the first memorial service in the Pentagon. This would not be the last.

Three days later, in that same auditorium, I again officiated at a memorial service for two more of our finest that were taken from us on 9/11. This time, we honored and remembered Major Wallace Cole Hogan, Jr., and Ms. Dianne Hale-McKinzy.

HONORING AMERICA'S FINEST

For me, the event in Iraq and the ones at the Pentagon share an important connection. Simply put, it is the need to remember and honor the sacrifices of those whose lives were cut short in service to their country. Too often, the actions of our fallen heroes are forgotten, and their memories become forever lost. Remembering them is not only the right thing to do, but doing so sends the right message to those needed heroes of tomorrow.

The ten years following 9/11, my duties as an Army chaplain carried me to such diverse places as the Pentagon, Guantanamo Bay, Cuba, Kuwait, Iraq, Qatar, Fort Bragg, North Carolina, and from Carolina to California. Much of that service involved "casualty assistance" in some form.

It challenges belief, but this is the twentieth anniversary year of 9/11. It was an honor for me to serve at the Pentagon in the aftermath of the attack—to encourage the living and remember the fallen.

THE BOOK'S INTENT

Throughout this prologue, I intend to provide what I believe is necessary and relevant background information important to the reader. The purpose of this book is rather straightforward.

Our intent is simply to make the following case: our nation's military heroes and veterans need to be appreciated, a strong military is justified in an evil world, our "all-volunteer" military must be sustained, and every citizen needs to contribute to the greater good.

From my experiences at the Pentagon, a year in Iraq, and three years at Fort Bragg, I witnessed many heroes who were an inspiration for this book. In each of these environments, I saw the unfathomable cost required to preserve the blessings of living in a free country.

It was my duty to officiate at services to remember and honor members of our military who died serving their country. In this book, as I recount some of those events, I share a profound part of my life story.

To accomplish the purpose of the book, I will incorporate my life experiences, interweave stories drawn from my personal heroes, and tell the stories of representative historical figures from various periods of American history.

It is easy for me to make the case for America to be a grateful nation. This gratitude can encompass many blessings, but I'm specifically speaking of gratitude for those who have honorably served in the nation's military. By design and purpose, those who serve in America's military always live in the shadow of "harm's way" on behalf of the country.

This topic is very personal to me. I've known too many fallen heroes to just let their memories fade away. I carry too many memories of walking alongside too many soldier's families, in too many cemeteries, as they paid their last respects.

Let me clarify something, I've conducted dozens of services for older veterans who died after a long life. It is an honor to remember the service of such individuals. But it is an entirely different thing to officiate at a memorial service for an eighteen, nineteen, twenty-year-old young American service member who gave his or her life.

Throughout our nation's history, some of our greatest military heroes were barely twenty years old, in the prime of life, when they died for their country. In reality, if someone dies in service to his or her country, whether at twenty or fifty, that person's future hopes and aspirations were sacrificed for the benefit of his or her fellow citizens. His or her family will forever suffer from his or her absence.

I have overseen well over a hundred memorial services or funerals for soldiers killed in action or died in the line of duty. Conducting an appropriate service, tailored for each one, allowed me an opportunity to "get to know" them as individuals, but it also magnified each one's personal sacrifice. Obviously, it's not difficult for me to feel a keen sense of gratitude for such sacrifices because I can attach a name and face to these heroes, and their deaths speak to me personally. This is certainly true for the families of these fallen as well. These loved ones can testify, "Freedom isn't free."

One of my concerns is that the great majority of my fellow Americans cannot personalize such sacrifices because they don't know anyone who was killed in action. Or, for that matter, many don't know anyone who served or is serving in our armed forces. I believe I have a unique perspective from which to help my fellow Americans feel and better understand the high cost that has been paid for their freedoms and liberty.

It seems America is always at a critical point in her history, and, certainly, that is true today. The world is a very dangerous place, with potential threats from nation-states, but also from terrorists of various ilks. Without question, America's security depends, in large measure, on having the appropriate resources and personnel to counter today's threats. This includes adequate personnel.

Honoring and remembering the over one million who died for this country can be a justifiable end in itself. However, doing so also helps address another challenge we have, and that's another reason for the book. We face an ever-growing, formidable challenge of filling an all-volunteer military. More than ever, our country needs our younger generation to appreciate America's unique freedoms and opportunities. In my mind, there is a direct link between filling the roles of an all-volunteer force and paying homage to previous generations of veterans. Our future volunteers need to see their country values the sacrifices made by those who serve.

From background reading, I was challenged by how many of our country's young men and women of all races, ethnic groups, socio-economic statuses, and religions have served their country from the pre-revolutionary period until the present. The country owes them a huge debt of gratitude.

STRIVING FOR A MORE PERFECT UNION

Like all countries, America has never been perfect and has always remained a work in progress, yet striving toward a more perfect union. Within the book, we address some of the shameful parts of America's history. However, we also remind the reader that, despite the inequalities and mistreatment afforded America's minorities, individuals from these minority groups have stepped up, time and again, to come to the aid of their country.

Despite decades of prejudicial mistreatment, Native Americans, Afro-Americans, Japanese, and Chinese citizens have been some of our nation's bravest, and most decorated military heroes. Many of these heroes, though deprived of many of the benefits of their fellow citizens, **volunteered** to serve. Their love of country was and is most inspiring. There is a chapter in the book on World War II, where we will share the stories of a number of these heroes. Their actions demonstrated, even with America's faults, these heroes viewed their country as worthy of their service, protection, and love.

Ironically, it was during periods of our nation's wars, including World War II, when tangible progress was made in becoming a more equitable society. As we shall see, our armed forces actually led the way.

For instance, in today's armed forces, every race and ethnic group in America is well represented, and many of the primary leadership are from minority groups. Our present Secretary of Defense, Lloyd Austin, happens to be Black. He is a West Point graduate, and retired as a four-star general.[2] He is an incredible leader, and at one time, when he was the commanding officer for the XVIII Airborne Corps at Fort Bragg, he was my senior rater, and actually recommended me for promotion to brigadier general.

It was a long time coming, but today's military reflects the demographics of America and welcomes recruits from all races. But there are still issues to solve.

A STEP AT RACIAL RECONCILIATION

I'm not in denial—we do face very real struggles with racial justice. As a country, we must solve the issue of a large number of our citizens being disenfranchised. These are real issues and have a direct bearing on the health of the nation and our nation's military going forward.

Since we are focused on maintaining a healthy military, I want to share something that Danielle Anderson, a former Naval officer and veteran said. She is Black, a graduate of the Naval Academy, and served for five and a half years as an officer on two guided missile cruisers.[3] Every American owes her a debt of gratitude for her service. During her years of service, America could sleep well because of her vigilance. She certainly earned the right to offer her opinions to help make us better going forward.

In the article, she shared numerous situations during her service where she experienced racism and a double standard. Her story makes it clear when any of our citizens are mistreated, then the entire country suffers. She is a patriot, fellow veteran, and I very much appreciated her thoughts on racial reconciliation.

For America to experience a healthier future, we must find a path forward to resolve those things that create our divisions. First, the resolving of divisive issues requires an agreement by all parties as to what the actual issues are. This is true for resolving small group's issues, as well as those of large groups, such as a family unit or a nation.

Part of my background is in family counseling. In 2007, I was honored to receive the Clyde M. Watson Jr. Distinguished Service Award for Pastoral Care and Education presented by the University of Virginia Health System. From my experience, I'm convinced a required step in resolving conflict begins with all parties committed to listening to one another and sincerely seeking to understand the positions.

On the topic of renaming American military bases that are named after confederate officers, Danielle Anderson said, "I certainly think that removing these confederate names is just the right thing to do, and it's just a step in the right direction."[4]

She went on, "It's a step at racial reconciliation with Black people who served this country before they were recognized for their service."[5]

Without question, as I have thought about it, I can certainly see the indignity of asking a Black soldier to serve on a base named after a proponent of slavery and one who fought to retain it. I believe this can be one of those steps our country can agree upon that will take us, as my fellow veteran Danielle Anderson said, in "the right direction."

Yes, this is just one step, but I appreciate concrete suggestions that we can work on together. I'm committed to being part of the solution in our country's pursuit of racial reconciliation. The investment of our veterans in the future of America is offered in the hopes of every American reaping the promise "all men are created equal."[6] Dr. King's visionary "I Have a Dream" speech was his hope and expectation of that day's ultimate arrival.

But, until that day is fully realized, the one institution that we must ensure stays strong, even during our nation's internal struggles, is our military.

We do have so much to be grateful for as Americans. We are a blessed people, with the right to choose our own leaders. We can celebrate those things that past generations went to defend so that our present and future generations will be willing to do the same. We can't afford for our younger, potential service members to give up on America.

> *"The ultimate foundation of our security rests—rests on the men and women who are willing to defend the nation."-GEN Colin Powell*[7]

THE ALL-VOLUNTEER MILITARY

Just to maintain our military's present force structure, 150,000 new recruits are needed each and every year.[8] Viewing recent trends, I am very concerned that, sooner not later, our military will fall woefully short in meeting its personnel needs. Without a draft, there must be a continual, unbroken line of volunteers stepping up in adequate numbers to fill every single position. I prefer an all-volunteer military for many reasons; however, the military's personnel needs are real. If critical positions are not filled, then our nation's security is threatened.

As I see it, a strong headwind to recruiting is the prevalent negativism about America that is espoused by many today. With so-called reality shows, social media, Hollywood, and sports shows on twenty-four seven, it seems every American has his or her list of "stars" in the entertainment and sports realms, and many spend hours keeping up with the rich and famous. A problem that I see is too many influential people focus too often only on America's shortcomings. It is, after all, the unique opportunities that America affords, which allows these "stars" to become so successful in the first place.

We need to ask ourselves an important question. Where will we be if the perception of America is disparaged to the point that America's young men and women don't see their country worth serving, or much less, dying for?

That's key, for our potential future soldiers, sailors, airmen, and Marines have to decide if they feel their country is worthy of their service, much less their lives. They see their fellow citizens, those on the national teams that represent the country, and even some of America's Olympic athletes, kneeling or turning their back to the flag when the national anthem is played. Yes, this is a display of our freedoms, but I assure you, this doesn't do much to encourage a young person to go talk to a recruiter so they can possibly have that flag laid upon their coffin.

The foundation for volunteers to join our military comes from love and esteem for the country. Our Department of Defense's strategy is predicated upon meeting the annual requirement of 150,000 new volunteers. To maintain these required levels, there must always be enough young Americans willing to put country before self.

This ultimately means these volunteers view America as an exceptional place that is worthy for someone to offer his or her life in service.

In our homes, schools, universities, and places of worship, we must instill in our younger generation that America is worthy of their love and devotion. I certainly can give testimony to that. I've been in thirty-six countries, and many of them are wonderful places, but there is no country in the world that offers what we have here in the USA. You see long lines of people trying to get into America, but you don't see long lines of people trying to leave.

I'm looking for a few more fellow Americans to join me in making sure our military members and veterans are never lost as the true heroes that they are. We need our youth to realize how blessed they are to be an American and the high price others paid on their behalf. And, if they choose to serve their country, they will have our full support.

In Robert Frost's poem, "The Death of the Hired Man," there is a line that says: "And nothing to look backward to with pride, And nothing to look forward to with hope."[9] As far as maintaining a volunteer military, we must ensure that our nation never arrives at either of those positions.

"Our Armed Forces are...our insurance policy for a hopeful future."-GEN Colin Powell[10]

THE BUSINESS OF PEACE AND DEMOCRACY

"All we ever asked for was the opportunity to raise up our former enemies, and to get back to the business of peace and democracy."-GEN Colin Powell[11]

Let me make something very clear, this book is not about glorifying war. If anything, it is to point out the sacrifices, suffering, and waste of lives caused by war. Spending a year in a war zone, I have seen the devastating results of war up close. My chaplain assistant and I often visited patients at the Baghdad ER and other hospitals in Iraq. In addition to seeing our coalition soldiers maimed and blinded, we saw innocent Iraqi men, women, and children in burn units and ICU units.

I'll reiterate, it's very difficult to experience the anguish of officiating at multiple memorial services and funerals for such fine young men and women. I've seen too many young spouses carry a flag in one hand and hold the hand of a child in the other, walking out of the cemetery. "Killed in action" or "died in the line of duty" are phrases that I am way too familiar with. I assure you, I will never take going to war lightly.

Chaplains don't serve or go to war to kill people; we are non-combatants. When we go to war, we go without a rifle or pistol. In Iraq, we assisted with civil affairs' projects designed to improve the lives of the Iraqi people. From my spiritual calling and personal convictions, I hate war. War is the ultimate dehumanization of persons.

I am convinced, however, there are times when a military intervention is morally justified and demanded. Evil will never place limits upon itself. In my view, war was necessary to establish our republic, end slavery, stop the Holocaust, and, when required, preserve liberty. Patrick Henry was not the only American to stand upon the principle of "Give me liberty, or give me death."[12] Some examples of pure evil became very real to me. In 1991, I visited Auschwitz-Birkenau and saw the remnants of its great horrors. I walked where over a million souls departed this world. These were not part of the multiple millions of combatants who died. No, these were the innocent and defenseless men, women, and children.

Of course, Auschwitz was emblematic, but in other camps and in many other places all around the world, millions more were intentionally murdered, died from the armaments of war, or died from starvation, lack of shelter, and disease. The world had never witnessed the level of killing and death that was unleashed by the Axis powers.

My chaplain assistant and I, in October 2006, attended Saddam Hussein's second trial in Baghdad. This one was for his genocidal gassing of thousands of Kurds. We heard his loud protestations of innocence, even as we saw the pictures of his victims' horrific suffering and painful deaths.

We visited several torture chambers operated by Saddam's sons, especially by his oldest son, Uday. One was in the basement of Adnan Palace. Uday tortured and murdered political enemies, players on the national soccer team when they lost, or random victims to torture, rape, and kill for his pleasure.

In Iraq, we witnessed the perverse evil of those who distributed hundreds of plastic toy guns to Iraqi children, hoping an American soldier would mistakenly kill a child. Al Qaida was willing to sacrifice those children if it would serve their purpose of creating hostility toward the Coalition Forces. Our soldiers swapped soccer balls for plastic rifles to help rid them from the streets.

Someone told me W. C. Fields once said, "You can't fool kids and dogs." I agree with him. As we traveled around Iraq, I saw Iraqi children approach American soldiers or Marines without fear when they entered their communities.

I saw the huge turnout in numerous neighborhoods when the civil affairs teams came in with medical clinics, school supplies, clean water projects, and other support services. The crowds came, though told the Americans were evil.

From world history, one can conclude most wars are simply about power. But history does record wars for a nation's self-defense or of good versus evil. There are those times when decent individuals cannot stand by and let evil go unchecked. And there are those times when nations, who value decency, cannot stand by and let evil go unchecked.

On the morning of 9/11, evil acts brought about the deaths of thousands. By the end of that day, responses to that evil brought forth amazing acts of goodness, courage, and selflessness. This was clearly demonstrated by the heroism of passengers on board Flight 93 and the deaths, later in the day, of hundreds of first responders in New York City. Within a few weeks of 9/11, many of America's bravest were in "hot pursuit" of the perpetrators.

America has frequently sent her sons and daughters off to war, and certainly, from World War I forward, the goal was never to expand the nation's borders, nor did it. Whether one agrees with the premises for engaging in any of these wars, I see them as based upon ideals, not conquest or to rob some other nations' coffers.

General Colin Powell spoke at West Point on September 15, 1998, with the following remarks:

*The world remembers well that several times in the course of this century, the United States was at the height of the world, the height of power. After World War I, or World War II, or even at the end of the Cold War, we could have imposed our will on the world but we didn't. All we ever asked for was the opportunity to raise up our former enemies, and to get back to the business of peace and democracy. The only other thing we ever asked for was **enough land to bury our dead**. We never wanted anyone else's land or sovereignty over anyone.*

*Our Armed Forces are number one and must remain so. They are our insurance policy for a hopeful future. And as we have seen repeatedly over our history, the premium on that insurance policy and **the ultimate foundation of our security rests—rests on the men and women who are willing to defend the nation.** The men and women who are willing to fight for the nation—to fight the nation's wars. Who are willing to go into harm's way, who are willing to give their lives for the country and for their fellow soldiers. They are the nation's warriors. They have come forward from city and farm whenever they have been needed for over 200 years. No group of Americans has a greater claim to the love, appreciation and respect of fellow citizens than the warriors of the nation. They are sons and daughters and brothers and sisters, husbands and wives*[13](emphasis mine).

This book seeks to honor the 1.3 million American servicemen and servicewomen who put their country's interest ahead of their own, to the cost of their lives. Our intent is to thank them and all of our veterans, as Colin Powell said, "…who are willing to defend the nation…who are willing to give their lives for their country…"[14]

If I learned anything from my research for this book, it is that men and women from every race, ethnic group, religious preference, and political persuasion valued America enough to put their lives on the line. My call is for their country to value them and those who continue to serve.

Within the book, we tell the stories of various individuals, whose war experiences are from different wars and under a number of different scenarios. It is my hope these "real-life" stories of young men and young women from all corners of America will help personalize and bring to life those who served. These individual Americans from the eighteenth, nineteenth, twentieth, and twenty-first centuries represent the multitudes from every generation who loved and valued their country more than life itself.

Within these pages are numerous accounts where someone gave his life for his country, but also, without hesitation, offered his life for his "battle buddies" of a different race, faith, and even politics. The spirit of unity between Americans is never seen more clearly than in combat when it's "all for one, and one for all."

Within the military, there is a special bond between brothers and sisters in arms. Not only will these die for one another, but they will go to great lengths to never leave a fallen brother or sister behind, and also ensure any fallen comrades are given proper military honors. We will explore certain aspects of this within the book as well.

In recognition of 9/11's twentieth anniversary, we will revisit the events of that tragic day. We will retell the stories of some of those first individuals that we lost. We will also discuss the very demanding and unsustainable tempo that's been placed upon our all-volunteer forces, and the challenges going forward to maintain a viable volunteer military.

Pulling it all together, I hope the final result will serve as a reminder to my fellow citizens that maintaining a healthy and strong military is the responsibility of all. It should be a national goal to help ensure that enough young men and women will see that serving their country, and even dying for their country, is worth their sacrifice.

History reminds us that every successive generation reaps the benefits or sorrows that come as a result of those who have gone before them. In America, we live free, and every day, enjoy those benefits earned by those, long passed, often nameless, heroes of the past.

As we remember and honor this generation of our military, we do so, realizing, they are "standing upon the shoulders" of their forbears. The freedom that was won in 1783 must be safeguarded by each generation that follows. In every period of American history, necessary heroes have arisen, and each deserves the nation's gratitude.

In a 1787 letter to William Stephens Smith, the son-in-law of John Adams, Thomas Jefferson noted, "The tree of liberty must be refreshed from time to time with the blood of patriots and tyrants."[15]

American history reveals this "refreshing" comes frequently. Some of our wars have come so close together that we have veterans who served in multiple wars. For example, some World War I veterans fought in World War II, and some World War II veterans also fought in Korea and Vietnam.

AMERICA'S CIVILIAN HEROES

Even though this book focuses upon honoring the service of our military, my purpose is absolutely **not to disregard** the national service and sacrifices made by America's civilian population. Throughout America's history, each generation of citizens worked hard and sacrificed to provide a better life for those who came after them. And certainly, the great majority of hardworking, dedicated, patriotic Americans never served in the nation's military.

President Kennedy called for an America where freedom and liberty is worthy of sacrifice by all her citizens. "There is work to be done and obligations to be met-obligations to truth, to justice, and to liberty."[16]

An example of an America with "all hands on deck," civilian and military, is described in Tom Brokaw's *The Greatest Generation*. Brokaw points out that practically everyone in America during the years of the Great Depression and up through World War II did their part to bring the nation through those perilous years.

As in our other wars, the victory in World War II was not possible without the vital contributions that America's civilian population made for the war effort. Such things exemplified this, such as the dramatic industrial productivity of war material, victory gardens, and ration cards. "The Rosie the Riveter We Can Do It" posters reflected the large number of women who replaced the men in the factories, allowing the men to pick up a rifle instead of a rivet.

Surely, many other World War II stories of exceptional civilian service remain hidden from history. Denise Kiernan's *The Girls of Atomic City* describes one such group whose essential service remained untold for generations.

No doubt, the greatest sacrifices made by the civilian population in World War II were from the deaths and injuries of sons and daughters who left home to take the fight to the Axis powers. Over 407,000 American service members died in World War II, and 670,000 received non-mortal wounds.[17]

The "Greatest Generation" stood tall, but every generation since our founding has demonstrated that being a patriotic citizen does not require a uniform.

Nevertheless, Presidents Harry Truman and Abraham Lincoln, commenting eighty years apart, agreed with Colin Powell that the country owes a particular debt of gratitude to our nation's service members. Truman and Lincoln were wartime presidents, each knowing the responsibility and weight of ordering young men and young women to their deaths.

President Abraham Lincoln called for the American people to remember the bravery and sacrifices displayed in that great battle at Gettysburg. Central to his two to three-minute "Gettysburg Address," he said, "It is altogether fitting and proper that we should do this."[18]

President Truman took a similar tone when he said, "Our debt to the heroic men and valiant women in the service of our country can never be repaid. They have earned our undying gratitude. America will never forget their sacrifices."[19]

****

I do not claim technical or grammatical expertise, but I will do my best to make this a readable manuscript due to the importance of the topic. For those readers who do not have a military background, I attempted to provide a few basic insights into America's military history, organization, and methodology.

I certainly don't see this book as a scholarly work or a historical work. Historical references that are used are limited and primarily serve as examples. I do introduce some of our military heroes to remind us that all who serve are "real people" with real hopes and dreams. Hopefully, these vignettes will be an inspiration for the reader to pursue further reading into the stories of sacrifice made by so many fellow Americans in behalf of their country.

It's obvious the American people do not hold that all of America's wars are equally justified. However, this book reminds its readers that the decision of when America goes to war is made by the politicians, not the war fighters. Thus, my call is to honor and show gratitude to all of America's sons and daughters who honorably served their country during all of our wars, and those brief years of peace between them.

Tennyson's "The Charge of the Light Brigade" captures this spirit: "…Theirs not to reason why, Theirs but to do and die, Into the valley of Death, Rode the Six hundred…"[20]

CHAPTER 1

. . . .

A WORLD OF HURT

"Are you guys ready? Let's roll."
-Todd Beamer, United Flight 93.[21]

O N THIS TWENTIETH ANNIVERSARY YEAR OF 9/11, I hope this book will serve as a tribute to our fellow Americans who died on that day; a tribute to them and a tribute to all American veterans, of all wars, who've offered their lives in freedom's defense.

The events of 9/11 changed many things, and among them, America awakened to a new sense of vulnerability. In all of our history, since the British were defeated, no foreign entity had ever wreaked such havoc upon our civilian population. Of the almost 3,000 persons killed on 9/11, over 2,600 of them were US citizens, who died for no other reason except they were Americans.[22]

After 9/11, America moved into a new era as the realization sank in that there were no Geneva Convention rules, nor any other rules for that matter, to insulate the noncombatant masses from the work of the so-called "terrorists." Jihadists loudly declared and demonstrated that anything and anyone associated with "the great Satan" of America needed to be destroyed.[23]

During an interview with Secretary of State Colin Powell on MTV back in 2002, a young lady from Norway asked him about America being perceived as "Satan." He replied, "Far from being the great Satan, I would say we are the great protector."[24] He said the United States had rebuilt Europe and Japan after World War II, defeated Communism and fascism, and "the only land we ever asked for was enough land to bury our dead."[25]

Obviously, Osama Bin Laden had not read that chapter on world history.

For decades, terrorists worldwide targeted and killed many, including Americans, but this was different because the attacks on 9/11 brought America into a protracted conflict that continues today; in essence, our longest war. Some of those serving in our military today were not even born on the day the planes were hijacked.

Some of my most indelible life experiences began on September 11, 2001. Any reference to 9/11 gets close to the heart for many of us. On September 25, 2001, in the Pentagon auditorium, I officiated at the first Pentagon memorial service of this "new" war.

Though the Pentagon was not my normal duty station, it became my home for the next several months. My life story is forever tied to the events of 9/11, and my service at the Pentagon that followed.

As a result of the infamous terrorist attack on 9/11, 2,977 innocent individuals perished. Among this number were the 184 Americans who died at the Pentagon. By 9:45 a.m., 125 military personnel and civilians working in the Pentagon, as well as 64 passengers and crew on American Airlines Flight 77 lost their lives. An additional 106 patients were received at local health facilities; 49 were admitted for treatments, and 9 patients were admitted to burn units.[26]

Here, I think it would be beneficial to share some background. The Pentagon is the world's largest office building,[27] housing approximately 25,000 military and civilian employees, in almost 4,000,000 square feet.[28]

One tragic irony forever intertwining the Pentagon and the World Trade Center is that the WTC, once fully operational, surpassed the Pentagon as the world's largest office building with over 10,000,000 square feet of office space for over 50,000 persons.[29] By the end of the day on September 11, 2001, the Pentagon sadly regained its previous premier status.

Another irony is the terrorist attack falling on the particular date of September 11. It seems incredulous, but the ground breaking for the Pentagon was September 11, 1941.[30] That ground breaking fell only a few months before America was officially in World War II, and was sixty years to the day from when death from the air would arrive on the scene.

The 77th Congress declared war on Japan on December 8, and Germany and Italy on December 11.[31]

Within a week of the 9/11 attacks, America was once again at war. The 107th Congress passed "The Authorization for Use of Military Force" (AUMF) on September 14, 2001, and signed by President Bush on September 18.[32]

Immediately after the attack on 9/11, the Pentagon personnel who experienced the attack did very heroic work. This included the contingent of active-duty chaplains and chaplain's assistants assigned to the Chief of Chaplain's office, from offices in the Pentagon as well as offices a few blocks away at the Crystal City complex. With smoke and fire billowing from America's defense headquarters, these chaplains and chaplain's assistants, like their fellow service members, rushed in to become frontline first responders assisting with recovery, triage, and engaging in around-the-clock pastoral care.

Soon, an urgent call went out from the Pentagon for reinforcements. It may seem strange that the Pentagon would need "outside" support following the attack. However, the reality is that everyone there already had a job to do, and now, more than ever, those individuals needed to be focused on his or her roles in this new paradigm of active conflict.

On the day of the attack and in the aftermath, Pentagon personnel went into action. Soon, help would be requested, and help would be received. Within twenty-four hours of the 9/11 attacks, plans were implemented to mobilize a number of National Guard and Reserve assets to assist at the Pentagon, and at "Ground Zero" in New York. As I was directly involved with the Pentagon, I will focus upon the Pentagon's response.

However, I must say, on several visits to Ground Zero in NYC, I was overcome with emotion as I thought of those thousands who died so tragically. Sometime around the first anniversary of 9/11, my wife and I accompanied a group to view the New York site. The day was damp and overcast, and the air still carried reminders of what happened there. It was as if the ground was saying, "I won't let you forget."

After the National September 11 Memorial and Museum opened, we returned to the location, walked among the displays, and again paid our respects to those who were taken.

For service at the Pentagon, personnel arrived from various Guard and Reserve military units, including medical staff, mental health staff, chaplains, and even a Casualty and Mortuary Affairs Army Reserve unit from Puerto Rico.

As ministry reinforcements arrived, the exhausted chaplains and chaplain assistants that were at the Pentagon on 9/11 could get back to their regular duty. Their jobs took on a new urgency of overseeing the big picture of training, staffing, and resourcing all chaplain assets, now on a war footing.

In addition to the necessity to call up supplementary personnel, the events of 9/11 revealed other aspects of the Pentagon's dependence upon outside assistance. Even with its highly restricted and secure status, when the fire alarms sounded, it was the nearby Arlington Fire and Rescue Department that went into action. Soon, other local departments joined the response, but Arlington FRD took the lead on fire suppression and search and rescue.

There are Pentagon personnel trained for immediate, localized fire response and other emergencies, but not for anything on the scale of a jumbo jet penetrating the building. There has long been an arrangement that in the event of a major fire, the Arlington Fire and Rescue Department are the first called.

Due to their proximity, most of the Army National Guard chaplains and chaplain assistants in the call-up came from Virginia, Maryland, West Virginia, and Pennsylvania. I'll never forget the phone call I received from Chaplain (Colonel) Robert Kohler (Ret.), then our Virginia National Guard STARC (State Area Command) chaplain. He was tasked by the Army Chief of Chaplains' Office to call up a number of Virginia chaplains and chaplain assistants to assist at the Pentagon. After we spoke, I packed my "kit bag," as the Brits call it, and cleared my calendar.

Once we reported, we were given our assignments. The newly arriving chaplains and chaplain assistants were assigned a wide range of duties. Some were assigned the sacred duty of assisting with the recovery, care, and disposition of remains. These duties were further complicated because the FBI had declared the Pentagon a crime scene, and everything had to be treated as evidence.

Other assignments included chaplain support to those hospitalized, including a number with critical injuries and severe burns. A team was assigned to the Pentagon Family Assistance Center at the nearby Crystal City Sheraton Hotel to support the families of the victims, as this was the "gathering place." Others were assigned inside the Pentagon to the Pentagon Chaplain's Office.

My assignment, along with other chaplains and chaplain assistants, was to the Pentagon Chaplain's Office. The Pentagon Chaplain's Office is not to be confused with the Chief of Chaplain's Office (the Army, Navy, and Air Force each have their own Chief of Chaplains, and each is a "two-star" command with staff personnel and offices in the Pentagon). In case you didn't know, the Navy provides chaplain support to the Marines and Coast Guard.

The Pentagon chaplain's position is an Army billet staffed by an Army chaplain (colonel). All larger military bases, posts, or commands have a chaplain's office established to coordinate religious activities and services on that base. The Pentagon Chaplain's Office is no exception, and thus provides religious support to all personnel assigned or attached to the Pentagon.

After being assigned to the Pentagon Chaplain's Office, I was introduced to the Pentagon chaplain, Chaplain (Colonel) Henry Haynes (whose wife was also an Army officer). By the time we arrived, several days had elapsed since the initial incident, and Chaplain Haynes had hardly stopped to catch his breath.

During the next several hectic months that we worked together, Henry became a good friend, and one of my Black "brothers." I've never met a finer individual, plus he was from North Carolina, which was my home turf. On a human level,

Henry was "no respecter of persons," and treated everyone in the building with equal respect, no matter one's rank or position.

Because of his position, but also because of his compassion, he was a true source of strength, and represented not just help, but hope as he walked the Pentagon halls with his infectious smile.

In addition to the great sorrow related to those killed and physically wounded, many others in the building that day were traumatized. PTSD was a common result. I'm still dealing with my own PTSD from a year in Iraq, and I can appreciate its impact on one's mental health.

Pentagon leadership advised that every person who was in the building that day should go through some type of mental health "cleansing" exercise.

Large numbers of personnel participated in intensive Critical Incident Stress Debriefings (CISD). Alongside psychiatrists, psychologists, and social workers, chaplains assisted with these debriefings. I assisted in a number of CISD sessions, and the pain and raw emotions were palpable. You might expect to come under attack on a far away battlefield, but not at your "nine to five" workplace.

Many Pentagon staff struggled on many levels, and this directly impacted the tasks the Pentagon Chaplain's Office faced. One frequent example of this was the number of persons that I spoke with who suffered from some form of "survivor's guilt." Over and over, I heard individuals struggle with the sense of "why was I spared?" Others described hearing someone's last words.

A number of personnel related they visualized "balls of fire" when they closed their eyes or tried to sleep. These are the scenes they couldn't escape that occurred when the plane hit and its fuel exploded. People in trauma were widespread.

In the midst of the anguish, great courage was evident as individuals pushed through their emotional pain and fears to continue the work at hand. I remember one afternoon the Pentagon's alarm system began blaring, and it was assumed there was another attack underway. It turned out to be a false alarm. Despite the anxiety that this false alarm caused, within a few minutes all were back at work.

As always, everyone's confidentiality was closely guarded, whether in CISD groups, or in individual counseling, but it was amazing to me that such a large number wanted their stories told, just in case it might help someone else struggling. There was truly the sense of, "we need to help each other through this."

Many individuals and groups all across America and the world sent cards, banners, and posters of encouragement, including a large ten-foot by five-foot poster from Columbine High School students. Eighteen months prior, Columbine High School lost twelve students and a teacher during the Columbine High School massacre.

Of all the large banners and posters that hung in the seventeen and a half miles of halls in the Pentagon, it seemed the one from these Columbine students drew the most attention. The poster had hundreds of individual Columbine student's signatures covering it. Many included a statement or verse offering support.

I was the highest-ranking reserve chaplain assigned to the Pentagon Chaplain's Office—recently promoted to lieutenant colonel, so Chaplain Haynes designated me as his deputy Pentagon chaplain. Chaplain Haynes asked me to organize and assign duties to this temporary cadre of reserve chaplains and chaplain assistants.

We immediately established a schedule whereby there was twenty-four seven coverage for religious support. The duties of our reserve chaplain teams included: individual counseling, participating on CISD teams, holding religious services, facilitating religious services for persons of divergent faiths, planning and conducting memorial services, and numerous other pastoral support duties.

On several occasions, some within our group were tasked to accompany casualty assistance officers (CAO) to visit family members of Pentagon victims. On one such occasion, I accompanied an Army major to visit a family to deliver a stainless steel urn containing the remains of their loved one.

The meeting had been prearranged with them, but that didn't make it any easier for them or us. He also presented them with certain personal effects of the individual. As we offered our condolences, they were very gracious despite their heart-wrenching pain. They invited us to sit with them around their kitchen table, and it was obvious whose chair remained empty, and would forever be so.

Prior to 9/11, at least in recent years, there were no regularly scheduled Sunday chapel services held in the Pentagon, as the great majority of the personnel didn't work on the weekends and could attend their own churches, synagogues, and mosques. After 9/11, the Pentagon was in a constant state of twenty-four seven hyper drive. Also, it's amazing how a "close call" affects one's spirituality.

After 9/11, as requests came in, the Pentagon Chaplain's Office offered support for religious activities and services across the board. Among those who requested assistance were members of the Muslim, Jewish, and Christian communities, and we worked hard to accommodate each request (the work of military chaplains is to ensure, as much as possible, the accommodation of each individual soldier's religious needs).

On Sunday, non-denominational Christian services were made available, and as our reserve team of chaplains included a Roman Catholic priest from Pennsylvania, Catholic Mass was offered. The attendance at the services confirmed that these services were most appreciated. Even in the "top-secret" Army Operation's Center, staff requested a brief Sunday chapel when it could be accommodated.

In my support of Chaplain Haynes, I was tasked to help coordinate and officiate at the first of the upcoming memorial services scheduled in the Pentagon auditorium. Chaplain Haynes's schedule, just like the rest of us, was usually a twelve-hour day. He, in particular, had a pressure-filled job. His schedule included a long list of requested counseling sessions, required staff meetings, requested funerals, memorial ceremonies, and other services.

We agreed that I would assume responsibility for the memorial services on September 25 and September 28. These turned out to be the first such services that were conducted in the building.

On October 11, one month after the attacks, over 20,000 people, including over a thousand family members of those who perished, gathered on the Pentagon's Parade Field for a Department of Defense Service of Remembrance. A chaplain accompanied each family group, and I accompanied the family of one of our civilian personnel. It was an honor to sit among her family, especially at that moment when her name was read and scrolled across the giant screen.

I'm certain that all who were present for that occasion will never forget the sense of unity, patriotism, and emotion felt as the combined military chorus sang "The Battle Hymn of the Republic," and spontaneously, everyone stood, waved small

American flags, and the tears flowed freely, including from President Bush.

Attending a service to support a grieving family is a special kind of honor. However, being responsible for planning and officiating a memorial service is far more challenging. I took this responsibility very seriously, and sought out the families' input.

Planning these services also required me to visit with personnel from the Deputy Chief of Staff for Programs (DCSPRO, now called Army G-8) and those from the Deputy Chief of Staff for Operations and Plans (DCSOPS).

I spoke with Lieutenant General Kevin Byrnes from Deputy Chief of Staff for Programs and his staff to prepare for the service for two of the DCSPRO staff members killed. That service was for Lieutenant Colonel Jerry Dickerson and Staff Sergeant Maudlyn White.

In preparation for the service, I became very familiar with these two individuals. These two soldiers held their respective positions at the Pentagon because of excelling in their Army careers.

Staff Sergeant White was born on February 20, 1963, on the island of Montserrat. At the age of twelve, her family moved to St. Croix, US Virgin Islands, which she called home. She had been in the Army since July 1985. Staff Sergeant White attended Bennett College and held a bachelor's degree from Strayer University in computer information technology.

She loved her work and was a consummate professional, but her greatest love was her precious little girl. Family and friends agreed that sweet Vielka was the love of Staff Sergeant White's life. Vielka was only six years old when her mother was killed. Staff Sergeant White was survived by her mother, Mrs. Priscilla Irish, and her daughter, Vielka.

Lieutenant Colonel Dickerson was a native son of Durant, Mississippi, born on July 29, 1960. In 1983, he was the distinguished military graduate of the year from Mississippi State University. He later received a master's degree in industrial engineering at Texas A & M University. He was a proud "Aggie," but he really loved his MSU bulldogs. His dad said he loved going back to Starkville "Bulldog" country.

Like Staff Sergeant White, Lieutenant Colonel Dickerson's greatest love was his family. He was survived by his wife, Page, and two children, Will, who was eleven at the time, and Beth, who was fifteen at the time.

It seems beyond belief, but Lieutenant Colonel Dickerson's best friend from childhood, Joe Ferguson, was a passenger on the plane that crashed into the Pentagon. Ferguson was a vice president of National Geographic.[33]

There was a full house that day in the Pentagon auditorium, and I'll never forget the feeling of love of country and a sense of unified purpose that pervaded the room as family members, friends, and coworkers concluded the service by singing, "God Bless America."

This war on terror was now personal to these two families. One little girl had the hugs of a mom taken from her, and a sister and brother had the hugs of a dad taken from them.

After the service, General Eric Shinseki, Chief of Staff of the United States Army, expressed his appreciation for the service.

A few days later, I received a very kind note from Lieutenant General Byrnes. He shared some encouraging words about the memorial service, but I focused on his words just above his signature, where he wrote: "Most importantly, was the spiritual support you provided to our soldiers and civilians. These are difficult times and your carefully selected words and prayers were very helpful. Thank you Chaplain for making a difference."

Later, I thought about those words. Yes, we as a nation were now thrust into "difficult times," and I was determined to be a "difference maker."

I appreciated the affirming words about the service, and I was grateful the service proved meaningful; however, my greatest affirmation came from the hugs and comments of the family members who were present.

After we closed the service on September 25, someone commented, "Chaplain, we are at war, and you just conducted the first memorial service of this new war, and I'm afraid many more such services will follow." How prophetic that turned out to be. Soon, this "war" would get a name, "the Global War on Terrorism," or sometimes called the "War on Terror."

Three days later, in that same auditorium, I again officiated at a memorial service for two more of our finest who were taken from us on 9/11. This time, we honored and remembered Major Wallace Hogan and Mrs. Dianne Hale-McKinzy. They, too, had precious families whose lives were forever changed.

This memorial service required a change in uniforms for those participating on the program. Major Hogan and Mrs. Hale-McKinzy were assigned to the office of the Deputy Chief of Staff for Operations and Plans (DCSOPS). The Deputy Chief of Staff for Operations and Plans was then-Lieutenant General Larry Ellis (later General Larry Ellis). At the time of the attack, then-Major General Phillip Kensinger (later Lieutenant General Kensinger) served as the direct supervisor for Major Hogan and Mrs. Hale-McKinzy. In the attack, Major General Kensinger's Class A uniforms were lost in the fire. Since he would be speaking at the memorial service, the uniform of the day became the BDU (Battle Dress Uniform).

In many ways, this seemed appropriate as the Pentagon was now on war-footing.

In preparation for this memorial service, I discovered many wonderful attributes of Mrs. Hale-McKinzy and Major Hogan. This was gleaned from spending time with family, friends, and coworkers, including conversations with Lieutenant General Ellis and Major General Kensinger.

Diane Hale-McKinzy was a Christmas gift to her family as she was born on December 21, 1962, in Lithonia, Georgia. She served on active duty for four years and then transitioned into civil service, where she served her country for over twenty years culminating at the Pentagon. Dianne was survived by her husband, Gary, her daughter, Connie Hale, and her stepdaughter, Ebony McKinzy. Diane was part of a large loving family, and she was survived by two sisters and four brothers.

It became very obvious to me that Dianne was very devoted to God and others. I was impressed that two of her ministries through her church included a nursing home ministry to the elderly and a "street" ministry to the homeless. I discovered she enjoyed drawing, loved singing, and brought joy wherever she went. Most of all, she loved spending time with her family.

MAJ Wallace Cole Hogan Jr., who went by Cole, was born on October 9, 1960, and shared a number of qualities with Dianne Hale-Mckinzy. Both were Georgia natives, he from Macon, and she from Lithonia, both were of the Christian faith, both loved to draw, and both loved their country.

Cole met his wife, Pat, when he fell ill at the Jungle Warfare School in Panama. In the hospital, he met Pat, a.k.a. Dr. Pat Phermsangngam. She was an Air Force doctor and was in charge of his medical care. Friends called it a storybook romance that began there in Panama.

Major Hogan enjoyed vigorous exercise and was known to ride his bike many miles at the time, including from his home to the Pentagon. Major Hogan was a "soldier's soldier," and his next assignment was to command a Special Forces company. He, too, was deeply loved by his family and wife, parents, and two sisters, and they would now face his absence for the rest of their lives.

These two memorial services confirmed that some of our best were taken from us way too soon. Notably, these four represented the diversity that makes America so special. This group included persons from different races, marital status, and genders, yet, these four were unified in purpose during their lives, and certainly unified in their deaths. Yes, real people staff the Pentagon.

It was a high honor to officiate at these early memorial services of what has become America's longest war. All who worked in the Pentagon on that fateful day would soon realize a new and deadly chapter of conflict for our nation had begun. No one could predict how protracted it would become, or the sacrifices ultimately required, because such sacrifices continue to this day.

. . . .

CHAPTER 2

WAR WITHOUT END

*"...What really counts is not the immediate
act of courage or of valor, but those who bear
the struggle day in and day out—not the sun-
shine patriots, but those who are willing to stand
for a long period of time,"-John F. Kennedy*[34]

THIS GLOBAL WAR ON TERRORISM IS NOW INTO
its fourth US president. This war far exceeded the length
of any other period of extended conflict in our nation's history.
Since 9/11, almost three million service members served on
deployments across the world, and at least a quarter of a million Army personnel deployed at least three times.[35] The great
majority of these deployments were to the combat zones of
Iraq and Afghanistan, and all of America's warfighters were
volunteers.

This present generation of warfighters, as those before them,
is heroic. They have spent more time, on average, in combat
than any other previous generation. "Roughly three-quarters
of post-9/11 veterans were deployed at least once, compared
with 58% of those who served before them.[36] And post-9/11
veterans are about twice as likely as their pre-9/11 counterparts
to have served in a combat zone."[37]

AFGHANISTAN—BOOTS ON THE GROUND— OCTOBER 2001

The military response in Afghanistan began in October 2001. In direct response to Osama Bin Laden and the Al-Qaida perpetrators of 9/11, on October 7, 2001, the US-led coalition began an intense bombing campaign. Soon thereafter, the first Special Forces were in country. The highest troop levels in Afghanistan peaked in 2011, at about 100,000, after President Obama authorized the surge.[38]

While I never served in Afghanistan, I saw, second hand, how dangerous a place it was. While with the 82nd Airborne Division, I officiated at memorial services for dozens of paratroopers who gave their lives in Afghanistan. Some of their stories will be shared later.

IRAQ—BOOTS ON THE GROUND—MARCH 2003

The Iraq War was unleashed on March 19, 2003, beginning with the air campaign. The ground invasion began the next day on the twentieth. Four and half years later, in October 2007, American troop levels for Iraq reached their highest level at 166,300. This came as a result of the surge President Bush ordered.[39]

COMMAND CHAPLAIN—MNSTC-I

My combat zone service was in Iraq during the "Operation Iraqi Freedom" period. I was the command chaplain for the Multi-National Security Transition Command-Iraq (MNSTC-I). My "boots on the ground" was mid-June 2006 until mid-June 2007.

I was there when President Bush ordered the "surge" that began in December 2006.

MNSTC-I was designed to develop, organize, train, equip, and sustain the Iraqi Armed Forces, Iraqi Police, Iraqi Courts, and other Iraqi security forces. By design, this command had coalition personnel embedded with Iraqi elements throughout the country.

Being multi-national, MNSTC-I's personnel included military forces from numerous countries; some of the major participants were: Americans, Brits, Australians, Koreans, Danes, Romanians, and Poles. The Koreans primarily limited their presence to the much more secure Kurdish region of Iraq.

Multi-national civilian contractors provided many of the needed services for operations. For example, at Phoenix Base, where my office was located, former Fijian Marines provided security and manned the checkpoints. Our housing area, called "Black Hawk" Camp, was secured by former Peruvian military. Many other support personnel for base operations, such as staffing for dining and custodial duties, were from India, Sri Lanka, and the Philippines.

There were also quite a few American civilians who worked for the US military, and State Department, assisting with the PX (post exchange), laundry, mail, dining facility management, and even American civilian firefighters worked the fire stations at a number of bases. These civilians were in harm's way, just like the rest of us. Even if their job did not require them to leave the relative security of their base, they were susceptible to the daily rocket and mortar barrages.

We sometimes dropped off our laundry at the Embassy laundry services, and we got to know the staff. These were non-military employees who were paid well and came over to Iraq simply to better support their families back in the States.

We spoke often to a sweet middle-aged lady from Tennessee who worked there. I remember she was a proud grandmother. One afternoon, she and several others were killed in a rocket attack aimed at the American Embassy in the Green Zone.

Rockets and mortars came frequently, and we often heard the incoming alarm, which sent us into a reinforced bunker. On several occasions, I counted as many as thirteen mortars coming in, one after the other (the artillery term is "walking them in"), and landing close enough to raise your blood pressure.

Most of the time, they didn't launch that many in a group because the more they fired, the easier it was for our counter measures and counter fire to find them. Those who were assigned in the Green Zone got more than their share of these regular encounters, but at every base or FOB that we visited, they were also targeted.

Several times, we visited an Iraqi military academy called Rustamiyah. Because of numerous incoming rockets, its nickname was "Rocketmiyah." On one trip to Rustamiyah, we escorted the USCENTCOM chaplain, Air Force Chaplain (Colonel) Jeffrey Dull, for a command visit. We were staying for a night, and he and I shared a room. Because of the frequent rockets, you always remained a little tense. During the night, his metal bed frame collapsed, with the bed falling to the concrete floor with a loud bang, and for a moment, we thought we had taken a hit.

An ability we soon picked up in Iraq was to distinguish the sound of an incoming rocket, as opposed to an incoming mortar. Fortunately, that's one gift I don't need anymore.

One evening, in particular, I remember a very surreal moment. We were at an outdoor birthday barbecue for one of our Indian D-FAC managers, and the "whiz" of rockets was heard flying high above our location. Hardly anybody even stopped eating, as it was obvious those were not for us.

Other times, it was obvious we were in the target zone. One very hot day, our then Army Chief of Chaplains, Chaplain (Major General) David Hicks, was in the American Embassy area in the International Zone (or Green Zone), meeting with Unit Ministry Teams located in that area. He received a "warm" welcome, as several rockets landed on the Embassy grounds, close enough to raise everyone's "hackle."

We lived in a housing area, called "Black Hawk," and it was made of "conex" boxes stacked on top of one another. They were comfortable, and we actually had a false sense of security living there. I say false sense because they were located directly beside a large pile of rubble from one of Saddam's bombed-out palaces. We had been told, based on the typical flight path of the rockets and mortars coming into our area, that the fifty-foot high pile of rubble kept us safe. A few weeks after I returned home, the chaplain who replaced me and took over my room e-mailed me to say a rocket hit the conexes and destroyed several rooms very near where I had lived.

Believer's Palace was the name of this particular palace, which was near Saddam's Republican Palace. An Iraqi told me the name had nothing to do with religion. Saddam named it that because anything he said, you must believe. Maybe, better said, you better say you believe it.

Underneath this palace was Saddam's huge command and control bunker. This palace was hit by three "JDams"(Joint Direct Attack Munitions) and totally destroyed, but the bunker remained intact. We toured the bunker one day, and alongside the huge Swiss-made, three-ton outer door were the names of the German company, "Boswau and Knauer," who designed and oversaw construction of the bunker.

American military personnel assigned to MNSTC-I were from the Army, Navy, Marine Corps, and Air Force. We also had a large contingent of civilian law enforcement officers. The military component trained their Iraqi counterparts, and the civilian police trainers trained the Iraqi police force. MNSTC-I was established in June 2004, and its first commander was then-Lieutenant General David Petraeus.[40] During my time with MNSTC-I, the commander was then-Lieutenant General Martin Dempsey.[41]

MNSTC-I certainly had great leadership. Generals Petraeus and Dempsey were two of the best military leaders of this generation. They were classmates at West Point, and each received a "fourth star," and would attain very prestigious roles within our national defense structure.

General Petraeus served, among other positions, as commander of US Central Command (USCENTCOM), commander of the International Security Assistance Force in Afghanistan, and eventually as director of the Central Intelligence Agency.[42] I only crossed paths with him once, and that was at the memorial service I officiated for Commander Murphy-Sweet.

General Dempsey served as deputy, and then acting commander of US Central Command (USCENTCOM), the commanding general of Army Training and Doctrine Command (TRADOC), and the chief of staff of the US Army. His career culminated with him serving as the eighteenth chairman of the Joint Chiefs of Staff.[43]

Since I was the MNSTC-I command chaplain, and we had MNSTC-I personnel scattered all over Iraq, my chaplain assistant Staff Sergeant Kyle Bennet and I made a point of often leaving our headquarters at Phoenix Base in the International Zone (Green Zone). We traveled on a weekly basis to visit our scattered, embedded, personnel in all parts of Iraq. We delivered care packages, provided morale support to our personnel, and conducted chapel services.

We touched all points of the compass in Iraq, from the Turkish border at Zacko in the north, to Umm Qasr, a port city in the south, to Al Asad near Syria in the west, to Diyala Province, in sight of Iran, to the east. During our time in Iraq, we made well over 150 ground and air movements to support MNSTC-I personnel.

While in Iraq, I became friends with Master Sergeant Nathan Franklin. He was an Army reservist assigned to MNSTC-I, and he lived and worked at Taji base. In his civilian life at the time, he was a police sergeant, later with the U.S. Marshall's Service. He had a son in Iraq at the same time he was there. His son was a paratrooper with the 82nd, whose battalion was located at COB (Contingency Operating Base) Speicher, near Saddam's hometown of Tikrit. Master Sergeant Franklin knew we traveled every week, and asked if we got to Speicher to look up his son, David. We made the trip to visit some of our police trainers and caught up with David's unit, and passed out some care packages for him and his 81-mm mortar crew. We enjoyed spending time with his mortar team.

Sergeant David Franklin was a squad leader for his team of six. When he completed this deployment his enlistment was up, and he was leaving the Army. Shortly after we visited, and since the unit was nearing the end of the deployment, his platoon leader asked David to stay behind on one of the last missions. The idea was to let his replacement take the team out and gain experience.

In combat, strange and unexpected things happen that change the course of a person's life. On that particular mission, as David stayed behind, his squad was ambushed and every single man in the squad was either killed or wounded. We had just met those guys, and they were eager to get back home to their families. The bottom line is, you just never know.

On that trip to Speicher, we also conducted an informal remembrance service for two civilian police trainers who had recently lost their lives.

When we traveled, due to distance, it was primarily in UH-60 Black Hawks. However, from time to time, we did fly in a wide variety of aircraft: CH-47 Chinooks, British MK2 Merlins, British Sea Kings, British AS 330 Pumas, C-23 Sherpas, Lockheed C-5A Galaxy, C-130 Hercules, and everybody's favorite, the C-17 Globemaster III.

As the "Offbase" column, formerly known as "Humor in Uniform," in *Reader's Digest* points out, there is humor in uniform. There were several things humorous about our flights out to the Al Kasik Iraqi training base. We always traveled on CH-47 Chinooks to get there.

One particular night (the Chinooks flew at night) as we were boarding, I overheard the crew chief talking to a wide-eyed soldier who was taking his first flight on a Chinook. Once the crew chief found out he had a "greenie," he played it up. He said, "Son, this aircraft is a CH-47C—look at the tail number, and it flew in Vietnam. If you ever get on this bird and you don't see leaking hydraulic fluid, then get off because it's out!"

On one visit to the Al Kasik base, we were shown around and informed the Russians originally built it, with quite a few comforts. The time came when the Russians were "disinvited" by Saddam and forced to leave. As they left, they intended to make the Iraqis regret it, and of all things, on their way out, "blew up" the Olympic-sized swimming pool.

Several times, while traveling in a Black Hawk, and once in a C-130, the aircraft automatically discharged counter measures of flares and chaff due to a perceived threat. On one occasion, we were on a C-130 flight from Baghdad making its approach to the Mosul airport, when it's counter measures, including flares, discharged. The aircraft was not struck, but once a C-130's counter measures were expended, it was not allowed to land in a combat zone. So, we diverted and flew directly to Kuwait. We vacated the aircraft, and all the passengers and crew boarded a different C-130 to continue the mission. No harm, no foul.

Many memories come to mind when thinking of our travels. In November 2006, we traveled out to the Ayn al Asad base to visit our "embedded" MNSTC-I civilian police trainers. This base also housed thousands of Marines from the III Marine Expeditionary Force (III MEF).

While there, I visited a friend, Chaplain (Lieutenant Colonel) John Weatherly. Chaplain Weatherly was the chaplain for an element of the 224th Aviation Regiment of the Virginia Army National Guard. They were assigned to Al Asad, and attached to Marine Aircraft Group 16 (reinforced) of the 3rd Marine Aircraft Wing. All of these air assets were to support the Marines of III MEF.

Our last night there, just prior to heading back to Baghdad, we sat in on the pre-flight briefing for the Black Hawk crews that were transporting us. It seemed rather routine to the two flight crews. But for us, it pointed out the very dangerous job of these aircrews. During the briefing, they received weather reports, "threat" reports, "hot spots" to avoid, and were shown photos of damage to the aircraft on the last mission.

The one part of the briefing that caused me the most concern was when they showed pictures of the multiple holes in the fuselage of both aircraft. These came from random, small-arms fire from "bad guys" along the flight path. They hoped to get lucky; occasionally, they did. For helicopters, however, most major damage from the ground came from either RPGs (rocket-propelled grenades), shoulder fired missiles, or machine guns.

When we made ground movements, we traveled in convoys made up of various up-armored military vehicles, usually escorted by a team of "rough riders" in gun trucks. MNSTC-I's rough riders were a convoy escort team whose mission was to provide security for ground movements of MNSTC-I personnel.

We did have an occasion, in southern Iraq, to travel with British troops in one of their Snatch Land Rovers. A British soldier told us the vehicle got its nickname, "Snatch," due to its heavy use in Northern Ireland in the 1990s. They were produced for counter terrorism and used to grab (or snatch) a terror suspect off the street. These would provide some protection from small arms, but they were not made to withstand the RPGs and IEDs (improvised explosive devices) so plentiful in Afghanistan and Iraq. At one point, some Brits began to refer to them as the "mobile coffin."

Even the best up-armored military vehicles could be compromised, but at least they brought the odds more into your favor. Other vehicles we rode in, but less safe, were the up-armored SUVs. We rode in these when transported by a civilian PSD (personal security detail) "shark" team. The shark teams were civilian contractors, mostly former Special Forces, who worked for companies hired by the US State Department, such as DynCorp, Triple Canopy, and Blackwater.

On a number of occasions, a shark team transported us through the "Red Zone" in up-armored Suburbans to the Baghdad Hotel to conduct memorial services. We provided memorial services for the multi-national civilian security contractors and multi-national civilian police trainers who were killed in Iraq.

Civilian contractors provided security forces, a QRF (quick response force), as well as an escort group that moved VIPs about the country. These VIPs included high-level diplomats, including the American Ambassador and members of Congress who visited Iraq. Blackwater "operators" had their own air assets, including the AH-6J "Little Birds" that provided air cover for the movement of ground convoys, and a QRF as needed.

I remember one afternoon, looking outside my office window at Phoenix Base, I watched a "Little Bird" engage in a firefight just outside the Green Zone. On my computer screen, I simultaneously watched this engagement, playing out on an American cable news channel.

REMEMBRANCE DAY IN IRAQ

MNSTC-I was a multi-national command, and British Brigadier Hugh Monroe was our deputy-commanding general. This meant I was his chaplain ("padre" to the Brits). In early November 2006, he asked in his pronounced Scottish dialect, "Padre, are you available to assist with our Commonwealth Remembrance Day Service on the eleventh at the Royal British Cemetery at Habbaniyah?" I immediately answered, "Absolutely." He replied, "Great, I'll make all the arrangements."

Staff Sergeant Bennet and I stayed on the move to different locations. But this trip to Habbaniyah was different. This trip was not about incurring risks to support the living, but instead about incurring risks to spend time in a cemetery to observe Remembrance Day and pay homage to the fallen.

That day came with a bright sky and warm temperatures; the two Black Hawks lifted up from Phoenix Base, Baghdad, at 0900 on 11 November 2006, and headed out toward the Iraqi

Base in the town of Habbaniyah, fifty-five miles to the west for the 1100 rendezvous. I was in the second Black Hawk, and seeing the AH-64 Apache attack helicopter pulling in behind us reminded me that we were heading into a dangerous place at a dangerous time.

I'll admit, I felt some additional anxiety because my very able chaplain's assistant and "body guard" was home on his two weeks of R & R. According to the Geneva Convention, chaplains are considered non-combatants, and thus do not carry weapons. Of course, to Al Qaida, the Geneva Convention guidelines meant absolutely nothing.

Habbaniyah lay almost equal distance between Fallujah and Ramadi. Both deserved their reputations as killing fields. Though there were risks in traveling from Baghdad to Habbaniyah, all of us were determined on this Remembrance Day to pay our respects to a group of fallen soldiers and airmen.

Brigadier Monro and I, along with those accompanying us, supported this mission because we valued it as one of duty and honor. Indeed, on that day, I would be the officiating padre who would stand over the graves of young men from England, Scotland, Australia, and New Zealand, who died a long way from home, never to return to see dear loved ones.

From my perspective, we would engage in one of the most significant acts of a free people. This was about honoring and remembering soldiers and airmen who gave their lives in defense of their country, and for the right to live as a free people. For the British and Australian military within our MNSTC-I command, I was their padre (chaplain), and it was my honor to be with them at one of their cemeteries on this special day.

Several of the British soldiers accompanying us on the trip informed us that the Habbaniyah Royal British Cemetery dated back to when the British had a Royal Air Force Base there from

1936 until 1959. Once the British left in 1959, the cemetery fell into terrible disrepair and suffered wanton destruction through the years. Yet, its ground still housed almost 200 fallen British and Commonwealth nation's airmen and soldiers, most dying in World War II.

Since early 2004, the coalition forces located at Habbaniyah worked hard to rehabilitate the cemetery from overgrown weeds and broken headstones.

We didn't take this flight to and from Habbaniyah lightly. In the weeks around this mission, either hostile fire or shoulder-fired missiles brought down over a dozen helicopters. In January, about six weeks later, there was a particularly dark day, as heavy machine guns and a shoulder-fired missile brought down a UH-60 Black Hawk, resulting in the deaths of all twelve crew and passengers.

Some may not understand why a band of British, Australian, and American soldiers assumed the risk to "go into harm's way" for the expressed purpose of holding a ceremony to honor fallen soldiers of an earlier generation. As part of the group, I can say the answer comes easy. It's because these dead deserved no less.

One reality became very evident to me. Whether or not a nation's civilian citizenry chooses to honor their fallen soldiers, for sure, the military community will do so.

These fallen brave souls answered their respective nation's call, left homes, families, their future dreams, and went to a foreign land to serve and die, never to return home again. Thus, this Remembrance Day was their day. We came with one purpose, to remember each sacrifice, and remember them as real persons, loved by real families. We came to mourn their passing.

In addition to prayers, poems, Scripture readings, and comments, there was a formal laying of wreathes adorned with poppies by British, Australian, and American soldiers. I was asked to read "In Flanders Fields," and found myself choking back deep emotions. Brigadier Monro's Scottish accent resonated across the cemetery as he brought forth a moving tribute.

The music included the solemn rendering of "Amazing Grace," played by two Scots on the pipes, and a final tribute by an American trumpeter playing taps. I borrow from President Lincoln, "It is altogether fitting and proper that we should do this."[44]

In case you weren't aware, Remembrance Day, for all British and Commonwealth nations, is the day they pay their respects to members of their armed forces who died in the line of duty. Initially, this day was set apart by King George V in 1919 to recognize the 886,000 British and Commonwealth military personnel killed in World War I.[45]

After World War II, Remembrance Day observances broadened to include honoring British and Commonwealth military personnel who died in the later conflicts. Remembrance Day is observed annually on November 11, acknowledging it as the anniversary date of the World War I Armistice. The Armistice was signed on November 11, 1918, stating the hostilities of World War I would end precisely "...at the 11th hour of the 11th month."[46]

In America, November 11 is our Veterans Day, when we honor all veterans. It was originally called Armistice Day, but President Eisenhower officially changed the name to Veterans Day in 1954.[47] America's day for remembering her uniformed military who died in service is Memorial Day, which is now observed on the last Monday of each May.

Juxtaposed to that November 11, in Iraq, ten years later to the day, on November 11, 2016, I was sitting on the platform at a community Veterans Day Ceremony and couldn't help but feel disappointed. Local American Legion Post 74 sponsored the event, and I was the post chaplain waiting to offer the invocation.

I would say the gathered audience was less than 250 persons in an outdoor arena that seats 3,500 in a surrounding community of over 150,000. Probably close to half of those in attendance were either in the local high school orchestra, participants on the program, or were there to present wreathes. Other than the high school students, clearly, the great majority of folks who were in attendance were silver-haired, and many of these were military veterans.

The Charlottesville High School orchestra was superb, the Charlottesville Fire Department had a huge American flag flown from a ladder truck, and a group of military re-enactors added a wonderful presence to the event. Yet, where were all those "grateful" Americans who would gather, on this one day, to remember and thank those veterans who served?

We know the unique differences between Veterans Day and Memorial Day, but both days afford each American an opportunity to express support to those who have served. Surely, on these two days, America can collectively say to her veterans, "Thanks for a job well done," a hard job at that!

At a minimum, there should be these special days of honor and remembrance, but as Abraham Lincoln reminded us, a grateful nation must also show tangible evidence of taking care of the soldier and the soldier's family.

CHAPTER 3

FORT BRAGG—HOME OF THE AIRBORNE

"...The Center of the Universe...The Home of Heroes..."

J UNE 2007 IS WHEN I REDEPLOYED FROM A YEAR IN
Iraq, and by October 2007, I received the orders that told
me to report to Fort Bragg, Fayetteville, North Carolina. My
wife joined me, and we relocated from Virginia. I joined a contingent of six other chaplains and a group of chaplain assistants
who were assigned to serve in Rear Detachment (Rear D)[48]
duty for units deployed from Fort Bragg. This group of "Rear
D" chaplains and chaplain assistants became a close-knit group.
From late 2007 until January 2011, I was a Rear D chaplain.

The first place we stopped when we arrived in Fayetteville,
North Carolina, even before going to our apartment, was the
local Krispy Kreme ("The Hot Light" was on—that's another
story). On the wall was a poster that read, "America can sleep
well tonight because the 82nd Airborne is on point." I made
sure I found one of those posters, and it remains prominently
displayed in my "man cave."

I'm sadly convinced that many Americans take their security for granted and never contemplate those individuals who
give up so much on their behalf. Even in a world with so many

"bad actors" who wish us harm, America can sleep well. Every American needs to keep in mind that we sleep well, because America's military is always on point!

During my years at Fort Bragg, other than one stint with the 44th MEDCOM, I served with the 82nd Airborne Division. For about a year, this was with two different brigade combat teams. For my last eighteen months, I served as the Rear D chaplain for the division. It was an honor to serve paratroopers and families of the 82nd, the "All American" Division, and America's Guard of Honor.

My last year of service with the division was somewhat of a "bonus" year, and came about due to some extenuating circumstances. I had been serving at Fort Bragg for over two years, and my retirement was about six months away. Following regulations, my MRD (Mandatory Removal Date) was to be the last day of the month following my sixtieth birthday, which was January 31, 2010.

The 82nd Airborne Division HHBN (Headquarters and Headquarters Battalion) was scheduled for a fifteen-month deployment back to Afghanistan, and there was, once again, the need for a division Rear D chaplain. I was requested to serve as the Rear D chaplain for the upcoming deployment. I related, I would be honored to do so, but my MRD would come during that period.

After concurring with me, then-Major General Curtis Scaparotti, the 82nd Airborne Division commander, made a "by name" request to the Army Chief of Chaplains, Chaplain (Major General) Douglas Carver, to give me an extension of my MRD. The waiver was granted, so I assumed the position of the 82nd's Rear Detachment chaplain and served out the entire deployment.

Since my MRD was delayed until January 31, 2011, I officially retired on February 1, 2011, at the age of sixty-one.

After two subsequent promotions, General Curtis M. Scaparotti eventually served as the Commander of United States European Command, and concurrently as NATO's Supreme Allied Commander Europe.

Providing rear detachment support for units deployed into combat zones is not an easy task. It proved very beneficial that I had previously deployed. There was a level of instant credibility if the chaplain and his family had "walked the ground" the soldiers and their families were walking.

I'll always remember one particular morning while serving as the division Rear D chaplain. It was barely sunup, and I was almost on post, headed to the 82nd Airborne Division Memorial Chapel. Then the voice on my car radio caught my attention, "As of this month [May 2010], the War on Terror exceeds the length of the Vietnam War." The War on Terror was now in its 104th month, and there was no end in sight.

Being reminded of this was sobering; my thoughts took me back to where I was in September 2001. I recalled those first Pentagon memorial services for Jerry Dickerson, Maudlyn White, Cole Hogan, and Dianne Hale-McKinzy. I will never forget those four individuals, how their deaths reflected the beginning of a new chapter of conflict for America, and of most importance to me, how my life became intertwined with theirs.

As I cleared the "All American" gate, Fort Bragg's main entrance, my mind returned to the task at hand. It was ironic, but here I was on my way to the 82nd Airborne Division Memorial Chapel to conduct a memorial service for two more fallen heroes. A critical part of my responsibilities as the 82nd Airborne Division Rear Detachment chaplain was to conduct monthly memorial services for division paratroopers killed in action during the previous month.

In preparation for the memorial service for these two paratroopers, I learned how special they were. On this particular day, we were remembering two 4th Brigade Combat Team (BCT) paratroopers, Staff Sergeant Scott W. Brunkhorst and Specialist Joseph Thierry Caron. They were both outstanding young men who had volunteered to protect and defend their country, and they, like many of their "brothers," made that ultimate sacrifice in the Arghandab Valley of Afghanistan. As of their deaths, twenty-one paratroopers from this one BCT had died in Afghanistan since the 4th BCT had deployed in August.

STAFF SERGEANT SCOTT BRUNKHORST, U.S. ARMY, AFGHANISTAN

Staff Sergeant Brunkhorst was killed by an IED on March 30, 2010. He was twenty-five years old, and was survived by his wife, Krystal, his three-year-old daughter, Kendall, and his parents, Rick and Linda Brunkhorst.

On her twenty-fifth birthday, Krystal answered the door, and there stood a casualty notification officer (CNO) and chaplain, who gave her the news she never wanted to hear, that the love of her life had been killed.

I met his sweet family, and a quote from his young wife was, "If I could dream up a guy, it would be him." Scott's parents said he told them if anything happened to him, he wanted to be buried in Arlington National Cemetery, and on April 13, 2010, this son of Bridgewater, New Jersey, was laid to rest in Section 60, site 9151, with full military honors.

Scott was a third-generation soldier. His father, mother, and grandfather were veterans, and his brother followed him into the Army.

SPECIALIST JOSEPH THIERRY CARON, U.S. ARMY, AFGHANISTAN

Specialist Caron was twenty-one years old, a native of Tacoma, Washington, and also an exceptional young man. He, too, was killed by an IED—this time, in Char Bagh, Afghanistan, on April 11, 2010. Specialist Caron was a third-generation soldier, just like Staff Sergeant Brunkhorst, and was named after his grandfather, Joseph "Joe" Caron, a Vietnam War veteran. Joey, as his family and friends called him, proudly served in Washington High School's Air Force JROTC unit. He was a determined and tough young man, and wrestled and played football in high school.

Joey Caron grew up being patriotic, and always said he wanted to be a soldier, but not just a soldier, a paratrooper. He planned at some point to use his GI Bill benefits to attend college, but instead, he gave his life for his country and was taken back home for burial in Lakewood, Washington.

This was our monthly memorial service in Division Memorial Chapel, and in the presence of fellow paratroopers and family members, we honored these paratroopers' service and sacrifice, followed by the final roll call, three round volley, and taps. Occasionally, if our monthly memorial service were for mass casualties, we would move our service from the chapel to the movie theater to accommodate the larger audience.

While I served as the Rear D division chaplain, I also served as one of the pastors for the 82nd Division Memorial Chapel. It was a special place, with a great deal of the division's history captured in the stained glass windows throughout the sanctuary. Even though many of my memories of the chapel are connected with memorial services, I also have good memories of weddings, enjoyable Sunday services, and fellowship meals.

Since the division included such a large and busy community, it became obvious the old chapel was inadequate. During my time with the division, I attended a few preliminary meetings to discuss the plans for the new chapel.

In January 2013, the new and much larger appropriately named "All American Chapel" was dedicated. It replaced the Division Memorial Chapel as the hub of the 82nd's religious activities. It also became the home of the division's memorial services. At the dedication, Major General John W. Nicholson, Jr., the division commander, said, "It was fitting that the dedication took place when all of the division's 21,000 soldiers are home for the first time in recent years."[49]

An often-used term for Fort Bragg by those who've served there is the "center of the universe." Actually, in terms of personnel, Fort Bragg is the largest military base in the world. "The current population stands at just over 140,000, made up of 77,000 active duty and reserve soldiers, and 63,000 dependents and family members."[50] I might add, while there, I was informed over 14,000 civilian personnel are also a vital part of the community.

But on a human level, Fort Bragg is just like all other US military installations; it is the home of a group of people who are either training for missions or engaging in missions. Too often, during either a mission or intense training, some will not make it home. Sadly, as I found out when I served there, the Fort Bragg Casualty Assistance Center (CAC) handles more casualty notifications than any other base.

During my time serving at Fort Bragg, on two occasions, the entire 82nd Airborne Division deployed at the same time. These were the first "full" deployments of the division since World War II. These deployments, with one exception, were rotations to Afghanistan and Iraq. Each time the entire division deployed, it represented roughly 21,000 paratroopers heading into harm's way for their country.

In early 2010, while I was serving as the division Rear D chaplain, one brigade still remained at Bragg, the 2nd BCT (Brigade Combat Team). However, following the January 12, 2010, catastrophic earthquake in Haiti, the 2nd BCT was quickly deployed to Haiti to provide humanitarian relief.

Our military provides a great deal of humanitarian relief, whether it's in war zones or during times of natural disaster. These humanitarian missions reflect the goodness that America is known for and why so many people risk their lives to come here.

When I served with the 505th Engineer Battalion (combat) (heavy), I participated in humanitarian missions in Ecuador, Honduras, and domestically after Hurricane Hugo. I also assisted with numerous humanitarian civil affairs missions while in Iraq.

The 2nd BCT was already packed and loaded when the call came to go to Haiti. At that time, 2nd BCT was designated as the "Global Response Force" of the division. By design, the GRF can be anywhere in the world in eighteen hours. The entire division is known as "America's Strategic Response Force," and there is always a brigade assigned as the GRF, and it stays ready to go!

The 82nd Division patch was designed when the division was constituted on August 5, 1917.[51] To fill this new division, its initial members had literally been "drafted" from all forty-eight states, thus the images of "AA," on the patch stand for the "All-American" Division.[52] In August 1942, the division was reconstituted as the first airborne division in the Army, and remains today as the sole airborne division.[53]

When the entire division of over 21,000 paratroopers is deployed, the Rear D not only supports "downrange" needs and responds to casualty situations, but is also left to care for the multiple thousands of dependents who remain. These dependents live in a state of constant stress and fear of losing a loved one, while at the same time, often struggling with financial, health, and childrearing issues of their own.

In a nutshell, as taken from myarmyonesource.com, "The rear detachment operations pick up the daily workload of the deployed unit and provide home-station support for the unit… the RDC's … work…to help families solve their problems…"[54]

A unit's Rear D is also responsible for making casualty notifications and coordinating the required memorial or funeral events. Of course, these duties fall upon the chaplain's section of the Rear D.

Earlier, I shared that one of my primary duties as the Rear Detachment chaplain of the 82nd Airborne Division was to ensure that all of our fallen paratroopers who were killed in action, in either Iraq or Afghanistan, were to be properly honored at memorial ceremonies, funerals, or interments, and their families supported. Of course, the support to the families began with the "Casualty Notification."

In addition to memorial ceremonies conducted at Fort Bragg, very often, our 82nd Rear D chaplains traveled all across the country to support funeral honors. One reason for so many funeral trips was because the 82nd Airborne Division motto was that we "bury our own." Often, many military organizations use assets from the closest military base to the fallen soldier's hometown to provide military honors, not the 82nd.

At the death of an 82nd paratrooper killed on active duty, a full burial detail, including an 82nd chaplain, was sent to the hometown and funeral site of the fallen paratrooper. This team handled everything, from the "Dignified Transfer" at the home airport, providing an honor guard for pre-funeral viewings, and culminating in presenting full military honors at the cemetery. Today, the 82nd still makes sure that we "bury our own."

It's amazing to me the various memories that recur as I think about my time with the 82nd. I remember being in Missouri for the funeral of a paratrooper, and we were waiting at the local airport for the jet to arrive to "return" the paratrooper back home. This was not that unusual, but what happened next was most unusual.

Our 82nd Funeral Honors team was on the ground and ready to make the "Dignified Transfer" from the plane, when an Air Force Funeral Honors team showed up to make the transfer. Initially, the Air Force lieutenant in charge of the AF detail insisted his team make the transfer to the hearse. He outranked the sergeant first class paratrooper supervising the 82nd detail, and told him to have the 82nd team "stand down."

When I saw what was happening, I intervened. I thanked the lieutenant for his team's presence and their willingness to provide support, and I was certain they were true professionals and would do an exceptional job. I told him I understood this miscommunication was not his fault. But I made it clear that it was in his and his team's best interest if they quietly excused themselves and departed. He got the message, and they packed up and left. He was wise to do so because, at all costs, the 82nd "buries our own."

CHAPTER 4

· · · · · · · · · · · · · · · · ·

A GRATEFUL NATION

"We can't all be heroes. Some of us have to sit on the curb and clap as they go by."-Will Rogers[55]

A S THE PREVIOUS CHAPTERS ILLUSTRATE, MUCH of my chaplaincy duty has been about honoring our fallen who died on 9/11, and those who died in response to it. It is also worthwhile for us to acknowledge the patriots of all generations who gave that last full measure for the cause of liberty. Those earlier generations of fallen patriots have no contemporaries left to miss them or remember their sacrifices, so now it is up to this generation to keep their memories alive.

The phrase, "on behalf of a grateful nation," is central to the recitation given when a folded American flag is presented to the next of kin at the graveside of a deceased service member or veteran. These honors may include the three-volley salute (not to be confused with the twenty-one-gun salute), playing of taps, prescribed folding of the flag, and the culmination with the leader of the military detail presenting the flag. This flag rests on the casket of the deceased, and is a tangible reminder of the deceased's honorable service.

The latest guidance from the Department of Defense on December 27, 2017, authorized the following standardized language for the presentation of the flag. The particular service branch of the deceased is used. For an Army veteran, one would hear: "On behalf of the President of the United States, the United States Army, and a grateful nation, please accept this flag as a symbol of our appreciation for your loved one's honorable and faithful service."

If we are a grateful people, then how could we ever take our freedoms for granted, or somehow feel worthy of them, or, for that matter, fail to display our gratitude to those who ensure them?

I have degrees in psychology and theology, and I have long felt there is an agreement in these fields of study that an "attitude of gratitude" makes a positive impact upon one's life at the deepest levels. Certainly, my faith in God informs my response to the many unearned "good things" that have blessed my life. I accept the fact that I am the recipient of unmerited goodness from God and my fellowman.

The following scriptures reflect my feelings:

> "Let them give thanks to the Lord for his loyal love
> and for the amazing things he has done for people."
> -Psalm 107:21

> "No one has greater love than this—that one lays
> down his life for his friends." -John 15:13

Even if one is not open to a theocentric worldview, the field of psychology has much to say about the benefits of having a grateful spirit. Many psychologists recognize the positive benefits one receives from being grateful.

An article published in the *Harvard Medical School Healthbeat* states:

The word gratitude is derived from the Latin word gratia, which means grace, graciousness, or gratefulness (depending on the context). In some ways gratitude encompasses all of these meanings. Gratitude is a thankful appreciation for what an individual receives, whether tangible or intangible. With gratitude, people acknowledge the goodness in their lives. In the process, people usually recognize that the source of that goodness lies at least partially outside themselves. As a result, gratitude also helps people connect to something larger than themselves as individuals — whether to other people, nature, or a higher power.

In positive psychology research, gratitude is strongly and consistently associated with greater happiness. Gratitude helps people feel more positive emotions, relish good experiences, improve their health, deal with adversity, and build strong relationships.[56]

If we accept the premise that gratitude is a good thing, then I suggest to my fellow Americans, the sacrifices of our nation's service members should be somewhere high on the list of things for which we are most grateful. If it were not for their sacrifices, the "pursuit of happiness" that we enjoy would not exist.

The following comes from a blog called, "Grey House Harbor."

From the beginning of the Revolutionary War in 1775 to present day, over 1.3 million Americans have paid for our freedom with their lives. During WW II nearly 12% of the American population was serving in the

*Armed Forces. As such, most citizens were related to
or personally knew someone in uniform.*

*Today less than 1% of our population has taken the
oath to protect the other 99%.*

*I fear this has created a culture of disconnected igno-
rance. Wars today require zero sacrifice from the
civilian population, and therefore zero understanding.
Zero understanding leads to zero awareness. Zero
awareness leads to zero gratitude. And zero gratitude
is a dangerous threat to those very freedoms so many
have died to defend.*[57]

This blog's conclusions remind us that gratitude doesn't just
happen. Being a grateful nation flows from an intentionality
that is definitely aided by an awareness of the "life and death"
demands that face our military. Since 9/11, America has been
engaged in the longest, protracted conflict in the nation's history, amazingly, with all volunteers.

The military draft finally ended on January 27, 1973.[58]
Since then, every member of our armed forces made a con-
scious decision to serve their country. And all who joined after
9/11 would have the expectation of going to war.

From my own association with so many of these fallen
heroes, and in light of the present struggles of our nation to
find a sense of unity, I offer to my fellow citizens a proposal.
Surely, we can be unified in our gratitude for those 1.3 million
who offered their lives for the rest of us. After all, those 1.3 million fellow Americans were male and female, and came from
every demographic, race, and religious persuasion from within
our society.

The difference between them and us is their enjoyment of the freedoms they secured was cut short.

In a broader sense, even apart from the military angle, surely, there can be agreement that every American has benefitted from the blood, sweat, and sacrifices of fellow Americans. The great majority of America's citizens will, rightfully so, never serve in the military. Yet, from our beginnings up through today, civilian Americans make personal sacrifices on a daily basis for the common good.

Since Covid-19 entered our vocabulary, a poignant demonstration of such sacrifice is seen in the valiant efforts of our medical providers and other "first responders" who put themselves in harm's way on a daily basis for complete strangers. Quite a number of these selfless servants would, themselves, succumb to the disease as a result of their service to others.

That same spirit of self-sacrifice was present on 9/11.

On 9/11, at 9:32 a.m., the hijackers had gained control of United Airlines Flight 93 on its way to San Francisco and announced they had a bomb on board and for the passengers to sit. A number of phone calls were made by passengers and several flight attendants to inform family and friends of their situation. Soon, the passengers become aware that three previous flights were hijacked and flown into the World Trade Center and the Pentagon.

Convinced that Flight 93 was also intended to crash into some important symbolic site, a group of passengers made the decision to thwart the hijackers and retake the cockpit. By their efforts, these passengers, even in the face of their own deaths, undoubtedly saved many lives and prevented the hijackers from claiming another major target.

Also on that day at the World Trade Center, 343 firefighters and 71 law enforcement officers died while trying to save others.[59] Many other first responders who survived that day incurred lasting injury to their health. Some studies say, "…as of 2014, over 1,400 additional 9/11 rescue workers died from 9/11 toxic exposure."[60]

An article written in 2019 in time.com says, "Within the next few years, the number of deaths caused by 9/11 related illnesses and injuries is expected to surpass the 3,000 deaths during the attacks."[61]

These brave first responders' actions reflect the adage, "As others run away from danger, first responders run to the danger."

Every day in America, a first responder puts his or her life in harm's way for a stranger. Too often, this job of alleviating other's pain requires a severe price from our EMTs, firefighters, and law enforcement. This personal cost is not just seen in the "line of duty" deaths but at an even higher level in the suicide rates of these first responders. There is an emotional weight that is borne by those who deal with so much pain and suffering.

In 2017, the Ruderman Foundation released a "White Paper," showing first responders are more likely to die by suicide than in the line of duty. In 2017, they found that 222 first responders died in the line of duty, and at least 243 first responders died by suicide. For firefighters, the suicide rate was 18 per 100,000; for police officers, the number was 17 per 100,000.[62]

These numbers were noticeably above the general population rate of 14 per 100,000. This study concludes that suicide can be one of the by-products of the trauma that our first responders face on a daily basis.[63]

Within our American family, many volunteers bear an oversized burden for the sake of others, most often, strangers. Doesn't this suggest, for our republic to survive, every citizen needs to contribute to the well-being of the republic, as we are always just one generation away from losing it.

President Kennedy said it so well, "Ask not what your country can do for you, but ask what you can do for your country."[64] When asked what sort of government the Constitutional Convention had created, Benjamin Franklin replied, "A republic, if you can keep it."[65]

Bearing the nation's burdens and sacrificing for strangers is exactly what our military has always been about. Just like our first responders, our military members pay a high price for carrying the burden of protecting others.

One tragic illustration is the alarming rate of suicide within our military community. The rate of suicide for our military members is even higher than for our first responders. For instance, the suicide rate for active duty troops in 2018 was 24.8 deaths per 100,000.[66] This is the highest on record since the DOD started tracking suicides closely in 2001.[67]

All forms of sacrifice for the greater good, even for strangers, has always been present in the American ethos, and certainly in our military. This comes not from a requirement of the state, as in Marxism, but flows from an individual's character, where service and beneficence toward others are valued above self-interests.

Dr. Martin Luther King Jr's vision held that a person's value and worth should be judged by their character, not by the color of their skin.[68]

His vision is fulfilled at its highest level when individuals risk their lives to save others without any consideration of that person's color or background.

An America that values those who make sacrifices for the greater good of all citizens moves us closer to a country where the words, "all men are created equal" is not just a catchphrase.

Those 1.3 million Americans who died in our wars made it possible for the continued existence of an American Republic, a work still in progress.

We quoted Gen. Colin Powell earlier, "Our Armed Forces are...our insurance policy for a hopeful future."[69]

Lives offered and given are the ultimate investment in America's future. They reflect a love of country, but also a hope for a better tomorrow. Such great sacrifices only reach their full worth when the nation reaches its full potential.

Using historical and personal experiences, I will present my premise that being a grateful nation for those whose exemplary service cannot be disregarded is not just the right thing to do; it is essential in preserving the spirit of America for future generations.

Having worn a U.S. Army uniform for twenty-seven years, I realize our military serves to protect the rights for each individual to hold his or her own disparate views. I respect and understand that every American enjoys this right.

If you choose to continue reading this book, then please read it from that perspective. I do not intend my positions to be judgmental of other points of view.

We are each entitled to our positions, but I do believe I can offer a unique perspective.

As for an individual, I'm convinced a nation's character reflects in the values revered and lived out. President Kennedy once said, "A nation reveals itself not only by the men it produces but also by the men it honors, the men it remembers."[70]

One's values are shaped by the people in one's life, as well as by one's experiences. Many of the values I hold dearest, spiritual and otherwise, were shaped by my wonderful, Greatest Generation parents, Rev. Joel and Joyce Jenkins, who instilled in me a love of God, a love of country, and a respect for all persons.

Along with my parent's guidance and example, there were many other individuals who invested themselves into my life.

It was during my service as an Army chaplain that I developed an intense awareness of the high price that so many individuals had paid in my behalf. It began to trouble me—there were too many of us who, too often, took our "good lives" for granted.

Primarily, this deepened awareness came as I provided chaplain support to a new generation of fallen heroes and their families. The most impactful moments came as we honored a brave young man or young woman whose life was given in service to country.

One reason it has taken me so many years to finally write this book is because of the faces of dozens of fallen American heroes and of their loved ones that stay fresh in my memory. My military service has brought me "up close and personal" to too many who paid the heaviest price that liberty could require.

How do you pay a debt to a soldier, sailor, airman, or Marine who gave up his or her future for your future, his or her chance for happiness for your happiness? Ultimately, I'm not sure what a proper response is to such a life, but I do know where that response must begin, with gratitude and a pledge never to forget them.

At Fort Stewart, GA, on November 26, 1962, President Kennedy was speaking to members of the First Armored Division who had been deployed during the Cuban missile crisis. President Kennedy shared that, years ago, the following poem was found in a sentry box in Gibraltar:

"God and the soldier, all men adore, In time of danger,
and not before, When the danger is passed, and

all things righted, God is forgotten, and the soldier slighted."[71]

Colonel James "Jim" O'Kelley, USMC (Ret.), a friend of mine, commanded an engineer battalion in Vietnam, was seriously wounded, and received the Bronze Star Medal for valor and the Purple Heart. Jim actually went to Gibraltar a few years ago and saw a plaque with those words inscribed on it. The plaque said that at one time, the poem had indeed been scrolled on the wall of a sentry box at Gibraltar.

· · · · · · · · · · · · · · · · ·

CHAPTER 5

THESE HONORED DEAD

"They have earned our undying gratitude. America will never forget their sacrifices."-President Harry Truman[72]

IN EVERY GENERATION, AMERICA HAS SENT HER sons and daughters off to war. Those Americans made many sacrifices for the good of other Americans. Those who served and did not come home were real people with aspirations of their own. The uniforms and armaments of our service members changed through the years, but one thing didn't change for those who served and died; they all forfeited their personal dreams in behalf of their country.

The soul stirring and reverent phrase, "these honored dead," is from President Lincoln's immortal, "Gettysburg Address." He was referring to the fallen soldiers of the Union who died at the crossroads town of Gettysburg, Pennsylvania, from July 1 to July 3, 1863. Those words equally apply for every American hero who has fallen on untold battlefields.

Maybe the more we tell each individual's story, the more we will appreciate what he or she has done. Within American history, the Battle of Gettysburg would set a new standard of suffering and death. Nearly a third of the 160,000 men who fought over those three days would become casualties, including over

7,000 killed.[73] Soon, days of even greater loss and sorrow would follow. The greatest losses of U.S. service members on a given day would come on June 6, 1944, D-Day. On that day on the beaches of Normandy, around 4,500 Allied deaths occurred, including over 2,500 American soldiers and sailors.[74]

For those thousands, the "D" in D-Day could stand for death. Within a few weeks, the Normandy soil would receive the remains of almost 10,000 of America's sons.

Another marker of indescribable losses comes from our nation's deadliest protracted battle, the Meuse-Argonne Offensive, which brought World War I to the Armistice. Over 1,200,000 U.S. troops fought in this six-week battle, and from September 26, 1918 until November 11, 1918, over 26,000 Americans died.[75]

Such catastrophic losses strain an effort to "humanize" or "personalize" these individuals whose lives ended.

President Lincoln tied America's purpose and sustainability, for that matter, to a proper response for those who put country before self. Gettysburg was a platform for him to do just that. President Lincoln was invited to the small Pennsylvania town of Gettysburg on November 19, 1863, four and half months after the battle, to help dedicate the National Cemetery, and at the same time, to call the nation to a renewed commitment to our national purpose.

To better appreciate those who died, I think it helps to try and put a face on some of those American heroes, across time, who gave "the last full measure of devotion."[76]

For the backdrop of President Lincoln's remarks, I share the story of one soldier who died at Gettysburg. Within the roll call of the thousands lost at Gettysburg, one finds the name of George Washington Sandoe. A monument at Gettysburg lists him as the first soldier killed at Gettysburg. He was a member of Company B Volunteers 21st Pennsylvania Cavalry.

On June 26, he was serving as one of two advance scouts for his unit when he unknowingly rode into Confederate pickets of Colonel Elijah V. White's 35th Virginia Cavalry. Trying to escape, his horse fell, and Private Sandoe received a mortal wound in the head.[77]

George Sandoe, like all others who died in battle, was a "real" person. George lost his life—better said, George offered his life before reaching his twenty-first birthday. He was cut down in his youth with everything going for him and with so much to live for. He married his childhood sweetheart Dianne Caskey at Mount Joy, Pennsylvania on February 19, 1863, and he voluntarily enlisted in the Union Army some four months later on June 18, 1863.[78]

Let me reiterate, George Sandoe voluntarily left home, his new bride, who was expecting their first child, and answered his country's call. George mustered into the Army on June 23, and was killed only three days later on the 26th. George had not served long enough to get his first pay. He was survived by his wife, but also by his unborn child, and other loving family.[79]

As we honor George Sandoe's act of sacrifice, we must equally honor the lifetime of sacrifices made by his wife and child.

George Sandoe's "volunteer" spirit brings to mind all of the millions of patriots throughout America's history who answered their nation's call to serve, and especially the 1.3 million who died.

President Lincoln honored George Sandoe and his fallen comrades. Lincoln's example serves as a reminder; it should be "the American thing to do" to honor those who go in harm's way for their country.

Often, President Lincoln returned to this theme of honoring the soldier's service. In his second inaugural address he made it clear there must be tangible demonstrations of gratitude for the soldier, as well as for the soldier's family.

This speech was given just six weeks before his assassination, and the President reemphasized the country's responsibility "... to care for him who shall have borne the battle..." This time, however, President Lincoln added, "...and for his widow and orphan." This "roll call" of widows and orphans includes the name, Dianne Caskey Sandoe, and her child.[80]

Now, the message was not just about Gettysburg's fallen, but for all soldiers, before and after Gettysburg, "who shall have borne the battle." Lincoln framed it as a debt the country owed to the fallen and their survivors.

He was a man of great empathy, and Lincoln realized great sacrifices for freedom do not just come from the soldier, but also from the families who offer a husband, wife, son, daughter, brother, or sister on the "altar of liberty," for their loss is forever.

This chapter's title, "These Honored Dead," comes from a phrase from President Lincoln's Gettysburg Address that sets apart a special group of individuals. This group had retired permanently from the battlefield and had answered their final roll call.

THE FOUR CHAPLAINS

In the limited space of this book, I think it is important to tell the stories of a representative group of our nation's military heroes who went "above and beyond the call of duty." Again, and I cannot emphasize enough, these are real persons, and I desire to continue honoring each sacrifice and to keep their memories alive.

In some ways, military chaplains often live close to the edge. I'm saying that as an Army chaplain who served in a combat theater and traveled in the "Red Zone" on over 150 occasions. According to the Geneva Convention's Rules of War, chaplains are considered non-combatants and do not carry weapons. Believe me, that carries no weight for Al Qaida, the Taliban, or ISIS, as they have no rules of war. The prescribed source of protection for a chaplain is the chaplain's assistant. For me, a special bond formed between my assistant and me.

There were reports in Iraq that Al Qaida had placed a "bounty" on chaplains and medical personnel as a way to affect troop morale. I must say, hearing that affected my morale. It's been confirmed, their captors ensured, that of all the Army chaplains captured in the Korean War, not one single chaplain survived captivity.[81]

Among the many heroic Navy and Army chaplains who have served in war, the story of four Army chaplains who voluntarily gave their lives for their troops is inspiring and needs retelling. World War II historians and all military chaplains are familiar with the story of the so-named "Four Chaplains." Annually, the American Legion and Civitan International clubs across America host programs to honor these four war heroes.

As noted, these four chaplains offered their lives to save the lives of other soldiers. The following article by John Brinstead tells their story:

> *It was Feb. 3, 1943, and the U. S. Army Transport Dorchester was one of three ships in a convoy, moving across the Atlantic from Newfoundland to an American base in Greenland. A converted luxury liner, the Dorchester was crowded to capacity, carrying 902 servicemen, merchant seamen and civilian workers.*

It was only 150 miles from its destination when shortly after midnight, an officer aboard the German submarine U2 spotted it. After identifying and targeting the ship, he gave orders to fire. The hit was decisive, striking the ship, far below the water line. The initial blast killed scores of men and seriously wounded many more. Others, stunned by the explosion were groping in the darkness. Panic and chaos quickly set in! Men were screaming, others crying or franticly trying to get lifeboats off the ship.

Through the pandemonium, four men spread out among the Soldiers, calming the frightened, tending the wounded and guiding the disoriented toward safety.

They were four Army chaplains, Lieutenant George Fox, a Methodist; Lieutenant Alexander Goode, a Jewish Rabbi; Lieutenant John Washington, a Roman Catholic Priest; and Lieutenant Clark Poling, a Dutch Reformed minister.

Quickly and quietly, the four chaplains worked to bring calm to the men. As soldiers began to find their way to the deck of the ship, many were still in their underwear, where they were confronted by the cold winds blowing down from the arctic.

Petty Officer John J. Mahoney, reeling from the cold, headed back towards his cabin. "Where are you going?" a voice of calm in the sea of distressed asked. "To get my gloves," Mahoney replied. "Here, take these," said Rabbi Goode as he handed a pair of gloves to the young officer. "I can't take those gloves," Mahoney replied. "Never mind," the Rabbi responded. "I have two pairs." It was only long after that Mahoney realized that the chaplain never intended to leave the ship.

Once topside, the chaplains opened a storage locker and began distributing life jackets. It was then that Engineer Grady Clark witnessed an astonishing sight. When there were no more lifejackets in the storage room, the chaplains simultaneously removed theirs and gave them to four frightened young men. When giving their life jackets, Rabbi Goode did not call out for a Jew; Father Washington did not call out for a Catholic; nor did Fox or Poling call out for a Protestant. They simply gave their life jackets to the next man in line. One survivor would later say, "It was the finest thing I have seen or hope to see this side of heaven."

As the ship went down, survivors in nearby rafts could see the four chaplains—arms linked and braced against the slanting deck. Their voices could also be heard offering prayers and singing hymns.

Of the 902 men aboard the USAT Dorchester, only 230 survived. Before boarding the Dorchester back in January, Chaplain Poling had asked his father to pray for him, "Not for my safe return, that wouldn't be fair. Just pray that I shall do my duty...never be a coward... and have the strength, courage and understanding of men. Just pray that I shall be adequate."

Although the Distinguished Service Cross and Purple Heart were later awarded posthumously, Congress wished to confer the Medal of Honor but was blocked by the stringent requirements which required heroism performed under fire. So a posthumous Special Medal for Heroism, The Four Chaplains' Medal, was authorized by Congress and awarded by the President on January 18, 1961.[82]

I am very moved by what Chaplain Poling said to his father, "Pray...not for my safe return, that wouldn't be fair. Just pray that I shall do my duty."

Yes, these, too, are "the honored dead."

The Four Chaplains Memorial Foundation shares the story of these selfless chaplains, and one of their missions is: "...to encourage selfless service in the tradition of The Four Chaplains"[83] For more information, visit fourchaplains.org.

CHAPTER 6

· · · · · · · · · · · · · · · · ·

SACRED DUTY

*"The Secretary of the Army has asked
me to express his deep regret…"*

T HE WORD *SACRED* IS OFTEN DEFINED AS SOME-
thing dedicated to a religious purpose, and I certainly
concur with that as one definition. However, Merriam-Webster
also defines *sacred* as "a purpose or person…entitled to rever-
ence and respect."[84]

It's that definition that describes the work of honoring the
deaths of America's military that were killed in the line of duty.

Thus, one of the most sacred duties for a military chaplain
is when he or she provides military funeral honors for a fallen
soldier. Obviously, this duty includes providing pastoral support
to the families, and it often includes assisting with a "casualty
notification."

FINAL HONORS

As mentioned, I had the responsibility at the Pentagon of officiating at what turned out to be the first memorial service of
the War on Terror. On that day, there was no way of knowing
just how many more such services I would support.

Providing services of "final honors" can take the form of a memorial service, a memorial ceremony, a remembrance service, a full military funeral service, an informal gathering, or a military honors burial service. The structure and purpose of each of these varies for the occasion, often depending upon whether the soldier's remains are present.

During my almost three decades in uniform, I have participated in all forms of military honors services for dozens of our bravest and best. "Killed in action," or "died in the line of duty" are phrases that I am far too familiar with.

No matter the soldier's rank or the location of the service, it is a high honor to participate in any type of service designed to render appropriate honors to the fallen. I was privileged to honor fallen heroes at such places as the Pentagon, Arlington National Cemetery, and Phoenix Base in Baghdad, Iraq, but I felt equally privileged the day we honored a fallen paratrooper at a family cemetery deep in the backwoods of Arkansas.

My military funeral duty has carried me all across the country. Performing these sacred duties, I've traveled from Carolina to California, from Florida to Iowa, to big cities, such as San Francisco, Los Angeles, Cleveland and Chicago, and smaller towns, such as Joplin, Galena, Masontown, and Bentonville. I personally knew some of the soldiers, sailors, airmen, and Marines, and I still see their faces. For the others, I still see the faces of the spouses, children, siblings, and parents.

These memories are seared into my consciousness and compel me to challenge my fellow Americans to keep faith with those who signed the contract for our freedom in their blood.

The majority of my honors and funeral duties came during the last three years of my military service, right up to my retirement at Fort Bragg on February 1, 2011.

CASUALTY NOTIFICATION

I need to address another type of sacred duty chaplains perform. Along with providing military funeral honors to the deceased, chaplains are also assigned to accompany CNOs in the performance of their duties.

Point of clarification: often, the term *casualty* is used to refer to both the wounded and killed. However, in the context of a CNO's duties, it only references those killed in action or killed in the line of duty.

It is the CNO's responsibility, accompanied by a chaplain, to make the official announcement to a family of the death of their loved one. It is very painful to recall those occasions when I was present and heard those words, "The Secretary of the Army has asked me to express his deep regret that ..."

Without a doubt, casualty notification duty is the most difficult duty of all, and it certainly qualifies as sacred duty. When two Army officers in Army service uniforms (or previously, Class As) knock on the door of a military family, that family knows before you speak why you are there. I've never met an officer or non-commissioned officer who wanted this duty.

There is nothing harder for a soldier than to tell another Army family their loved one is not coming home. It is considered the most important duty of all, so serious effort is made in selecting a CNO.

My first occasion to assist with a casualty notification came during Desert Shield/Desert Storm. Little did I know then that during my years of chaplaincy, this would be the first of many such missions. After experiencing so much of this soul-piercing duty, I assure you, you could not pay me enough money to do this duty. I would do it, however, as my duty to honor a fallen hero and provide a compassionate presence to his or her family.

As I share memories of that first experience, I shall intersperse information about the process used by the military in making "casualty notifications."

At the beginning of the Gulf War, I served as the battalion chaplain for the 505th Engineer Battalion (combat) (heavy) of the North Carolina National Guard. Due to our unique heavy engineering capabilities, our battalion was considered for mobilization to the Theater of Operations.

As our BN's possible deployment was discussed through various command channels, it was noted the 505th was already scheduled to support a humanitarian mission to Honduras later in 1991. Ultimately, since some of our heavy equipment was already headed to Honduras, there would be too many "moving parts" to change those orders. Thus, for 1991, Honduras became our BN's mission, and another Engineer Battalion deployed to the war zone.

Despite that, certain personnel from our headquarters company were put on stand-by for stateside duty. I was one of those from our BN HHC (Battalion Headquarters and Headquarters Company) who was put on stand-by for casualty notification duty. Our first call came on a Sunday evening, February 17, 1991, that two soldiers from our area were killed in the Theater of Operations, and we were to make the notification.

I was told where to meet Captain Eddie Pollard, our BN S-1, who was assigned as the CNO. We linked up, and prepared ourselves to make the notification to the next of kin (NOK). In this case, the primary NOK was the soldier's wife. Captain Pollard's job was to make the notification, and I was to provide emotional and spiritual support to the family.

Specialist Bobby L. McKnight lost his life in service to his country in a foreign land. Our job was to inform his family of this worst of news. Specialist McKnight was an older soldier with almost twenty years of service. He was killed as he and his co-driver were hauling fuel from Saudi Arabia to an Iraqi staging area.

As an African-American soldier, his death confirms, once again, that America's heroes come from all races and all corners of the country. He was assigned to the 1454th Transportation Company, 540th Quartermaster Battalion out of the North Carolina National Guard.

Once Captain Pollard and I were briefed on the situation and received the proper paper work, we headed out to do our duty. The protocol is that the primary next of kin (PNOK) must be notified first, then secondary next of kin (SNOK) notifications are made. The soldier's DD93, "Record of Emergency Data," listed his wife as the PNOK, and provided us with the soldier's home of record. It was almost 10 p.m. (2200) by the time we knocked on her door.

Even with protocols in place, there is no guaranteed formula for walking up to a family's door to deliver a death notification. Specifically, the chaplain is assigned to accompany the CNO to offer support and consolation to the family, but what I found was that the chaplain was also there to offer support to the CNO. Chaplains, due to their vocations, deal with death on a far more frequent basis than a "regular" line officer or non-commissioned officer. I'm not saying it is ever easy or that this duty ever becomes nonchalant, but I am saying there are good reasons why a chaplain is to accompany a CNO.

Several times, I had accompanied a CNO, and as the door opened, the CNO "froze" and couldn't say anything. Technically, the actual notification was not my job, but if necessity required, I would then proceed to make the notification to the family. I was never hard on those CNOs who stumbled because, as one told me, when he saw the wife holding a child in her arms as the door opened, in his mind, he saw his wife and children. It was actually better under those circumstances for me to make the notification than for him to struggle through it.

Dealing with death is a difficult yet expected responsibility for a chaplain. My experience has been that an effective chaplain is one who feels a definite "call" into service to God, and whose life reflects a willingness to put others' needs ahead of his or her own. The military does a good job of reinforcing and training chaplains in their respective duties, but ultimately, the best work of a chaplain is done in those hardest and harshest moments when the chaplain comes alongside the suffering.

Chaplains are human, and most are empathetic by nature and thus do struggle with their own emotions. However, when assisting with "notification" duty, it is very important for the family that the chaplain remains self-controlled.

The chaplain has to remember, this is "not about me," this is about them. I found, during such occasions, chaplains need to draw deep from their own faith reservoir and keep the focus on helping a hurting family.

Once a death is confirmed through the closest CAC and a notification team is dispatched, the casualty notification is to be done within four hours, between the hours 0500 to 2400 local time, unless otherwise directed. The goal is to move quickly to try to preempt inadvertent word from getting back to the family before the official notification can take place.

While in Iraq in December 2007, I remember waiting at the Mosul airport, awaiting a Blackhawk flight up to an Iraqi Military Academy in Zacko, in the Kurdish region. While sitting on the tarmac, word came down an OH 58 Kiowah pilot, flying out of Mosul, was killed in flight by a sniper. Immediately, orders were given that all outgoing, non-essential phone and e-mail traffic was suspended until the family was notified.

Commanders have the discretion to hit the so-called communication "kill switch" as needed. Every effort is made to afford the families as much dignity and respect as possible, and to guard the process of notifications. Even so, with mobile phones and laptops readily available, there were occasions when word got back to families before the CNO could get there.

Getting back to our notification, let me say something here. In the following paragraphs, you are going to read what transpired that evening and the period shortly after. I found the circumstances of that notification most unique and very powerful, to the extent that I recently reconnected with Mrs. Pat McKnight and asked and received permission to share her story.

Immediately, after Captain Pollard rang the doorbell, Mrs. Pat McKnight opened the door to let us in. I'll always remember her first words after opening the door, even before Captain Pollard could confirm that we were at the right place. She spoke up with, "Well, I've been waiting for you." There we were, two officers in Class As, and she had been waiting for us. Looking back, the brightly burning front porch light was probably a clue that she was indeed expecting us.

My first thought was that somehow, someone from "downrange" had made a call back home and broke the news. But she informed us that no such call had been received. In a quiet, yet strong voice, she described having heaviness in her spirit at the time he died. She went on, "I knew before you gentlemen got here." In our recent conversation by phone, she said that once the notification was confirmed, she actually felt relieved.

Captain Pollard still needed to give his official statement, and began with, "The Secretary of the Army has asked me to express his deep regret ..." Captain Pollard handled the notification very professionally and with genuine empathy. After the notification, Captain Pollard related what was known about the circumstances; simply, his tanker was involved in a collision, overturned, and both crew members were killed.

Sometimes families are in shock and don't raise any questions. In this case, the wife did have questions that we couldn't answer, so she was informed that the event was under investigation and more details would follow.

Captain Pollard then deferred to me, and after offering my condolences, I asked if there was anything we could do for her or someone we could call to come over. Mrs. McKnight informed us, she and her husband were Christian people with strong faith and asked if I would call her minister. During our conversation, she told us that she and "Bobby" were high-school sweethearts. Their closeness was very evident. We also shared a prayer together.

Just as with Mrs. McKnight, on every notification visit that I made, we never left a family until we insured that a friend, minister, or someone of their choice could provide them support. If they desired, we would always make that first outreach for them. While we waited until her minister and his wife arrived at the home, Captain Pollard explained that a casualty assistance officer would be coming over the next day to assist her going forward.

During a later conversation with Mrs. McKnight, she mentioned my assisting her pastor with the funeral service. I replied that it would be an honor. The beautiful brick church was filled to capacity, and all who were present were challenged by the sacrifices and courage of Bobby and Pat McKnight. Both will be forever remembered, for each, in their own way, paid a very high price for freedom's sake.

At the funeral, I met the children and other family members, and realized this entire family had an exceptional bond of shared faith, hope, and love.

As I learned more of their story, it became very obvious these were very special people. They were devoted to God, one another, and to country. Mrs. McKnight, an obvious patriot herself, commented, "I feel he was doing what he should have been doing. I have no regrets of him doing what he did." During our recent conversation, she once again confirmed her sentiments about his service.

Specialist Bobby McKnight, age fifty-two years old, answered when his country called. His life truly mattered! Why not add Bobby McKnight, his widow, children, and family, to your "thank-you" list!

We owe it to families like the McKnights to do our best, "to get it right," as we support them in their loss. That's one reason every time I provided chaplain support in a death situation, I realized the importance of our Army procedures. These procedures are designed to ensure consistent, proper respect and care is given.

For the Army, the CNO and the CAO are not the same individuals. This is important for several reasons, including emotionally. Once the CNO makes the casualty notification, then he or she becomes identified with that message. I agree with the process of bringing in a different individual to assist the family going forward.

The CNO's responsibilities to the family are fulfilled when the notification is completed and he reports back to the CAC, in this case, the Fort Bragg CAC.

Following a completed notification, the Department of Defense's Casualty Assistance Program has a CAO ready to immediately begin his or her work to advise and assist the PNOK. If there are secondary next of kin (SNOK) on the DD93, then they will be assigned a separate CAO.

AR 638-8 (Army Regulation 638-8) (7 June 2019) gives a synopsis of the duties of a casualty assistance officer, but basically, the CAO assists the PNOK during the difficult period immediately following a casualty, eliminate delay in settling claims and applying for benefits, and assists the PNOK in resolving other personnel-related affairs.

The duties of the CAO fall into two distinct phases: Phase I is the period from notification to completing funeral arrangements (burial); Phase II is the period from burial through approximately ninety days after when entitlements and benefits are processed and started. A CAO may be an officer, a warrant officer, or a non-commissioned officer in the rank of staff sergeant or above. While performing this duty, the CAO is relieved of all other duties.

Having participated in this firsthand, I can vouch for the fact that each of our military branches works very hard to honor the fallen and show compassion and assistance to their survivors. The protocols in place for this are far better than in previous periods.

For instance, in World War I, World War II, Korea, and even early in the Vietnam War, death notifications were made by telegram. As late as 1965, for soldiers killed in action in Vietnam, a telegram was sent through a Western Union office that would simply hand the telegram over to a yellow cab driver to deliver. Even though the eventual message is still just as devastating, at least now, the survivors are never alone when the news arrives.

Within this discussion of casualty notifications, I recall a conversation I had with my youngest daughter while her Army sergeant husband was on his first deployment to Iraq. She asked some very pointed questions, so I clarified the casualty notification process to her. I reminded her "death notifications" are never made over the phone. If she ever received a phone call about her husband being injured or wounded, then she would at least know, he was still alive.

Sure enough, one day her phone rang, and the voice started out: "Is this the wife of Sergeant William Underwood?" After affirming, she then heard, "I regret to inform you…"

The voice went on to say Sergeant Underwood had been wounded in action and was at the Baghdad ER (at the time, it was operated by the 28th CSH [Combat Support Hospital] out of Fort Bragg). She shared with us later, as she heard the words, "I regret to inform you…" she told herself, "at least he's alive" because it was a phone call.

An RPG struck the Buffalo MPRC (Mine Protected Route Clearance Vehicle) that my son-in-law was operating on a route-clearing mission. In the vehicle, two soldiers were wounded while a battle buddy, Specialist Thomas Caughman, was killed instantly. Our son-in-law did recover from his shrapnel wounds, though he still carries a few pieces, and eventually served a second tour in Iraq.

Specialist Caughman's family, like many others, had a CNO and chaplain show up on their doorstep. In his letters home, Specialist Caughman always signed off with: "freedom isn't free." He and his family should know!

General of the Army George C. Marshall knew the importance for the military to support military families who had suffered a casualty. He said in 1944, "There's no more effective way of creating bitter enemies of the Army than by failing to do everything we can possibly do in a time of bereavement, nor is there a more effective way of making friends for the Army than by showing we are personally interested in every casualty which occurs."[85]

CHAPTER 7

· · · · · · · · · · · · · · · · ·

SACRED PLACES,
SACRED MEMORIES

*"...We need...citizens willing to...sacrifice
for... freedom." -John F Kennedy*[86]

O NE PLACE THAT BRINGS TOGETHER AMERICA'S
military heroes more than any other is the grounds of
our national cemeteries. There are over 200 sacred national
cemeteries whose only purpose is to hold America's deceased
military members.

Two of these cemeteries are maintained by the Department
of the Army, Arlington National Cemetery, and nearby in
DC, the United States Soldiers' & Airmen's Home National
Cemetery.[87]

Other national cemeteries are under the auspices of dif-
ferent departments. The Department of the Interior National
Cemeteries comprises fourteen cemeteries that are maintained
by the National Park Service. In addition, the Department of
Veterans Affairs National Cemeteries number 153, and the VA's
National Cemetery Administration maintains them.[88]

The overseas United States military cemeteries fall under
the American Battle Monuments Commission Cemeteries.
This Commission oversees twenty-six American cemeteries

in eleven countries, ranging from Europe, Tunisia, Mexico, Panama, and the Philippines. Almost 218,000 US servicemen and servicewomen are interred at these cemeteries, and over 94,000 missing in action or lost at sea are memorialized on the cemetery's "Tablets of the Missing."[89]

It's easy to see that America not only owes her fallen service members, as President Truman said, "a debt of gratitude,"[90] but also a place of final rest.

ARLINGTON NATIONAL CEMETERY

As far as all of our repositories that hold the remains of our fallen, there is one place in particular that stands out. Among all of our national cemeteries, Arlington National Cemetery is unique. While at ANC, I learned, though not the largest in acreage, ANC holds the most remains at over 400,000.

Arlington National Cemetery's history is America's history. Since the beginnings of the USA, the story of this property is closely tied to America's story and can be traced back to President George Washington's family. On August 24, 1814, as the British sacked and burned the Capitol and the White House, the inferno was clearly visible from the heights of what was then Arlington Estate.[91]

On September 11, 1941, within walking distance of Arlington, America's strategic defense center, the Pentagon, had its groundbreaking.[92] Exactly sixty years later, from those same heights, one could clearly see another inferno as American Airlines Flight 77 crashed into the Pentagon.

The nation's connection to this property began during the middle of the Revolutionary War, when, in 1778, George Washington's adopted stepson, John Parke Custis, purchased the property. In 1802, George Washington Parke Custis,

Washington's step-grandson, inherited the property and dedicated part of the 1,100 acres to become a living memorial to President Washington.[93]

Another interesting story from Arlington's history is that George Washington Custis's daughter, Mary, married U.S. Army Lieutenant Robert E. Lee in 1831. Following her father's death in 1857, Mary inherited a life interest in the estate. The Lee's made this their home until Virginia seceded from the Union on May 24, 1861. Once they departed from the property, they never returned, and it was seized by the Union. In March 1883, the Lee family ultimately received $150,000 from the federal government as compensation for their loss.[94]

On the heels of the Lees' abandonment of the property, the Union Army moved in, primarily due to its high ground overlooking the Capitol. Three forts were built on the property during the Civil War, including today's Fort Myer and Fort McPherson.[95]

It was under the presidency of Abraham Lincoln that Arlington would assume its ultimate purpose. The first military burial at Arlington was on May 13, 1864, and on June 15, 1864, President Lincoln's Secretary of War Edwin Stanton declared 200 acres of the property as a national cemetery, which it has permanently remained.[96]

Found among the rows of burial sites is that of Robert Todd Lincoln, President Lincoln's son, two presidents, and other governmental officials.[97]

Arlington is also the final resting place of sixty-four individuals who died at the Pentagon on "9/11." Fifty-seven of them are buried in Section 64 in the southeastern part of the cemetery closest to the Pentagon.[98]

"... I COULD STAY HERE FOREVER..."

During the one hundredth anniversary year of Arlington National Cemetery, the thirty-fifth president of the US, President John F. Kennedy, was buried among his fellow service members.

On March 3, 1963, the spring before he died, President Kennedy made an unscheduled visit to Arlington. While walking the grounds near the Custis-Lee Mansion, President Kennedy was so taken with the view of the Potomac that he commented to a friend, it was "so magnificent I could stay here forever." On March 14, 1967, his body made its final move and was permanently placed at that very site.[99]

If there was ever a president who could speak from the "high ground" on calling Americans to a patriotic duty, it was President Kennedy. John F. Kennedy volunteered to go to war on behalf of his country, volunteered for hazardous duty, and put himself at death's door to save his crew.

President Kennedy's life and words have given us much to think about. There is a line in President Kennedy's Roosevelt Day commemoration message of January 29, 1961 that states: "Today we need a nation of minute men; citizens who are not only prepared to take up arms, but citizens who regard the preservation of freedom as a basic purpose of their daily life and who are willing to consciously work and sacrifice for that freedom."[100]

President Kennedy saw the necessity of every citizen accepting the call to share in required sacrifices. He went on to say, "The cause of liberty and the cause of America cannot succeed without such shared sacrifices."[101]

The call for sacrifice by President Kennedy was grounded in his own understanding and experience of just what that might look like. In World War II, he almost made that ultimate sacrifice, and eventually, Lincoln and Kennedy would pay that ultimate price while in service to country.

President Kennedy tried to join the Army in 1940, but he was rejected for ulcers, asthma, and his bad back. Using his father's influence, he was allowed to use a private Boston doctor to certify his "good health."[102]

Thus, in July 1942, he entered the Naval Reserve Officers Training School in Chicago. After completing this training, Kennedy voluntarily entered the Motor Torpedo Boat Squadrons Training Center in Melville, Rhode Island. He was originally posted in Panama, and against his father's wishes, pulled strings and made it to the Pacific.[103]

After arriving in the Solomon Islands, on 23 April 1943, he took command of PT-109, and on 2 August, PT-109 was rammed and sunk by the Japanese destroyer, Amagiri. Kennedy's heroic efforts were credited with the ultimate survival and rescue of his crew, minus the two who were killed by the collision.[104]

One remarkable irony about Lieutenant (junior grade) Kennedy's heroism was that he never received a combat award for his efforts. He was awarded the Navy and Marine Corps medal, a non-combat award for heroism. He did receive the Purple Heart, which requires combat action, so the correct award, many believed, should have been the Silver Star.

President Kennedy, a true combat hero, never received the Silver Star medal, that many thought he deserved, but Lyndon Johnson was awarded a Silver Star that was verified to be a sham.

On the day of President Kennedy's assassination, Vice President Johnson was wearing a miniature lapel Silver Star medal. As Jackie Kennedy stood by, he wore it on Air Force One while being sworn in as president. President Johnson wore the Silver Star lapel pin on his suit coat throughout his tenure as president.

In 1942, LBJ was a young congressman from Texas and a lieutenant commander in the Navy Reserve. As a member of Congress, he lobbied President Roosevelt to send him on an inspection tour of the southwestern Pacific. In Australia, he met General Douglas MacArthur, who allowed Johnson to go on a single bombing mission as an observer.[105]

On June 9, 1942, eleven American B-26s left Port Moresby, New Guinea, to attack a Japanese base at Lae. The plane that Johnson was on developed engine trouble and returned to base, never encountering any enemy. The other ten bombers suffered great damage with several crews lost.[106]

In Johnson's account of the bombing run, he said he watched as the crew valiantly fended off a withering attack by Japanese fighters. The problem was that it was not true. Later, crew members on the plane said on that flight they never saw an enemy fighter.[107]

General MacArthur authorized the award, and though the citation noted the plane had to turn back, yet it went on to state: "He evidenced marked coolness in spite of the hazard. His gallant action allowed him to obtain and return with valuable information." It was said one reason for MacArthur to push this was his hope Congressman Johnson would go back to Roosevelt and persuade him to send more resources and personnel to the South Pacific.[108]

Johnson's biographer Robert Caro said, "It is surely one of the most undeserved Silver Stars in history."[109]

Kennedy never forgot his fallen comrades, and never fully recovered from his own injuries. The motto for the PT boats was simply, "They were expendable," yet this is the duty he sought.

Kennedy loved the Navy, and once remarked while speaking at the Naval Academy, "Any man who may be asked in this century, what he did to make his life worthwhile can respond with a good deal of pride and satisfaction, I served in the United States Navy."[110]

A great resource on President Kennedy's life and death is Larry Sabato's *The Kennedy Half-Century: The Presidency, Assassination, and Lasting Legacy of John F. Kennedy.*

THE HONOR FLIGHT NETWORK

There is another story from Arlington National Cemetery that holds a very dear memory for me. I often reflect upon that day at ANC when I spent some very quality time with a ninety-year-old World War II veteran. That veteran was my dad.

In early October 2015, I stood behind my ninety-year-old father as he sat in his wheelchair at the Tomb of the Unknown Soldier. We were there for a wreath laying ceremony and a changing of the Tomb guard.

We were there as part of a group of over 150 World War II and Korean War veterans who had come to Washington for the day, and this was part of our tour. The tour was designed to visit memorial sites, including the World War II, Korean War, and Vietnam War memorials, the US Marine Corps War Memorial, and especially to pay a visit to Arlington National Cemetery.

The trip was made possible because of an organization called the Honor Flight Network. Earl Morse and Jeff Miller cofounded the Honor Flight Network. Earl was a former Air Force captain and the son of a Korean War and Vietnam War veteran, while Jeff was the son of a World War II veteran.

Their respective visions of such a program arose separately, but in February 2007, they merged their ideas into what would become the Honor Flight Network. As their website points out, "The mission of Honor Flight is to transport America's veterans to Washington, D.C. to visit the memorials dedicated to honoring those who have served and sacrificed for our country."[111]

Every year since 2007, the Honor Flight Network has transported over 20,000 veterans to our nation's capitol, at no cost to the veteran. Prior to the Covid-19 interruptions, over 240,000 veterans had participated in these trips. Since spring 2020, all trips have been put on hold with the hopes of beginning again sometime in 2021.[112]

Our particular group from SC totaled about one hundred individuals, which included around fifty World War II and Korean War veterans, one of which was a female World War II nurse, and around fifty of us who served as guardians. We flew out of the Greenville, SC airport, and less than two hours later, landed in DC.

At Reagan National Airport, our group linked up with other groups for our day tour. After the six buses were loaded, we proceeded behind a police motorcycle escort for the rest of our appointed stops. A guardian accompanied each veteran, and I served as my father's guardian.

At the World War II Memorial, there was a prearranged patriotic concert by children from one of the local schools. Then, the children mingled among the veterans, giving them flowers and notes. Members of Congress sent some of their staff over to greet constituents from their districts. Active duty military personnel were also walking around, greeting their forbears in uniform.

Witnessing what a great experience this was for these World War II and Korean War veterans, I would encourage my fellow Americans to support honorflight.org.

Our final event was at the Tomb of the Unknown. After the wreath laying, but prior to the Changing of the Guard, the "relief commander" informed these elderly veterans that the Sentinel who was guarding the Tomb could not give them a hand salute, but as he approached their viewing area, he would slide his shoes on the ground and the sound of the taps on his shoes was his salute to them.

What an honor to see the Tomb guard give his salute to these heroes of another era. I'm very grateful that all of the Tomb guards are the best of the best. And rightfully so, they "... honor the fallen, unidentified U. S. service members from each major war in their appearance, in their movements, and in how they steadily watch over the Tomb grounds."[113]

There is a powerful article on army.mil that describes this duty from the perspective of a Tomb guard. The article also describes a recent documentary series called, *Honor Guard*, and a separate documentary called, *The Unknowns* (available on Amazon and Apple TV).[114]

My father died less than a year after we made that trip, and I will always cherish those memories and be thankful for Jeff Morse and Earl Miller.

CHAPTER 8

. . . .

SECTION 60

"...Ross McGinnis joined the U. S. Army
on...his 17th birthday..."[115]

M ANY MEMORIES COME TO MIND AS I THINK OF
the hallowed Section 60 of Arlington National
Cemetery. I have personal heroes whose remains lie under this
part of Arlington's manicured lawn. Through these courageous individuals, I developed a deep appreciation of the selfless acts that are offered on a daily basis by this generation of
our military.

Every grave at Arlington houses the remains of someone
who made a difference with his or her life. And every person
buried there still has a story to tell. Many of the more recent
graves are found in Section 60. For more information, I recommend Robert Poole's book, *Section 60: Where War Comes Home*,
and Senator Tom Cotten's book, *Sacred Duty*, as great resources.

On the corner of Halsey and York are the fourteen acres
of Section 60. From Section 60, one can see the side of the
Pentagon that was struck on 9/11. Ironically, it was from that
day that Section 60 began its expansion. Even though Section
60 was opened in 1972, it is primarily known for housing the
gravesites of those who have been killed since the War on Terror

began. Section 60 holds over 10,000 graves, and includes the most group burials. These are for those who died together in battle or those who requested burial with friends.[116]

Until a war memorial is built for the Global War on Terror, many families and recent veterans say Section 60 is their War on Terror memorial. This is true for me as well.

Below are the stories of some of the heroes whose resting place is Section 60. As we remember them, we remember their families who continue every day of their lives to pay a heavy price on our behalf.

CAPTAIN RUSSELL B. RIPPETOE, SECTION 60, SITE 7860

My path never crossed with Captain Rippetoe's, but his death and burial became significant in the history of Section 60. Captain Russell "Rusty" B. Rippetoe, an Army Ranger, was the first casualty from Iraq who was buried in Section 60.

Almost immediately after 9/11, Captain Rippetoe was one of America's first soldiers to see combat in the War on Terror, as his Special Forces unit was ordered to Afghanistan.

At the time of his death, he was assigned to the 75th Ranger Regiment, and he and two fellow Rangers were killed in Iraq on April 3, 2003, by a suicide detonated VBIED (vehicle borne improvised explosive device).[117]

Rusty's father, Lieutenant Colonel Joe Rippetoe, US Army (Ret.), said, "My son's big heart got him killed." A pregnant Iraqi woman had begged him for food and water, and as he approached her vehicle to offer help, someone in the vehicle detonated a suicide car bomb, killing the three terrorists and mortally wounding Captain Rippetoe, along with his fellow rangers, Staff Sergeant Nino D. Livaudais and Specialist Ryan P. Long.[118]

Lieutenant Colonel Joe Rippetoe is also an Army Ranger and two-tour combat veteran of the Vietnam War. Due to war injuries, he struggles to raise his right arm, but at his son's burial, there is a moving photo of him offering a final salute.

Joe and Rita, Rusty's mother, make the trip from Colorado several times a year to visit their son's grave in Section 60. The Rippetoes make these trips to "keep his memory alive."[119]

Captain Rusty Rippetoe chose to live a life of service. The phrase, "for God and country," certainly described him. He had a deep love of country, and was also a man with deep faith in God. Inscribed on the back of his dog tags was the verse, "Have I not commanded you? Be strong and courageous. Do not be afraid; do not be discouraged, for the Lord your God will be with you wherever you go" (Joshua1:9 NIV)

Captain Rippetoe is survived by his parents, Joe and Rita, and a sister, Rebecca.

SPECIALIST ROSS A. MCGINNIS, SECTION 60, SITE 8544

Specialist Ross A. McGinnis was killed on December 4, 2006. He and I were in Iraq at the same time. To my knowledge, I never met Private First Class McGinnis, but I heard about his decision to throw himself upon a fragmentation grenade to save four of his comrades.

The following biographical information concerning Specialist Ross Andrew McGinnis is taken from the army. mil website:

Posthumously promoted to Specialist, Ross McGinnis was also posthumously awarded The Congressional Medal of Honor which was presented to his parents at a White House Ceremony on June 2, 2008.

Ross A. McGinnis joined the U. S. Army on June 14, 2004, his 17th birthday, on a delayed entry program. This young man, the day before he joined the Army was a 16 year old teenager, doing what 16 year old teenagers do. While many of his peers were hanging out at the mall, or playing the latest video games, Ross was volunteering to serve his country. America was in a "two front" war in 2004, and Ross knew, full well, that joining meant he would end up in combat, in Afghanistan or Iraq or both.

On December 4, 2006, nineteen year old PFC Ross McGinnis was serving as an M2 .50 caliber machine gunner in 1st Platoon, C Company, 1st Battalion, 26th Infantry Regiment, 2nd BCT, 101st Airborne Division (Air Assault) in support of operations against insurgents in Adhamiyah, Iraq. While on patrol, an insurgent threw a fragmentation grenade through the Humvee turret opening where PFC McGinnis was serving as gunner.

Without hesitation, PFC McGinnis threw himself upon the grenade, pinning it between his body and the Humvee's radio mount. His actions absorbed all the lethal fragments and the concussive effects of the grenade, allowing all four of his fellow soldiers to survive.[120]

Ross is survived by his parents, Tom and Romayne McGinnis, and his two sisters, Becky Gorman and Katie McGinnis of Knox, Pennsylvania. Specialist McGinnis's dedication to duty and love for his fellow soldiers were embodied in a statement issued by his parents shortly after his death:

> *Ross did not become our hero by dying to save his fellow Soldiers from a grenade. He was a hero to us long before he died, because he was willing to risk his life to protect the ideals of freedom and justice that America represents. He has been recommended for the Medal of Honor... That is not why he gave his life. The lives of four men who were his Army brothers outweighed the value of his one life. It was just a matter of simple kindergarten arithmetic.*
>
> *Four means more than one. It didn't matter to Ross that he could have escaped the situation without a scratch. Nobody would have questioned such a reflex reaction. What mattered to him were the four men placed in his care on a moment's notice. One moment he was responsible for defending the rear of a convoy from enemy fire; the next moment he held the lives of four of his friends in his hands. The choice for Ross was simple, but simple does not mean easy. His straightforward answer to a simple but difficult choice should stand as a shining example for the rest of us. We all face simple choices, but how often do we choose to make a sacrifice to get the right answer? The right choice sometimes requires honor.[121]*

Clearly, this young man was reared in a home that shaped an incredible human being. In a world where many people call musicians, athletes, or movie stars their heroes, Ross McGinnis displayed what a real hero looks like.

As his parents said: "He was a hero to us long before he died, because he was willing to risk his life to protect the ideals of freedom and justice that America represents."

COMMANDER PHILLIP A. MURPHY-SWEET, SECTION 60, SITE 8616

Navy Commander Phillip A. Murphy-Sweet's earthly life ended on Saturday, April 7, 2007, in the Rusafa District of Baghdad, Iraq. In the afternoon of the 7th, I received word a convoy was ambushed and four personnel were killed, including my friend, Phillip Murphy-Sweet. Death was frequent in Iraq, but this time, it was personal, as this was a friend and associate. I knew his life story. I knew about his deep love of his wife, Cheryl, and his three precious children.

Phil and I spoke often, especially around trips to the D-FAC (dining facility) and I knew he completed his original six-month tour and had voluntarily extended to finish a very important project. Phil was a friend to many of us on Phoenix Base, and for me, his death would forever be a fresh memory.

Phil loved life and enjoyed people. We had a lot of laughs together, and it was a running joke that all of the "negligent" discharges at the D-FAC were from the Navy guys (there was some truth to that). To enter a dining facility in a combat zone, each person had to "clear" his or her weapon before entering. If an M-16, M-4, or 9-mm was not cleared properly in the clearing barrel, then the weapon would discharge, and such a thing in a combat zone raised everyone's "pucker" factor.

Many of these discharges reflected the fact that most of the Navy and Air Force personnel in our joint command were not used to the "daily" carry of a loaded weapon required in a combat zone. Phil was "squared away," and this did not happen to him, but the Army vs. Navy rivalry led to razzing each other about such things anyway, especially since after the 2006 game, Navy football had a five-game win streak over Army.

Commander Murphy-Sweet was not killed by the frequently employed IEDs but by an EFP (explosively formed penetrator). For clarification, the EFPs proved far more deadly than the IED when deployed against armored vehicles. The "up-armored" SUV that Commander Murphy-Sweet and three others were traveling in was no match for such a device, and we lost all four.

The EFP was of Iranian engineering, and the late Iranian Major General Qasim Soleimani's Quds Force provided the training and logistics for this weapon to militants in Iraq.[122] Commander Murphy-Sweet had seen the results of the frequent EFP ambushes, and he certainly knew the deadly threat that he faced traveling on the roads of Iraq. To fulfill his mission, Commander Murphy-Sweet traveled almost daily to many of the most dangerous places within Iraq. He felt he had a job to do, and he found the courage and bravery required to do it.

The courage and depth of commitment to his country that was exemplified by Commander Murphy-Sweet's voluntary extension of his tour in Iraq cannot be overstated. It was not just death that threatened Commander Murphy-Sweet in that environment, but even more fearsome possibilities than death.

Our soldiers operated with an understanding of what would happen to them if they were captured alive. Recovered remains of captured Coalition military, as well as captured Iraqi civilians who worked with the Coalition, revealed untold horrors and the slow torture inflicted upon these individuals before they died. I realize it sounds ghastly, but one typical form of torture included the use of an electric drill. It was in that environment that my friend, Commander Phillip Murphy-Sweet, volunteered to "finish" the job.

Much like Phil's job, my job called for extensive travel across Iraq. I was the MNSTC-I (Multi-National Security Command-Iraq) Command chaplain, and my chaplain assistant Staff Sergeant Kyle Bennet and I made over 150 air and ground movements throughout Iraq. During that period, I often thought, "Is this my day?"

At the end of my tour, General Dempsey presented me the Bronze Star medal. Part of the inscription on the medal states: "He put himself in harm's way without hesitation by traveling throughout some of the more dangerous regions in Iraq to attend the needs of service members located in base camps and forward operating bases."

I appreciated those words, and I am grateful I found the courage to do my job, but believe me, I'm not sharing this to suggest that what I did made me unique or a hero. I'm sharing this because I experienced real fear, and I dealt with the nightmares that seemed oh so real. When "you put yourself in harm's way" on a daily basis and you do your job despite your fears, I think this qualifies for what courage looks like. I saw a lot of that over there.

Being completely honest, it wasn't death that I feared, except in the sense of missing family, but my greatest fear was to be captured alive by such a sadistic enemy. Many soldiers confessed to me, "Chaplain, I hope God understands because if I'm down to my last round, I'm saving it for myself."

An incredible chaplain's assistant, Staff Sergeant Kyle Bennet, accompanied me in Iraq. Everywhere I went, he went. He actually made all the arrangements. By the Geneva

Convention Code, military chaplains are considered "non-combatants," and do not carry weapons. The problem was, the Coalition honored the Laws of War, but the people seeking to kill us were beyond ruthless, and they wouldn't even honor the Marquess of Queensbury rules, much less the Geneva Convention Code.

I'll readily admit, my faith was tested, traveling in a war zone for a year unarmed. My comfort was God's very real presence, and the fact my young assistant was heavily armed. He carried an M-4 carbine equipped with an advanced combat optical gunsight (ACOG), and a Beretta M9, 9 mm, service pistol and plenty of ammunition for both.

Despite such effective weapons, Staff Sergeant Bennet's armaments were only intended for our self-defense. My first question to him when we met at our pre-mobilization station was, "SSG Bennet, how good are you with an M-4?" Let's just say he reassured me.

I'm relating a bit of my story to reinforce just how brave and courageous Phil Murphy-Sweet was. When my chaplain assistant and I made ground movements, we were usually in an up-armored Humvee. These Humvees were not impregnable, but they were a degree safer than the up-armored SUV that Phil always traveled in.

I know the context and battlefield environment at the time of Phil's decision to extend. This was during the surge, and there was intensity on the battlefield and on the streets. I know somewhat of the commitment and courage that was required for him to say, "Count me in, I'll stay and finish the job." Phil knew if he didn't stay, then someone else would have to complete that project. In reality, Phil's life wasn't taken, for he had a flight home weeks earlier; no, Phil's life was given, given for his country. "No greater love than this..."

This man had volunteered three times for his country. He had voluntarily joined the Navy, volunteered to go to Iraq, and he had voluntarily extended his tour in Iraq. Certainly, Lincoln's words apply, and we remember Commander Murphy-Sweet's sacrifice because "It is altogether fitting that we do so."[123]

Present at his service were many of his American, British, Australian, and Iraqi coworkers, as well representatives of many of the Command groups in Iraq. Among those attending were at least five general officers, including General David Petraus (later becoming a CIA director), then-Lieutenant General Martin Dempsey (later becoming General Martin Dempsey, Chairman of the Joint Chiefs of Staff) and Air Force then-Major General Daryl Scott, later retiring as Lieutenant General Scott.

I officiated at the memorial service on Phoenix Base, Iraq, and we tailored it for a proud US Navy officer. Air Force Major General Daryl Scott shared remarks since Phil worked for him in the Joint Contracting Command, Multi-National Force-Iraq.

The most moving moments in the service were when I read inspiring words from Phil's wife, Cheryl. Cheryl emphasized that Phil believed in what he was doing, and he felt that he was making a difference. She also reminded everyone that Phil's six-month deployment had been completed, and with her full support, he voluntarily extended. Phil wanted to complete a particular project that he had been working on. It was during that extension that he lost his life.

Shortly after the service, I received very kind notes from Major General Scott and Lieutenant General Dempsey that I have saved, expressing appreciation for my leadership in the memorial service. I couldn't help but reflect back to that first memorial service I officiated at the Pentagon, when someone asked, "I wonder how many more memorial services would follow."

Here we were again, honoring another great American who volunteered to serve, and gave his life for his country. We must also remember liberty's heavy cost, forever charged, to his widow and three children who lost their dad.

There's no question, Commander Phillip Murphy-Sweet understood the pride in President Kennedy's words, "Any man who may be asked in this century, what he did to make his life worthwhile can respond with a good deal of pride and satisfaction, I served in the United States Navy."[124]

Today, Commander Phillip Murphy-Sweet's earthly remains lie just a few hundred yards away from those of President John F. Kennedy, his fellow naval officer.

You can pay your respects to Phil in Section 60, Site 8616. When you do, put up a good word—he deserves it!

Phil's survivors included his wife, Cheryl, and his children, Olivia, Seth, and Lauren, his father, mother, and two sisters.

STAFF SERGEANT LAURENT J. WEST. SECTION 60, SITE 8554

On March 26, 2008, I traveled up to Arlington with a team from Fort Bragg for the graveside service for fallen 82nd Airborne Division paratrooper, Staff Sergeant Laurent J. West. Staff Sergeant West was assigned to the 3rd Squadron, 73rd Cavalry Regiment, 1st Brigade Combat Team, 82nd Airborne Division. Staff Sergeant West died from wounds sustained when an IED (Improvised Explosive Device) struck his vehicle near Kishkishkia, Iraq, on March 11, 2008.

Arriving for Staff Sergeant West's internment, I checked into the ANC Administration Building, spoke with the family, and met the ANC representative, an "Arlington Lady" assigned to the family, and the OIC (officer in charge). I also paid a courtesy call to see the senior Arlington chaplain. I knew him from prior assignments.

Soldiers from the US Army's 3rd United States Infantry Regiment (the Old Guard) provided a military funeral escort from the Administration Building to the gravesite in Section 60.

The Old Guard is America's oldest active-duty regiment, dating back to 1784. The Old Guard is the Army's official ceremonial unit and the escort to the president. In time of national emergency, this regiment also provides security for Washington, DC.[125]

Soldiers from the Old Guard are the ones who maintain a twenty-four-hour vigil at the Tomb of the Unknowns.

Our family takes pride in the fact that our son-in-law, Staff Sergeant William "Bill" Underwood, US Army (Ret.) served in the Old Guard. After his time in the Old Guard, he began a career as a fireman and law enforcement officer.

He continued his military service in the Virginia Army National Guard and the Army Reserves. He eventually served two tours in Iraq. On his first tour, he received the Purple Heart while supporting the 1st Cavalry Division. On his second tour in a Joint Command, he received the Bronze Star medal for his actions in helping compromise an enemy sniper.

Though the Old Guard takes the lead, provides the escort, and presents the honors, the 82nd would always send a team from the fallen paratrooper's unit to participate in the service. I was the chaplain tasked by the 82nd to support the family and officiate at the service for Staff Sergeant West.

On that chilly March morning, with traffic zooming by on I-395, and surrounded by over 400,000 grave markers, war had become very personal. Staff Sergeant Laurent West was deeply loved, and survived by his wife, two daughters, his parents, other family, and many friends.

He was a few weeks' shy of his thirty-third birthday, in the prime of his life. He volunteered to go into the Army and into harm's way, and during his fifteen years of service, he had deployed often, including Bosnia, Afghanistan, and Iraq. Staff Sergeant West knew what he was getting into when he joined the Army because he was the son of a career soldier, Lieutenant Colonel Larry West, U.S. Army, (Ret.).

Staff Sergeant West was a "real" person and true hero. And yes, "...It is fitting and proper..." he be remembered. Now his remains will forever lie in sacred ground alongside President John Kennedy and other Americans who arrived to this place from all conflicts, all ranks, and all parts of our national fabric.

As the flag was presented to Staff Sergeant West's wife, I again heard those words, "on behalf of a grateful nation." That day, I committed to never forget him. Since then, I broadened my promise to remember all of our fallen American heroes. I often restate my pledge that I am very grateful for what they have done, and I will never forget what they have done.

After the military honors had been rendered, I spoke individually to each member of his family. In their tears, I saw, up close and personal, the price of freedom that had been paid by Staff Sergeant West, and the price his loved ones must pay for the rest of their lives.

As I stepped aside, a gentleman in a dark suit leaned over to me and said, "The Secretary would like to speak to you when you have a minute." As I turned around, a tall, dignified gentleman, who had just finished speaking with the family, took my hand and placed something in it. Then he expressed his appreciation to me for the service that we had just completed. I thanked him for his kindness, and as he walked off, I asked his aide, to whom I was speaking. He said, "That's the Secretary of the Army, Pete Geren."

His aide told me that Secretary Geren attended every burial of an Army soldier at Arlington who was killed in action in either Iraq or Afghanistan. He said the Secretary put this duty above all else. What Secretary Geren had placed in my hand was his Secretary of the Army coin. When I pick up that coin, I think of Staff Sergeant West and his family. I also think of Pete Geren. Without pretense, Secretary Geren faithfully set the example of what a grateful citizen looks like.

Staff Sergeant West, "Airborne! All the way!"

STAFF SERGEANT SCOTT W. BRUNKHORST, SECTION 60, SITE 9151

Staff Sergeant Brunkhorst was assigned to 2nd Battalion, 508th Parachute Infantry Regiment, 4th Brigade Combat Team, 82nd Airborne Division, and was killed March 30, 2010, in the "death valley" of the Arghandab River Valley of Afghanistan. Scott joined the Army right after graduating from Bridgewater-Raritan High School in Bridgewater, New Jersey.

Staff Sergeant Brunkhorst could have left the Army in August 2010, at the end of his enlistment, but instead, he reenlisted and continued to serve his country despite regularly going into harm's way. He was a squad leader, and took good care of his men.

Scott Brunkhorst, like many other military service members, came from a family that believed it was a good thing to serve one's country. His mother, father, grandfather, and brother all served. He was a very good soldier, and was assigned, for a time, at the United States Military Academy.

In May 2010, I officiated at the monthly 82nd Airborne Division memorial service in which we honored Staff Sergeant Brunkhorst and Specialist Joseph Thierry Caron. More comments about Staff Sergeant Brunkhorst and the memorial service are found in the Fort Bragg chapter.

Staff Sergeant Brunkhorst was survived by his wife, Krystal, his three-year-old daughter, Kendall, his parents, Rick and Linda Brunkhorst, brothers Adam and Richard, and a sister, Danyella. His brother Adam served in the US Army.

Forever changing her life, it was on her twenty-fifth birthday that Krystal answered the door, and there stood a CNO. At Arlington, Krystal also received a flag and heard, "on behalf of a grateful nation."

Staff Sergeant Brunkhorst, "Airborne! All the way!"

SPECIALIST LORI ANN PIESTEWA, U.S. ARMY, IRAQ WAR

Before concluding this chapter on some of America's newer heroes from the Iraq and Afghanistan War zones, we have three more stories to add to this group. None of these three heroes were buried in Section 60, though they earned that honor.

On March 23, 2003, within three days of the Iraq war's beginning, two "firsts" took place. The first female service member was killed in the Iraq War, and she was also the first American Indian woman to die in combat in the history of the U.S. military.

U.S. Army Specialist Lori Ann Piestewa was a Hopi Indian. Köcha-Hon-Mana, her Hopi name, means White Bear Girl.[11]

When Specialist Piestwa left for Iraq, she was twenty-three years old and a third-generation Hopi warrior. "As is the case in many Indian homes, both her grandfather who served in World War II, and her father, who served in Vietnam, embraced the warrior tradition, a pride they instilled in their children."[126]

Her parents, Terry Piestewa and Priscilla (Percy) Baca-Piestewa raised their children in a modest but loving home with respect for family and cultural values.

On the day Specialist Piestwa died, she was driving a Humvee as part a convoy of 600 vehicles. They were leaving Kuwait and heading north into Iraq. Eventually, some of the 507th Maintenance Company's vehicles, including hers, became separated from the main convoy. Mistakenly, they ended up in the middle of Nasiriyah, Iraq, where they were ambushed.

Private First Class Jessica Lynch was in the same Humvee, and she later said that as bullets flew, Specialist Piestewa never wavered, kept her wits, and drove hard to push through the ambush. Before they could clear the area, their vehicle was struck by an RPG and subsequently crashed. Specialist Piestewa received head wounds and died in an Iraqi civilian hospital.[127]

An article in *Indian Country Today* stated: "Her heart, spirit, and undaunted courage made her an icon for Indians and non-Indians alike." In the article, her brother Wayland said: "My parents have been visiting tribes all over the nation, Lori's death ... is a symbol of honor and pride among all Indian people."[128]

After her death, Specialist Piestewa's body was returned home and now rests on the Hopi reservation near Tuba City. In addition to her parents and siblings, Specialist Lori Piestewa is survived by her children, Brandon and Carla.[129]

It has been an incredible process of discovery for me as I have read the accounts of so many brave Americans, like Lori Piestewa, who left family and the comforts of their homes, and put themselves at the "tip of the spear," in defense of our country. She honored her country, family, and as her brother said, "All Indian people." She died a brave warrior.

Her service brought to mind an American Indian friend of mine that I served with in Iraq. Gunnery Sergeant Ronnie

McOmber, USMC, was from the Chinnewa Tribe. We became friends, and since I was his chaplain, he made me an olive wood, "Chinnewa Shaman prayer stick." It is one of my prized possessions.

The dove feathers attached to the prayer stick represent "a messenger of peace," in the midst of the chaos. That description was included on the Chinnewa Shaman prayer stick, information page that was included with the prayer stick. On the page, it also explained the "Tri-Braid." The relationship of the Tri-Braid is for the Earth, Wind, and Fire, or Father, Son, and the Holy Ghost."

The prayer stick is beautifully and intricately made, and each of its various parts: olive wood, feathers, leather, and colored beads carry an important meaning. My Chinnewa friend offered me something from "his world" that added great meaning to mine. This act is another reminder that all of us who share this land are part of a great family.

PRIVATE FIRST CLASS MARCUS ALLAN TYNES, U.S. ARMY, AFGHANISTAN

Marcus Tynes joined the US Army just one month after graduating from Valley View High School in Moreno Valley, California. He became a paratrooper and served in Company C, 2nd Battalion, 508th Parachute Infantry Regiment, 4th Brigade Combat Team, 82nd Airborne Division. On November 22, 2009, he and another paratrooper, Sergeant James M. Nolen, of Alvin, Texas, were killed in action when an IED exploded near his vehicle.[130]

Sergeant Nolen had recently been informed that he was an expectant father. One of these soldiers was Black, and one was White, but they served as brothers and died as brothers.

Due to mass casualty incidents within 4th BCT, several Rear D chaplains were needed to support families located in different parts of the country. I went to California as part of a funeral honors detail to assist with the funeral and interment for Private First Class Tynes. Once there, our team met the family, and the first thing they did was invite all of us over to the home for a barbecue. We had gone to support them, but in the midst of their great pain, they chose to extend to Marcus's fellow paratroopers a most gracious reception.

This was an amazing family, and they took well-deserved pride in Marcus's service and sacrifice for his country.

We learned a lot from this family about the type of home that produces heroes, like Private First Class Marcus Tynes. Marcus's mother, Dana Atlas, a nurse, said, "He was very happy about being there. It was what he wanted to do. He enjoyed serving his country, he loved traveling, he loved the Lord, and he loved life."

From his obituary in the Los Angeles Times:

> *As he grew, one uniform followed another. One for football at Valley View High School...and another for track. A favorite was one he wore as a Riverside County Sheriff's Explorer. He put on the Explorer's green slacks and tan shirt, complete with badge and "rocker" insignia, and a new version of himself emerged. He had his heart set on someday wearing the navy blues of a Los Angeles Police Department SWAT officer. [He] was encouraged...to do a stint in the military... standard career advice for a would-be police officer.*[131]

Marcus would have been a terrific police officer because he obviously put others ahead of himself. His death is a great loss to the profession, the community, the country, and mostly to his family.

Marcus's parents, Bruce and Dana Atlas, established the "Marcus' Heart Foundation" in honor of Marcus. This foundation supports youth with scholarships, mentors youth, and is dedicated to helping soldiers and veterans. For more information visit: http://marcussheartfoundation.org.

1ST LIEUTENANT SALVATORE "SAL" CORMA II, U.S. ARMY, AFGHANISTAN

In my position as the Rear D chaplain, I learned the life story of another amazing young man. On April 29, 2010, Salvatore and Trudy Corma lost their only son, and her only child, First Lieutenant Salvatore "Sal" Simplicio Corma II. First Lieutenant Corma was killed by an IED in Zabul Province, Afghanistan.

Lieutenant Corma was a 2008 graduate of the United States Military Academy and was serving as an infantry platoon leader in Afghanistan. He was assigned to the 2nd Battalion, 508th Parachute Infantry Regiment, 4th Brigade Combat Team, 82nd Airborne Division, Fort Bragg, North Carolina. He was not physically imposing, at around five foot four inches and 140 lbs, but he certainly stood tall in the eyes of the men in his platoon.

On May 13, 2010, his parents, Salvatore S. Corma and Gertrude H. Corma, were present as their son's body was returned to his alma mater for burial at West Point Cemetery.

Within a month, "Big Sal" Corma and Trudy Corma made the trip down from Wenonah, New Jersey, for our June 2010, 82nd Airborne Division monthly memorial service for fallen paratroopers. "Big Sal," so called to distinguish him from his son, was confined to a wheelchair as a result of his amputated leg. It was very moving to be with these very gracious and loving parents whose son gave his life for the members of his platoon and his country.

During the service, members of his unit shared the circumstances of Lieutenant Corma's death. His death came near the end of a combat patrol. On the way back to the platoon's forward operating base, the lead vehicle was monitoring the road for possible IEDs and noticed disturbed ground just beyond a bridge they needed to cross. This led to the discovery of an IED buried in the roadway.

Lieutenant Corma ordered the nineteen paratroopers under his command to clear the area. He then proceeded, alone, to mark the IED with a bright orange VS-17 panel. Placing these panels was a common procedure to warn local Afghans and other coalition forces to avoid the site until the IED could be diffused. As he approached the IED with the panel, his foot struck the pressure plate, which triggered the explosion that took his life. In comments to Lieutenant Corma's parents, the men in his platoon credited their son's actions for saving their lives.

All of our monthly collective memorial services were quite meaningful. For each of them, we brought together comrades of the fallen paratroopers and family members of the fallen. In one real sense, everyone in the 82nd Airborne Division Chapel was part of the same family anyway.

We always had a reception for the families after the memorial service, and this gave us a chance to spend some time with them. Mr. and Mrs. Corma were very proud of their son, and grateful for our remembering him on that day. They emphasized it was Lieutenant Corma's goal to go to Afghanistan and lead paratroopers in combat. They related that he finished near the top of his class at West Point and had other options but still chose to be an infantry officer and even extended his commission two years.

After graduation, when he got orders to South Korea, he traded assignments with another officer so he could go to Afghanistan. "He was thrilled," Trudy said. "We weren't, though. But we didn't say anything. What were we going to say?" His dad said, "It was what he wanted to do. He wanted to lead men in combat."

Due to his father's critical illness, a few months before Lieutenant Corma's death, he came home on a short emergency leave. Trudy Corma said the whole time he was home, his thoughts remained with his men. He called to check on them every day, and sent his platoon a pallet of 300 cans of Monster Energy drinks.

A few weeks after they were with us at Fort Bragg, I received a personal thank-you note from Trudy Corma. She was so gracious in expressing her and her husband's appreciation for the many kindnesses shown them. She also thanked us for everyone's participation in the memorial service. Here was a mother whose only child had died; not only was he gone, but her hope of someday having grandchildren was gone, and she was thanking us.

Below is part of a very moving article from the *Camden Courier-Post*:

> *Outside the Corma's home in the town of Wenonah in Gloucester County, NJ, two dozen America flags ring the shrubbery garden and the tree mounds.*
>
> *The Rev. Father Paul Galetto, president of St. Augustine's Preparatory School, where Corma*

graduated in 2004, presided over the funeral Mass. It was a day when faith and mission convened, where the "Ave Maria" was immediately followed by "The Star-Spangled Banner." That's because Corma loved the church and the military, friends and family said.

Father Galetto said Corma embodied the spirit of service and good deeds, not for his own sake, but to earn the honor of friends, family and "a grateful nation who gives thanks for men and women like Salvatore Corma."[132]

On December 31, 2011, Salvatore "Big Sal" S. Corma died at the age of seventy-nine. But a large part of him died on April 30, 2010, in Afghanistan.

Trudy Corma, maintaining her gracious spirit, continues to honor her son's memory. A grateful nation can do no less than stand with her!

Army National Guard chaplains and chaplain's assistants mobilized to the Pentagon after 9/11. Pentagon chaplain, Chaplain Henry Haynes is front row second from left. His chaplain assistant, Staff Sergeant Monge is front row to his right. I'm on the back row, second from the left.

This is a screenshot of Lieutenant General Burns speaking at the First Memorial Service at the Pentagon on September 25, 2001.

Screenshot of First Memorial Service in Pentagon
Auditorium following 9/11, on September 25, 2001.

Screenshot of Memorial Service on September 25, 2001 for Lieutenant
Colonel Jerry Dickerson and Staff Sergeant Maudlyn White.

Note from Lieutenant General Burns following the
Memorial Service on September 25, 2001.

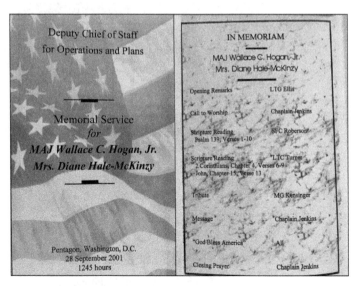

Program for Memorial Service for Major Wallace C. Hogan, Jr.
and Mrs. Dianne Hale-McKinzy on September 28, 2001.

Screenshot of Memorial Service on September 28, 2001.
This was conducted in BDU's due to then-Major General
Kensinger's Class A's lost in the fire on 9/11.

Screenshot of then-Lieutenant General Ellis speaking
at Memorial Service on September 28, 2001.

Certificate of
RECOGNITION

This certificate is awarded to

LIEUTENANT COLONEL JOEL JENKINS

in recognition of the comfort and assistance you provided to the family members of the heroes who died in the line of duty at the Pentagon. Your efforts have made a positive difference in the lives of these family members during their darkest days. Your generous contributions during this national tragedy will always be remembered with utmost gratitude within the Department of Defense.

DONALD H. RUMSFELD
SECRETARY OF DEFENSE

Certificate from Secretary of Defense Rumsfeld for Pentagon Service.

DEPARTMENT OF THE ARMY

THIS IS TO CERTIFY THAT THE SECRETARY OF THE ARMY HAS AWARDED

THE ARMY COMMENDATION MEDAL

TO

LIEUTENANT COLONEL JOEL P. JENKINS
1ST BRIGADE, 29TH INFANTRY DIVISION

FOR   outstanding performance while assigned to the Pentagon Chaplain's Office during the period of the Pentagon attack. Chaplain Jenkins tirelessly contributed by providing support to Pentagon personnel. He coordinated the work of five Chaplains and two Chaplain's assistants. He counseled many, and conducted numerous Memorial Services. His meritorious service reflects great credit upon him, The Chaplain's Corps, and the United States Army

FROM: 17 SEPTEMBER 2001 TO 29 OCTOBER 2001

GIVEN UNDER MY HAND IN THE CITY OF WASHINGTON
THIS   DAY OF   2001

PERMANENT ORDER   338-08
Office of the Administrative Assistant
Personnel Administrative Center
Washington, DC

Joel B. Hudson
Administrative Assistant to the
Secretary of the Army

Army Commendation Medal for Pentagon Service following 9/11.

IN MEMORY OF

PHILIP A. MURPHY-SWEET

Commander, Supply Corps, USN

5 November 1964 - 7 April 2007

14 April 2007

The final test of a leader is that he leaves behind him in
other men the conviction and the will to carry on.

~Walter Lippman

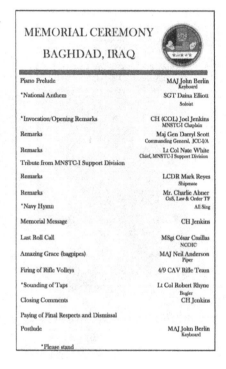

MEMORIAL CEREMONY

BAGHDAD, IRAQ

Piano Prelude	MAJ John Berlin Keyboard
*National Anthem	SGT Daina Elliott Soloist
*Invocation/Opening Remarks	CH (COL) Joel Jenkins MNSTC-I Chaplain
Remarks	Maj Gen Darryl Scott Commanding General, JCC-I/A
Remarks	Lt Col Nate White Chief, MNSTC-I Support Division
Tribute from MNSTC-I Support Division	
Remarks	LCDR Mark Reyes Shipmate
Remarks	Mr. Charlie Abner CoS, Law & Order TF
*Navy Hymn	All Sing
Memorial Message	CH Jenkins
Last Roll Call	MSgt César Casillas NCOIC
Amazing Grace (bagpipes)	MAJ Neil Anderson Piper
Firing of Rifle Volleys	4/9 CAV Rifle Team
*Sounding of Taps	Lt Col Robert Rhyne Bugler
Closing Comments	CH Jenkins
Paying of Final Respects and Dismissal	
Postlude	MAJ John Berlin Keyboard
*Please stand	

Program for Memorial Ceremony for Commander Phillip Murphy-
Sweet at Phoenix Base, Baghdad, Iraq on April 14, 2007.

Memorial Ceremony for Commander Murphy-Sweet on April 14, 2007.
I'm on the left. On the front row, third from the right is General
Dempsey, and on the front row, sixth from the right is General Petraeus.

14 APR 07

Dear Chaplain,

My compliments and thanks for your efforts in conducting the memorial service for Phil Murphy-Sweet. It was a very moving experience for us all and fitting tribute

to a great sailor and great American.

Thanks for all you do for MNSTC-I and for your country every day.

Martin E. Dempsey
LTG, US Army
Commanding General
Baghdad, Iraq

Note from General Dempsey following Commander
Murphy-Sweet's Memorial Ceremony.

Getting ready for the Remembrance Day Service at the
Habbaniyah Royal Air Force Cemetery, Habbaniyah, Iraq,
on November 11, 2006. I'm on the first row on the right.
Brigadier Hugh Monroe is to my immediate right.

Remembrance Day at Habbaniyah Royal Air Force Cemetery. An Australian officer prepares to lay a wreath in memory of the fallen.

Scottish Pipers playing "Amazing Grace" at the Remembrance Day Ceremony on November 11, 2006.

General Dempsey presenting me the Bronze Star Medal
at Phoenix Base in May, 2007. To my right is my chaplain
assistant, Staff Sergeant Kyle Bennett, having received a
well-deserved Defense Meritorious Service Medal.

Getting ready for a "road trip." Protected by our
MNSTC-I "Rough Riders" security escort team.

Staff Sergeant Bennett and I posing with some
Kurdish children in Zacko, Iraq.

Some of the Iraqi children we met at a Civil Affairs visit in Besamya,
Iraq. The visit included medical check-ups, delivery of school
supplies, shoes and clothing items, and of course new soccer balls.

Staff Sergeant Bennett at the post office picking up one shipment of the over five thousand pounds of care packages that passed through our office.

Staff Sergeant Bennett and I speaking with Ambassador Crocker at the American Embassy.

Staff Sergeant Bennett and I, on one of the 150 trips we made outside the Green Zone. This time we were traveling on a C-130.

DIVISION MEMORIAL CEREMONY
82D AIRBORNE DIVISION MEMORIAL CHAPEL
FORT BRAGG, NORTH CAROLINA

1100 Hours	14 October 2009

Prelude...Sheila Aderhold

Entrance of the Official Party.........................Official Party

*Invocation..Chaplain Jenkins

Reading of Names & Lighting of Candles.............SFC Frans
                                        SGT White

Commander's Remarks................................MAJ DelaCruz

Scripture Reading............. Psalm 23.................SFC Frans

Soldier's Remarks......SGT Lynch, SSG Lane, SPC Vasquez

Special Music..SGT Odom

Memorial Meditation...............................Chaplain Jenkins

*Benediction...Chaplain Jenkins

*Firing of Volleys.......................................Honor Guard

*Taps..Honor Bugler

Individual Honors..........................Friends and Comrades

Postlude...Sheila Aderhold

*Please Stand

IN MEMORY OF

SGT Tyler A. Juden
C Troop, 4th Squadron, 73rd Cavalry Regiment
508th PIR, 4th Brigade Combat Team

BORN: 18 Jan 1988   DIED: 12 Sep 2009

SPC Corey J. Kowall
A Company, 2nd Battalion
508th PIR, 4th Brigade Combat Team

BORN: 1 Feb 1989   DIED: 20 Sep 2009

SPC Damon G. Winkleman
HHC, 2nd Battalion
508th PIR, 4th Brigade Combat Team

BORN: 25 Feb 1986   DIED: 20 Sep 2009

Almighty God, Father of all mercies and Giver of all comforts, deal graciously with us who mourn, that casting all our cares on You, we may know the comfort of Your love and presence. Make us all aware of the brevity of life and the need to live it with a noble purpose. Keep us in this hour of need and enable us to find your strength sufficient. AMEN

Memorial Ceremony program for the October 2009 82nd Airborne Division Monthly Memorial Ceremony. Some months we honored much larger losses and moved the ceremony from the chapel to the movie theater.

Screenshot of participating paratroopers for a monthly 82nd Airborne Division Memorial Ceremony. I'm leading the procession.

Here I was performing a wedding ceremony in the 82nd Airborne Memorial Chapel for a paratrooper and his new bride.

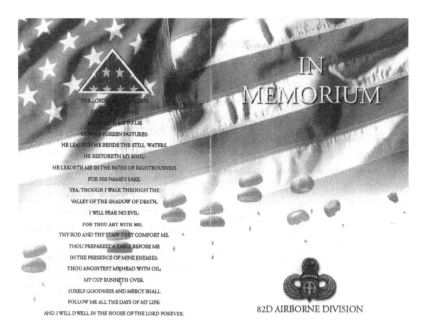

THE LORD IS MY SHEPHERD
I SHALL NOT WANT
HE MAKETH ME TO LIE
DOWN IN GREEN PASTURES:
HE LEADETH ME BESIDE THE STILL WATERS
HE RESTORETH MY SOUL:
HE LEADETH ME IN THE PATHS OF RIGHTEOUSNESS
FOR HIS NAME'S SAKE.
YEA, THOUGH I WALK THROUGH THE
VALLEY OF THE SHADOW OF DEATH,
I WILL FEAR NO EVIL:
FOR THOU ART WITH ME;
THY ROD AND THY STAFF THEY COMFORT ME.
THOU PREPAREST A TABLE BEFORE ME
IN THE PRESENCE OF MINE ENEMIES:
THOU ANOINTEST MY HEAD WITH OIL;
MY CUP RUNNETH OVER.
SURELY GOODNESS AND MERCY SHALL
FOLLOW ME ALL THE DAYS OF MY LIFE:
AND I WILL DWELL IN THE HOUSE OF THE LORD FOREVER.

82D AIRBORNE DIVISION

Bulletin cover for monthly division memorial ceremonies,
and a reminder of all of America's fallen heroes.

Standing behind my father at the Tomb of the Unknown,
watching the changing of the guard. This was with the large
group of WW II and Korean War veterans who traveled to
DC through the efforts of the Honor Flight Network.

121

Offering the Invocation at the annual Charlottesville Dogwood
Festival's Vietnam Memorial annual rededication.

My wife Donna and I after I spoke at a church in New Bern, NC.
At Fort Bragg she worked with the chapel children's programs,
assisted with hosting families for our monthly Division Memorial
Ceremonies, and worked with the "Strong Bonds" program to
support families during periods when units were deployed.

CHAPTER 9

· · · · · · · · · · · · · · · · ·

9/11 AND THE NEW PARADIGM

"Post-9/11 veterans...twice as likely as...
pre-9/11 counterparts to...serve in...combat"[133]

For many, Section 60 represents the high cost required of this generation of our military for the nation's defense. Over 7,000 of our finest have given their lives, over 50,000 physically incurring wounds, and much larger numbers incurring "injuries" to their mental health in this cause. All who have served and still serve since 9/11 have faced an unrelenting challenge. This chapter tries to illustrate just some of the demands they have faced.

Since 9/11, many within our military, active and reserve, and their families, have literally not stopped. That's a long time, twenty years, for less than 1 percent of the population to bear the burden for the safety of the other 99 percent.

During the years, 2007-2011, while at Fort Bragg, my wife and I saw, up close and personal, what a "very tired" Army looks like. When we say Army, we are always thinking of the total Army team, which includes the soldier, his or her dependents, and the Army civilians who help sustain base operations. While America's service members make personal sacrifices while deployed, their families make their own sacrifices on the home front.

At Fort Bragg, we saw the stressors that face every military family. These military families are very strong and resilient, but they pay a heavy price for their country's security. They do very much appreciate all outside support and well wishes.

On a day-to-day basis, however, they find their greatest support comes from others within the "military family." They understand each other like no one else possibly could. At a minimum, America must remind them they are not forgotten.

Particularly, after the Iraq invasion, the tempo of the War on Terror quickly became unsustainable for our active duty forces. The first deployments went into Afghanistan within weeks of 9/11, and by March 2003, the war in Iraq had begun. As I write this, this war isn't over.

While at Fort Bragg, it was not unusual to see someone in an Army uniform with "Overseas Service Bars," indicating five or more years of tours into a theater of war. During every one of those years, someone was at home, anxious they would never see that loved one again. Give that some thought!

As noted, my service at the Pentagon was as a mobilized Army National Guard chaplain. My experience, along with thousands of others, demonstrates that from the very beginning of the War on Terror, there have been Guard and Reserve forces involved. This was absolutely required to offset some of the deployment pressures on the active force.

Without getting into the "weeds," I thought it might be helpful to offer some limited historical context as to the use of the National Guard (Air Force and Army) and other reserves (Air Force, Army, Navy, Marines, and Coast Guard) in our present conflict. From early on in the War on Terror, there was a shift in the use of America's military reserves. The new approach was really a rebalancing of forces under the Total Force Structure.

My focus will be upon the Army's piece. The Army's new model became the "Army Total Force Policy." "The Army Total Force Policy is an on-going effort by the service to transition its reserve component forces, both the Army Reserve and the National Guard into an operational force. The intent is to create a seamless and holistic 'total force' governed by the same interchangeable policies and procedures."[134]

Jules Hurst elaborates on this:

> *During the later periods of the Cold War and during Operations Desert Shield and Desert Storm, the relative stability of the operational environment and large active-duty force made the Army Reserve a strategic reserve—only to serve in major wars, with significant notice. That changed in the years after 9/11, when the active Army's small size caused the Army Reserve to become more of an operational reserve—one routinely tasked to deploy to meet limited demand on known, stable timelines. Now, the increasingly multipolar nature of the international order, relatively small size of the Regular Army, and concentration of combat enablers inside the Army Reserve has caused the Army to continually rely on it to conduct operations.[135]*

At the height of the war, America had over 100,000 troops in Afghanistan and over 150,000 in Iraq. During those heaviest years of conflict, deployments for many active duty Army combat and combat support units were almost on an every-other-year basis. The manpower shortages were so challenging that many Army units were seeing fifteen-month deployments. The stress and toll this takes on those forces and their families are unimaginable.

As recently as January 8, 2021, our total military forces stood at 1,385,000 active duty and 849,000 reserve personnel.[136] Since 9/11, according to the Congressional Research Service, "1,007,061 reservists were involuntarily or voluntarily activated as of June 9, 2020."[137]

If you read those numbers closely, you will notice that many of our reservists were activated more than once. Together, America's military members comprise of only .8 percent of our total population.

During this period, of the 7,000 deaths in either Afghanistan or Iraq, 1,500 of them were Guard and Reserve personnel.[138]

The following statistics from a Pew Research Center study confirms this generation of our uniformed services has paid their dues:

Roughly three-quarters of post-9/11 veterans were deployed at least once, compared with 58 percent of those who served before them. And post-9/11 veterans are about twice as likely as their pre-9/11 counterparts to have served in a combat zone.[139]

> *Because they are more likely to have been deployed and to have seen combat, post-9/11 veterans are also more likely to bear the scars of battle, whether physical or not. Roughly half say they had emotionally traumatic or distressing experiences related to their military service, and about a third say they sought professional help to deal with those experiences.*

In addition, 36% say that—regardless of whether they
have sought help— they think they have suffered from
post-traumatic stress (PTS).[140]

Even with the "drawdowns" in Iraq and Afghanistan, almost 200,000 of our military are still stationed overseas in 177 countries.[141]

Where will we be if the day comes when no one desires to join the military because it is seen as a difficult and thankless job?

·····················

CHAPTER 10

LESSONS LEARNED: AMERICA'S MILITARY SINCE 9/11

*"...recruiting and retention problems...the active
and reserve components... scale back..."[142]*

F OR THOSE WHO HAVE NOT KEPT UP WITH THE PER-
sonnel issues facing our nation's defense needs, I hope this
will be informative.

Our nation is truly blessed that we continue to have so many
of the best of our young men and women step forward to
serve. However, it is starkly evident that even as our population
increases, the number of volunteers that our military requires
is becoming insufficient.

Mark Cancian illustrates this in an article for the Center
for Strategic and International Studies. Concerning the Army,
he writes:

> *FY 2019 plans called for expansion to 1,040,000 by
> FY 2023, and Army officials had talked about much
> higher levels. As recently as July 2017, General Milley
> said: "[B]ased on the tasks that are required, I believe*

*that we need a larger Army...it's not just some arbi-
trary number. We've done the analysis, and we think
we need to be bigger." Army officials had implied a regular force of 500,000 to 510,000.* **However, recruiting
and retention problems have forced both the active
and reserve components to scale back their plans.**

*In FY 2020 the total Army will have an end strength of
1,005,500 and by FY 2024 will grow to only 1,016,500.
Thus, the Army in the 2020s will be at about the level
that it was before the post-9/11 expansion. To its
credit, though, the Army did not reduce its standards
but rather accepted a smaller size.*[143] (emphasis mine)

Did you catch that last line? "The Army did not reduce its
standards but rather accepted a smaller size." For me, this is just
one more way of saying that though we will continue receiving
some of our best into the military, the burden of protecting
America will fall on the shoulders of even smaller numbers of
individuals and families. In other words, the size of our military
is not just about right-sizing our fighting forces, but also about
providing enough personnel to fill this new right size.

For fifty years, every person who has served in any of our
military components has been a volunteer. Since the implemen-
tation of the all-volunteer military, we have seen these volunteers fight and die in places, such as Grenada, Lebanon, Panama,
Somalia, Yemen, Afghanistan, and in two wars with Iraq.

During the last twenty years, our military has been engaged
in America's longest period of sustained conflict. In addition,
to these years of exceptionally high tempo and continual
combat in Iraq and Afghanistan, our armed forces performed
numerous other missions throughout the world. On any given

day, America's military is eliminating some threat, providing humanitarian aide, leading a training mission for allied countries, or patrolling the skies and the world's oceans, seeking to deter some aggressor.

The requirement to fill all of our military personnel needs is not just about projecting or sustaining combat power. Typically, our military is thought of in terms of a war-fighting capability, but the truth is our military is constantly involved in supporting vast efforts of humanitarian relief. These efforts require large numbers of personnel that add to the strain on our forces and their families.

During my time at Fort Bragg, thousands of combat arms personnel were sent to New Orleans, Haiti, Thailand, Japan, the Caribbean, and other places to assist with devastating natural disasters. All of this was in addition to their regularly scheduled deployments.

On two occasions, I experienced such efforts firsthand. First, in 1987, following a major earthquake, I accompanied my National Guard Engineer Battalion on a mission into the jungles of Ecuador. A few years later, I went with this same battalion to Honduras on a humanitarian mission to improve infrastructure in an isolated part of the countryside.

It should be pointed out, even in combat zones, our military doesn't just send trigger pullers but also sends thousands of personnel whose mission is to improve the lives of the local population. A major purpose of these humanitarian missions in a war zone is to alleviate human suffering, but another purpose is to help create environments where the need for combat presence is lessoned.

In Afghanistan and Iraq, great efforts have been made to improve the living standards of the population. I experienced this in Iraq as I worked with civil affairs teams in setting up medical clinics and dispensing school supplies, clothing, food, and clean water operations.

America can take rightful pride in her sons and daughters who continue to step up to defend the country but who also demonstrate to the world the goodness of America.

This generation of our military is as good as any before them, but their morale and willingness to continue serving hinges, in large part, on their country's support. This generation is courageous, skilled, formidably equipped, and this, along with their constant preparation, serves as a deterrent to any potential enemy.

But going forward, maybe more than ever, honorable service to the nation must be seen as a worthy profession, and those potential, future service members must see America as "worthy" of their service.

In any discussion about our military's personnel needs, several concerns become evident. One is the disconcerting trend that fewer and fewer families are bearing a disproportionate burden for our national defense.

In 2013, a Pentagon report detailed that anywhere from 77 percent of Marine recruits to 86 percent of new Air Force recruits had a close relative who had served (Army and Navy numbers were around 80 percent).[144]

A *New York Times* article published in 2020 said these percentages were much the same, with the Army percentage in 2019 at 79 percent.[145]

America is very dependent upon these generational families that continue to fill the roles of our uniform services, but these numbers reinforce the potential separation gap between the average civilian and his or her nation's soldiers.

Speaking for the chief of Naval personnel on this subject, Navy Commander Nate Christensen said, "We believe that this limits both the talent pool from which the Navy draws, as well as the diversity of background in our force, and ultimately could lead to a civil-military divide."[146]

You may have noticed the generational trend in some of the short bios that we included in the book:

Captain Russell "Rusty" B. Rippetoe, an Army Ranger, was the first casualty from Iraq, and had already served in Afghanistan. His father is Lieutenant Colonel Joe Rippetoe, U.S. Army (Ret.), also an Army Ranger, and a two-tour combat veteran of the Vietnam War. That's four combat tours from this one family.

Staff Sergeant Scott Brunkhorst, a paratrooper with the 82nd ABN DIV, killed in Afghanistan, was a third-generation soldier. His grandfather, father, mother, and brother served in the military. Specialist Joseph "Joey" Thierry Caron, also a paratrooper with the 82nd ABN DIV, who lost his life in Afghanistan, was a third-generation soldier. He was named after his grandfather, Joseph, who was a Vietnam War veteran.

Specialist Lori Ann Piestewa, U.S. Army, was the first Native American woman killed in U.S. military service. She was a Hopi Indian and a third-generation soldier. Her grandfather served in World War II, and her father, Terry Piestewa, was a Vietnam War veteran.

Staff Sergeant Laurent J. West, a paratrooper with the 82nd ABN DIV, killed in Iraq, was from an Army family; his father is Lieutenant Colonel Larry West, U.S. Army (Ret.).

Captain John S. McCain III, U.S. Navy (Ret.), from a third-generation Navy family, volunteered to go to war; the son of Admiral John S. McCain Jr. and grandson of Admiral John S. McCain Sr.

Later, the fourth generation of McCains went to war, as two of Senator McCain's sons, one a Marine, and one a Navy pilot, served in Afghanistan.

These are poignant examples of how some families carry such an oversized burden for liberty's sake, and the trends are getting worse. Within the general populace, many of our citizens don't know a single person in the military. A comment I have heard more than once is, "The military went to war, and America went to the mall."

Robert Poole, in his article, "Where the Modern Wars Hit Home," writes, "For most Americans, the longest war in the history of the United States...that began with the Sept. 11 attacks, has taken place largely out of sight, the casualties piling up in Afghanistan and Iraq while normal life continued on the home front, with...none of the shared sacrifice of the country's earlier conflicts."[147]

I'm certainly not making the point that every American should or could serve in our nation's military. For one thing, most Americans couldn't qualify for the age and physical standards required. However, I am making the point that those who do serve in our military cannot be taken for granted, and as President Kennedy said, "If freedom is to survive...it will require the sacrifice...of every citizen."[148]

· · · · · · · · · · · · · · · · · · ·

CHAPTER 11

FORSAKEN HEROES

"Private First Class Johnson...
threw himself upon the grenade."

O
N ONE LEVEL, THIS BOOK IS A SIMPLE REMINDER
that true patriotism includes remembering the patriots. Expressing gratitude to those who fight our wars is the absolute least we can do.

"Forsaken heroes" is an anguished thought. Yet, those words describe an entire generation of our nation's war fighters; specifically, a generation of returning Vietnam War veterans who were horribly mistreated by many of their fellow Americans. It's the politicians, not the soldiers, who choose when our nation goes to war, so how is it ever fair that the soldier should bear the burden of a nation's disdain over political decisions?

Many descriptions of the Vietnam War focus far more upon its detractors than upon its heroes. Many of those heroes were young Americans who volunteered their service to their country. **Two-thirds of the soldiers, sailors, airmen, coast-guardsmen, and Marines who served in Vietnam were not drafted, but volunteered.**[149]

Even in the face of their fellow Americans spewing hate toward them and trying to negate their sacrifices, literally tens of thousands of young men and young women continued to step up.

Certainly, the Vietnam War was one of our longest and most difficult conflicts, and as of now, compared to the War on Terror, it incurred far more casualties; over 58,000 deaths compared to around 7,000 up to this point.

In some very important ways, the fighting of the War on Terror, with the heavy use of National Guard and Reserve assets, more resembles our military structures from World War I, World War II, and Korea than that of our military structure in Vietnam.

Many believe politics contributed to the eventual lack of support for the Vietnam veterans. It was primarily for political reasons that President Johnson made a deliberate decision not to call up the National Guard or the Reserves, with few exceptions, to serve in Vietnam. Some say this was a combination of domestic politics, concern for his reelection and international politics, and concern of bringing the Chinese into the war.

He made this decision against the strong objections of Secretary of Defense McNamara and the Joint Chiefs of Staff. Johnson was "…bucking 200 years of precedent. In every war since the American Revolution, the militia—which evolved into the National Guard and Reserves—was mobilized to fight."[150]

Many felt that not using the Guard and Reserves contributed to the lack of support that our Vietnam combatants received. "Gen. Creighton Abrams, who commanded U. S. forces in Vietnam from 1968 to 1972, wanted to ensure the guard was not sidelined in future conflicts."[151] Professor Andrew Wiest said, "he [General Abrams] felt that one of the great failings of the Vietnam War was that the National Guard was never called up, and the nation was never engaged."[152]

Whatever the reasons, the generation of Vietnam War veterans were not just the forgotten by so many fellow citizens, they were the forsaken by so many fellow citizens. All Americans who value liberty should see the undeserved, despicable treatment that Vietnam veterans received as a grave travesty that must never happen again.

World War II produced 473 Medal of Honor recipients. The Vietnam War saw 261 Medals of Honor awarded.[153] Both reflect very heroic actions. But based on the far fewer veterans of the Vietnam War, compared to the 16,000,000 World War II veterans, a much higher percentage of Medals of Honor were awarded to Vietnam veterans. This statistic is another validation of the heroic service of those Americans who fought in Vietnam.

Many see the Vietnam War as the most "unpopular" war in America's history. Even if that's true, what is often overlooked is the patriotism of those who did serve. It is an amazing statistic that only one-third of the Vietnam-era veterans were drafted into service, while **two-thirds of World War II veterans entered service through the draft.**[154]

Whatever else one might say about the veterans of the Vietnam War, they were indeed a courageous and patriotic lot who did their duty.

Answering a draft call is certainly a patriotic thing to do (my own father was drafted into the Army in World War II). Yet, **two-thirds of the US military wh served in the Vietnam War, and approximately 70 percent of the names on "The Wall" volunteered for duty**.[155]

No segment of the American family was more committed to serve in Vietnam than Native American Indians. Of the 42,000 American Indians who served in Vietnam, 90 percent were volunteers.[156] "Approximately one of every four eligible

American Indian people served, compared with one of 12 in the general population. Of those, 226 died in action and five received the Medal of Honor."[157]

Many of our Vietnam War vets endured intense and extended combat. "The average infantryman in the South Pacific during World War II saw about 40 days of combat in four years. The average infantryman in Vietnam saw about 240 days of combat in one year thanks to the mobility of the helicopter."[158]

In addition to the over 58,000 who died, three times that many were wounded, many incurring devastating wounds, not counting all of the damaging effects of the Agent Orange exposure, which has killed many more.

If there is any shame tied to the Vietnam War, it certainly does not belong to the vets who fought the war; the shame lies upon their fellow citizens who either treated them in disgraceful ways or condoned such disgraceful behavior. Despite such disdain, the American combatants in Vietnam exhibited incredible bravery and should forever hold their heads high.

All of the many folks and those I would later get to know who served in Vietnam certainly are great Americans. I had an uncle and two cousins who fought in Vietnam, as well as a number of close friends, and all were incredible individuals. They were the "give you the shirt off their backs," kind of folks.

A high school classmate and friend of mine was killed in Vietnam in 1971. Army Specialist Donald Hamrick was a terrific person, and the world lost a bright light when he was killed. Donald was a non-pretentious guy, and kept everyone around him in good humor with his easygoing nature and his laughter. Donald Hamrick was smart, hard working, and had great plans for the future, including college. Donald's bright future ended at age twenty-one because his country said they needed him to go and defend freedom, and he answered the call.

THE VIETNAM WAR: A WAR OF HEROES

It is often said in combat that when the battle starts, you are not necessarily fighting for some grand purpose, but you are fighting for the guys on your right and left. Many a soldier has given his or her life attempting to protect buddies or died trying to rescue a wounded or fallen comrade.

The quintessential example of this is when a soldier jumps on a live grenade to save his fellow soldiers, as we saw in the actions of Specialist Ross McGinnis in Iraq. There is a reason why this example is so often mentioned. I believe it's simply because this act is easily visualized and has indeed been repeated over and over. Even the phrase "jumping on a live grenade" has almost become a metaphor for other types of life and death sacrifices.

Often in our society, there are events that challenge our unity and separate us between races, politics, sub-cultures, religion, and socio-economics. From personal experience and much reading, I have discovered that of all places, it is in the heat of battle where our nation's war fighters show us what "one nation, under God" look like. This is seen most readily in those instantaneous decisions when an American warrior gives his life to save his fellow American combatants, regardless of race, politics, or other differences.

PRIVATE FIRST CLASS JAMES ANDERSON JR., USMC, VIETNAM WAR

The first African-American Marine to be awarded the Congressional Medal of Honor fits this mold. Private First Class James Anderson Jr. left college, and on February 17, 1966, at the age of nineteen, **voluntarily** enlisted in the US Marine Corps, and a year later, was mortally wounded on February 28, 1967, in Quang Tri Province, South Vietnam. Private First Class Anderson gave "the last full measure" in service to his country and for his fellow Marines. He was assigned to 2nd Platoon, Company F, 2nd Battalion, 3rd Marines, 3rd Marine Division.[159]

His platoon was sent to extricate a besieged reconnaissance patrol when they came under heavy enemy small arms and automatic weapons fire. During the fighting, a grenade landed near Private First Class Anderson's head, and without hesitation, he pulled it under his chest and curled around it. He was killed instantly, but because of his actions, other fellow Marines, Black and White, were saved.[160]

Private First Class Anderson was posthumously awarded the Congressional Medal of Honor on August 21, 1968, by President Lyndon Johnson. Another reminder from Private First Class Anderson's heroic service is that Americans of all races have voluntarily served and offered their lives on the belief their country was worthy of their sacrifice. His body was returned to Los Angeles, and his burial was at Lincoln Memorial Park, Los Angeles County, where his parents, James Sr. and Aggiethine Anderson were presented the flag that covered his coffin.[161]

"Semper Fi," Private First Class James Anderson Jr.! May your country be "always faithful" to you!

PRIVATE FIRST CLASS RALPH H. JOHNSON, USMC, VIETNAM WAR

1ST LIEUTENANT PATRICK C. "CLEBE" MCCLARY, USMC, VIETNAM WAR

In the mid '80s, I had the personal privilege of meeting a Vietnam vet whose life was saved by a fellow Marine who jumped on a live grenade to save his fellow Marines. The life stories of Clebe McClary and Ralph Johnson were forever intertwined on March 5, 1968.[162]

The short version of this story points out that 1st Lieutenant Clebe McClary and Private First Class Ralph Johnson were both "low country" natives of South Carolina; Johnson from Charleston, and McClary from Georgetown. In the midst of the growing death tolls in Vietnam, both had **volunteered to join** the Marines, and eventually, each was assigned to Company A, First Reconnaissance Battalion, First Marine Division.

It is a known fact that United States Marine Corps Force Reconnaissance is one of the Marine Corps' special operations capable forces. Their missions are "behind the lines," and done with stealth and in small teams.

My son-in-law, Roger W. Johnson Jr. is the son of a "Recon" Marine. Recon Marines have a unique skill set, and his dad, Roger Sr., developed those skills in the Corps. He had an ability to analyze, design, and solve complex mechanical or construction issues. I had the opportunity to work with him once on a project, and his ability to visualize solutions to problems was uncanny. He could build anything, and he could fix anything. My son-in-law gained those abilities from his father. At one time, they worked together at Roger W. Johnson and Son Contractors.

Roger Sr. died young, at only fifty-four years old. In his mid-forties, he underwent a heart transplant, and eventually died from heart-related issues. But from his time in the Corps until his death: once a Marine, always a Marine.

Roger Jr. also developed other skills from his father. In addition to his professional engineering career of designing institutional computer infrastructure and cyber security, our son-in-law coaches a university "shotgun" team. At the 2021 National Collegiate Clay Target Championships in San Antonio, he coached the team, which included his son, to a second place in the nation in their division. The children of military parents do indeed benefit from their parents' service and experience.

In the early morning hours of March 5, 1968, a fifteen-man reconnaissance team, led by Lieutenant McClary on his nineteenth recon mission, was manning an observation post on Hill 146, overlooking the Quad Duc Duc Valley of Vietnam, deep in enemy territory. They came under heavy attack by a well-equipped enemy platoon, and during the engagement, a grenade was thrown into the three-man fighting hole occupied by Private First Class Johnson and two fellow Marines.[163]

Private First Class Johnson shouted a warning, and without hesitation, threw himself upon the grenade, absorbing most of the blast. His actions saved the lives of two fellow Marines, one of them was Lieutenant Clebe McClary. Private First Class Ralph Johnson, for his selfless actions, was posthumously awarded the Congressional Medal of Honor.[164]

I didn't know Private First Class Johnson, yet, what he did has become personal to me. That's because I do know 1st Lieutenant Clebe McClary, USMC (Ret.), one of the Marines who survived due to Ralph Johnson's selflessness. It is a most somber feeling to be in the presence of a man who is alive because of another's self sacrifice. On several occasions, I felt the emotion in his voice as Lieutenant McClary described that day when his fellow Marine died so he might live.

Lieutenant McClary's recovery was long and hard, and he almost succumbed to his wounds, among which were internal injuries, the loss of an eye, his left arm, and damage to his right hand.[165]

Private First Class Johnson offered the sacrifice of himself instantaneously, without a second thought. He died for fellow Marines, fellow Americans, without any thought that they were of different races.

Ralph Johnson's actions and the depth of his love for others is a call to every American to strive for a new day in race relations in America. If more Americans had the vision of a Ralph Johnson, we could see beyond the things that divide us and see one another's value. Private First Class Johnson's example demonstrates it's possible to put aside our prejudices and seek the well-being of others before self.

Obviously, since he didn't have time to think about it, Ralph Johnson's quick actions confirm what was already engrained in his heart, even before that fateful moment came. He is an American that must not be forgotten. It was not just his fellow Marines for whom he died, but he died for all his fellow Americans.

Clebe McClary is not the only American who owes a debt to Ralph Johnson. America's gratitude for him can never be reduced to a one day a year, a Memorial Day event. Each time, I am privileged to recite the Pledge of Allegiance "...to the flag, and to the Republic for which it stands..." and every time I stand for our national anthem, I believe I'm bringing honor to Ralph Henry Johnson and those like him who have given me that privilege.

For his actions, Private First Class Ralph H. Johnson became one of the 261 Vietnam veterans awarded the Medal of Honor. His picture hangs in the Ralph Henry Johnson VA Medical Center in Charleston that was named after him in 2009.[166] On March 24, 2017, a new Navy guided missile destroyer, the USS Ralph Johnson, was commissioned.[167] Now, once again, Private First Class Ralph Johnson is on patrol.

CLEBE MCCLARY AND BILLY CASPER

Another hero in Clebe McClary's life is a man named Billy Casper—yes, that Billy Casper. During last year's Masters Golf Tournament television coverage, I saw excerpts of the story describing an encounter in 1968 that Lieutenant McClary had with professional golfer, Billy Casper, in a military hospital in Japan. Wanting to hear more about this, I found an article by Jim McCabe in golfweek.usatoday.com.

I highly recommend you find and read the entire article. But the story is so powerful I'm sharing some excerpts from the article. This story reminds us a well-placed word in a given situation just might be life-changing or life-saving.

Though the two had never met, this article is about one man's words of hope that were offered to another man who had no hope. Here are highlights:

> It was 1968, the height of the Vietnam War, and Casper, in the prime of his golf career, was off to Japan to play some offseason tournaments.

> While he was there, did he want to visit some wounded American troops, who had been convalescing from Vietnam? Casper said yes, because, well, that's his

warm-hearted nature. "I was recently asked by a man what I want to be remembered for," Casper said. "I told him, 'I want to be remembered for how I loved my fellow man.'"

That day at a hospital in Japan may have shown Casper at his warmest because when he looked over at a bed and saw a young man who had been wounded to a point where he could barely be recognized, the golfer moved closer. A doctor told him not to bother, that Marine 1st Lieutenant Patrick Cleburne "Clebe" McClary "was ready to die," said Casper, but something made him approach the man.

"I will never forget that day," said McClary, who on March 3, 1968, had been wounded during his 19th reconnaissance mission in Vietnam. McClary lost his left arm and his left eye and laid in that bed that day thinking one thing. "I'd given up," he said. "I wanted to die, and I'd have died right there if not for him."

Casper, by 1968 a two-time U.S. Open champion and one of the most prolific winners on the PGA Tour, sensed McClary's hopelessness as he approached the man.

He put his arm around me, leaned in and said, "God could use you today. Don't give up," McClary said. "Then he thanked me for what I had done for our country and said, 'God bless you.'"

Somehow, McClary found the resolve to fight. Somehow, he survived, left that hospital in Japan, and settled in his native South Carolina, near Myrtle Beach. Years went by and he often wondered about this gentle golfer who had brought out the fight in him, but there was nothing more than that. "I mean, I didn't know golf from polo," McClary said.

But one day more than a year ago, McClary was down at his beach house talking with a neighbor, a guy named Jay Haas, telling him his life story. The left arm and left eye had been lost in 'Nam, and his life should have been ended in a hospital in Japan, if not for a golfer. With that, Haas' ear perked up. "I said, 'Who was the golfer?'" Haas said. "He said, 'Billy Casper. Do you know him?'"

Haas smiled, then made it his mission to reunite McClary and Casper. The Masters would offer the perfect opportunity. Casper, the 1970 champion, would never miss the pilgrimage. Neither would Haas, who competed 22 times at the Masters and whose son Bill is a regular participant these years and whose uncle, the irrepressible Bob Goalby, won in 1968.

The first chance fell apart Monday when rain washed out the day's action at Augusta National, but on Tuesday the story unfolded to perfection. Haas met McClary up behind the clubhouse, found Goalby, who tracked down Casper and then ... well, it is said that Augusta National is a magical place, and here was proof positive that it is.

"You never know what effect you're going to have on another human being," said Cervantes, who watched the emotions unfold alongside her mother, Shirley, other family members, Haas and Goalby.

When finally the long, emotional hug was over and the pictures were taken, Casper and McClary had so much to say to each other. Forty-six years is a long, long time, but the Marine told the golfer that he had thought of him often. The golfer nodded, because he felt similarly.

McClary told Casper that he was proud of his life. Not because of the Silver Star or Bronze Star or the three Purple Hearts that he had been presented. It wasn't for the book he had written, "Living Proof," either. No, he was proud because he had heeded Casper's advice to stay strong and find faith in God.

But make no mistake about it: "You're the reason he's living. He was ready to die," one of McClary's friends said to Casper.

McClary, a motivational speaker who has given talks in all 50 states, smiled, wiped away tears, and nodded his head. "My guardian angel," he said, pointing to Casper.

McClary reached into his pocket and handed his business card to someone standing nearby. It read: "I'm just a nobody, that wants to tell everybody, about somebody, that can save anybody."[168]

Traveling all over the world and to all fifty states, Clebe McClary and his wife, Deanna, have made it their life calling to pass on those same "life-saving" words of encouragement that Billy Casper shared with Clebe. If you would like to know more about the McClary's unique journey, they have each written inspiring books: *Living Proof* by Lieutenant Clebe McClary and *Committed to Love* by Deanna McClary.

Fortunately for America, after returning home, many Vietnam veterans pushed aside their country's rejection and became some of America's greatest leaders nationally and within their respective communities. That is certainly true in my community where many of our local service organizations, and civic clubs, are led by Vietnam vets.

LIEUTENANT COMMANDER JOHN S. McCAIN III, U.S. NAVY, VIETNAM WAR

"HONOR-DUTY-COUNTRY"

The Vietnam War produced thousands of heroes, and everyone who served honorably has a story worth telling. But, for me, when thinking of a hero from this war, I keep coming back to John McCain. The one word summary of his Vietnam service is the word *honor*.

The first time I heard the story of John McCain's refusal to accept early release from the "Hanoi Hilton," I thought to myself, *that man is the real deal.* In my thinking, this is what a true war hero looks like. Politics aside, this man, while he was a prisoner of war in Hanoi, was offered the opportunity to leave imprisonment at the Hanoi Hilton ahead of his fellow POWs, and he flatly refused. I'm convinced his Vietnam War sacrifices are not as appreciated as they should be.

John S. McCain, III was truly a "Navy brat." If, for some reason, you are not aware, this is not a pejorative term, but actually an affectionate way of describing a child who grew up within the military culture; in this case, the Navy culture. John McCain was a namesake of both his father and grandfather. His grandfather, Admiral John S. McCain Sr., and his father, Admiral John S. McCain Jr., retired as four-star admirals in the Navy, which was a first for a father and son.[169] Another family tradition was to attend and graduate from the Naval Academy. For the youngest John, the graduation part was the challenge. John McCain, from early in his naval career, often challenged the system, and this is evident in his low class rank of 894 out of 899 at the Academy.[170]

His earlier years in uniform were not necessarily exemplary, but I want to focus upon his service during the Vietnam War. In 1967, Navy Lieutenant Commander John McCain, by then an A-4 Skyhawk pilot, and "...his deep-rooted sense of duty compelled him to specifically request a combat assignment."[171]

He had only flown five missions when he almost died on the deck of the super carrier, the Forrestal. On July 29, 1967, as he was preparing for takeoff, a missile was accidentally fired from a nearby fighter, striking the fuel tank on McCain's Skyhawk. That set off explosions that would kill 134 crew members and damage the Forrestal so severely it took two years to make repairs. McCain put himself in harm's way and saved the lives of multiple fellow pilots.[172]

Later that year in October, he volunteered again for a combat tour, and this time, he was assigned to the smaller and undermanned Oriskany. His squadron was called the Saints, and during a one-year period, one-third of its pilots were either killed or captured.[173]

On October 26, 1967, on his twenty-third mission, and his first over Hanoi, his A-4 was shot down. He was injured from the ejection and a hard landing in a lake, which resulted in both arms and his right knee broken.[174]

He was dragged from the lake, beaten with a rifle butt, and bayonetted in the foot. He was taken to the Hanoi Hilton, a French-built prison, where his captors refused to treat his wounds. Lieutenant Commander McCain spent five and a half years as a prisoner of war. He almost died shortly after his capture due to his wounds being untreated.[175]

When his captors realized his father was Admiral John McCain Jr., the war commander for the Pacific, for propaganda purposes, offered Lieutenant Commander McCain an early release. John McCain refused to accept freedom before those who had been held longer because that was the military's code. His refusal to accept the offer meant another three and a half years in captivity and added torture.[176]

"For the next several years, the high-profile POW was subjected to prolonged brutal treatment and spent two years in solitary confinement in a windowless 10-by-10-foot cell."[177]

"His torturer, known as Cat, singled him out for what was probably the harshest sustained persecution of any prisoner at the plantation. For over a year, he was trussed with ropes and/or beaten for two to three hour stretches at a time."[178]

He said his lowest point came after extensive beatings that broke his ribs and broke his left arm again, that he finally signed a vaguely-worded "confession." Even though he was beaten and tortured daily, and though the document he signed really didn't say anything specific, McCain described it as his disgrace. "I was ashamed," he wrote in his 1999 memoir, *Faith of My Fathers*. "I shook, as if my disgrace were a fever."

John McCain had much to gain if he had accepted the early release offer, and the only thing he had to lose, if he accepted it, was his honor. But **his honor was worth more to him than his freedom.**

After the Paris Peace Accords were signed, the prisoners were finally released in the order in which they had been captured. When John McCain made it home, he was thirty-six years old and emaciated. Once home, he could never raise his arms high enough to even comb his hair, and he would forever walk with a noticeable limp.[179]

One may agree or disagree with Senator McCain's politics, but John McCain's service in Vietnam as a combat volunteer and the torture he endured as a prisoner of war qualifies him as another of our great patriots who deserve our respect.

Along with many others, this man put country and others above self. Captain John S. McCain III, U.S. Navy (Ret.) is not buried at Arlington National Cemetery, alongside his father and grandfather, but at the United States Naval Academy Cemetery in Annapolis, MD.

NEVER AGAIN: "...VETERANS... DISRESPECTED."

Despite seeing their service unappreciated by so many, the majority of Vietnam War veterans remain some of America's most patriotic citizens. During the years 2007–2011, I traveled across the country conducting funerals for fallen paratroopers. Whether in northern California, the suburbs of Chicago, the small towns of Ohio, or Arkansas, I always witnessed an outpouring of support from Vietnam War veterans. These vets were determined, as many of them often said, **"Never again will one generation of veterans let another generation of veterans be disrespected."**

The "Patriot Guard Riders," a group of Vietnam veterans, continue to provide support at the funerals of active duty service members killed in action. The motto of this group is simply, "Standing for Those Who Stood for Us." This organization was founded in 2005 as their website says, "to shield families of fallen heroes from those that would disrupt the services of their loved ones."[180]

Contingents of these Patriot Guard Riders, themselves great patriots in my view, would often provide inspiring motorcycle escorts from funeral sites to burial sites. Sometimes these motorcycle escorts would wind through a community for over a mile, paying respect to a fallen hero.

On several occasions where I was present, the Patriot Guard Riders shielded families from a small but loud group of protesters. In Joplin, MO, I remember them putting their motorcycles between the protestors and the family as the family processed to and from the local high school auditorium where the funeral service was conducted.

Another organization established by Vietnam veterans is Rolling Thunder Washington, DC, Inc. This origination, founded in 1987, started as an annual motorcycle demonstration to bring attention to the POW/MIA situation. "The first run (Memorial Day) in 1988, had roughly 2500 motorcycles and riders demanding that the U. S. government account for all POW/MIA's."[181] With over a million riders and spectators combined, it has become the world's largest single-day motorcycle event.[182]

Their Mission Statement emphasizes that they remain committed through their annual Memorial Day ride to ensure those "…service members that were abandoned after the Vietnam War…" will never be forgotten. Their Mission Statement adds: "The Rolling Thunder Washington, DC First Amendment

Demonstration Run has also evolved into a display of patriotism and respect for all who defend our country."[183]

· · · · · · · · · · · · · · · · · ·

CHAPTER 12

THE WAR TO END ALL WARS, OR MAYBE NOT

"The sign over the gate still reads Arbeit macht frei."

B EFORE WE DISCUSS AMERICA'S PARTICIPATION in World War II, I want to establish some historical reference points. World peace following the "Great War," or the "war to end all wars," lasted less than twenty years. Once World War II finally got its name, the "Great War," would pick up the title of World War I.

The next world war had somewhat of a staggered start. Apart from various border clashes and the Manchurian invasion of 1931, the second Sino-Japanese War began in earnest on July 7, 1937, with the Japanese invading China.[184]

By September 1, 1939, Germany invaded Poland, which brought in France and Britain; Europe was embroiled in another war.

World War II truly became a "world war" in 1941. On June 22, 1941, Hitler declared war on the Soviet Union and opened the eastern front. When the Japanese attacked Pearl Harbor on December 7, 1941, Germany also declared war on the United States. The Japanese also attacked British and Dutch assets, and the battle lines were drawn in the Pacific.

The world was truly at war as never before, and the opposing sides were settled; the Axis powers: Germany, Italy, and Japan versus the Allies, chief of which were: the United States, Great Britain, France, the Soviet Union, and China.[185]

THE FINAL SOLUTION TO THE FINAL SOLUTION

From my experience, no one who has seen war up close and personal wants war. However, using World War II as an example, I believe war can become a necessary imperative. From my perspective, the Allies' response to the Axis was absolutely justified and required of civilized nations.

The loss of over seventy-five million human beings as a result of the war, most of them civilians, is absolutely horrendous.[186] Without a doubt, war is hell!

These tens of millions of lives were lost due to the megalomania of Hitler, Tojo, and Mussolini. Most of the civilian deaths were not just collateral to the fighting, but their deaths were the intended goal.

Mussolini was a minor player compared to Hitler and Hideki Tojo, but he was responsible for murdering over 100,000 Ethiopians, including the "infamous 3-day massacre of up to 20,000 in ...Addis Ababa."[187]

The Japanese had their own genocidal episodes. "From the invasion of China in 1937 to the end of WW II, the Japanese military murdered ...over 10,000,000 people."[188] The "Nanking Massacre" alone saw between 200,000 and 300,000 Chinese slaughtered.[189] The "Final Solution" of the Nazi's "...envisioned killing 11 million Jews. They succeeded in murdering 6 million."[190]

"In addition to the six million Jews, an additional five to six million ethnic Poles, other slavs...and other ethnic and minority groups..." were exterminated.[191]

One way the Nazis justified their wanton murders is seen in their coining phrases for persons they deemed not fit to live. The terms "Lebensunwertes Leben" ("life unworthy of life), and "Untermensch" (subhumans) entered the Nazi vocabulary.[192] Either of these descriptions reflected the Nazi view the world was better off without such persons.

The nomadic Romani people were so classified and Hitler authorized the murder of as many as 500,000 of these Roma and Sinti people.[193]

Our so-called ally, the Soviets, was also complicit in the great loss of millions of innocent civilians during this period, including Poles, Ukrainians, and their own Russian people.

Another irrefutable justification for World War II was the fact Hitler had scientists working on a nuclear bomb. His possession of such weapons, along with his emphasis on long-range rockets, would have put him a position to wipe out Moscow, London, and even New York, as well as hold the world hostage to his demonic plans to reshape humanity. It's simply unimaginable to think of such a maniac having an arsenal of atomic weapons.

"The United States government became aware of the German nuclear program in August 1939. The United States was in a race to develop an atomic bomb believing whoever had the bomb first would win the war."[194]

It required tremendous sacrifices, but an intervention became necessary to stop the evil that had been unleashed in the world.

I cannot grasp the point of view that under no circumstances can war ever be justified. My answer is simplistic, but

I believe analogous. I might ask someone who holds that point of view: "If a family member of yours was being assaulted or murdered, would you think it inappropriate if a policeman came to their aid?"

When innocent millions are being assaulted, or worse, and cannot defend themselves, how can it be wrong for someone to rescue them? In my world construct, it would have been immoral if there were no intervention during the Holocaust. Self-preservation is moral for an individual, and also for a people or nation. And when the defenseless innocent of the world cry for help, surely, civilized people cannot let such cries fall on deaf ears.

I'm absolutely not saying all wars are fought for virtuous or moral reasons. I am saying there can be circumstances where going to war is the only moral option.

Slavery ended in America as a result of a war, not from dialogue.

Hitler proved to Chamberlain and Reynaud that verbal demands and diplomacy would not end his ambitions.

If Hitler had not been stopped, does anyone honestly think he would not have completed the "Final Solution" and who knows what else? His plan was to totally eradicate every Jew and other "undesirables" from Europe. He had killed six million, but he had his eyes on the surviving five million Jews in Europe.

History's purveyors of great evil have arisen often, and have much in common. They are easily recognizable by their actions of inflicting wanton death and atrocities upon the defenseless for their own egotistical agendas.

While in Iraq, in late October 2006, my chaplain assistant, Staff Sergeant Bennet, and I attended the trial of Saddam Hussein. The trial that day focused upon Saddam's genocidal gassing of the Kurds in March of 1988. Five thousand men, women, children, and even infants in their mother's arms, died a painful death, and thousands more were wounded.[195]

We listened to survivors tell of the horrible suffering from the effects of the gas and watching their loved ones die. Some showed their scars from beatings and shootings from Saddam's soldiers; others testified to seeing entire families, from infants to grandparents, slaughtered.

This is the same Saddam Hussein who orchestrated the Iran-Iraq War that resulted in the deaths of "an estimated one million Iranians, and ...500,000 for Iraq."[196] This man sacrificed untold numbers of innocent human beings' lives for the sake of his political ambitions.

At the trial, he stood up in his white shirt and suit, holding a large copy of the Koran, and declared his innocence. It was difficult to envision, but this man, obviously, felt he was justified when he tried to eliminate those he saw as impediments to his power.

Hitler may not have convinced all seventy million Germans in 1940 that whatever he said was good for the country, but the sad truth is many millions did go along with his plans. Somehow, he convinced the nation that due to their "superiority," it was in their best interest to eliminate millions of "lesser" human beings.

Three of my experiences allow me to better visualize the tremendous anguish caused by the actions of Hitler and persons of his ilk.

KING DAVID HOTEL

In 1988, I visited Israel, and since I was a Rotarian, I wanted to attend a Rotary meeting. I discovered there was a Rotary Club having their monthly meeting at the King David Hotel in Jerusalem, and I attended. One of the Jerusalem Rotarians was an older gentleman who invited me to sit with him. Over the luncheon meal, he shared some of his life story. He was Jewish and was born in Germany in the 1920s. Sometime in the mid 1930s, his entire family was sent to a concentration camp, and each was given a numbered tattoo on the arm.

"In the early years of existence of concentration camps, in Germany, …prisoners …had a chance of leaving the camp after three months, or at the most after a year."[197]

My new friend told me that after some months in the camp, he and his sister were allowed to leave. The hope was his parents could join them later. That never happened. They never saw or heard from their parents ever again.

He and his sister made their way out of the country and eventually to Palestine, later becoming Israeli citizens in 1948. I saw the numbers tattooed on his arm, and heard his wrenching story of remembering his father and mother's sobs as he left them. I realized one of Hitler's victims, whose life was forever changed, was standing in my presence.

AUSCHWITZ-BIRKENAU

As I noted earlier, another personal encounter that I had with Hitler's "new world order" came in 1990. I visited the site of the Auschwitz concentration camp, not far from Krakow, Poland. "Auschwitz, also called Auschwitz-Birkenau, was Nazi Germany's largest concentration camp and extermination camp."[198]

When I entered the main gate, like the 1.3 million before me, I passed under the large gate sign that reads, "Arbeit macht frei" ("work makes one free").

As I entered, the feeling of a heavy darkness was overwhelming and pervasive. Seeing the preserved artifacts, viewing the photographs, and reading the accounts of those who died here created a sense of grief and despair, and the question for humanity, "How was this ever allowed to happen?"

The Holocaust Memorial Museum in Washington, DC, estimates that 1.3 million people were sent to this combined concentration and death camp in Poland. Of this number, 1.1 million were Jews, of which, close to a million died in the camp.[199]

MISKOLC SYNAGOGUE

In 1996, I had the opportunity to visit the Hungarian city of Miskolc. Four of us spent the night there on our way to visit Bratislova, Slovakia. Miskolc is a city in northeastern Hungary, near the Slovakian border. Prior to World War II, there was a large Jewish community of over 10,000 who resided there.

"Between May 15 and July 9, 1944, some 438,000 Hungarian Jews were shipped on 147 trains to Birkenau."[200] It was during this roundup of Hungarian Jews in 1944 that "Miskolc's Jews were rounded up and deported to Auschwitz...of the approximately 10,000 Jews deported from Miskolc, 400 survived."[201]

While we were in Miskolc, our group of four visited the large, beautiful synagogue in the city that was built in 1861. This synagogue is often called the Kazinczy Street Synagogue. Inside the synagogue, huge decorative columns supported the vaulted ceiling, and the walls and ceiling were covered with incredible geometric designs.

But the most moving aspect of our visit was seeing the pictures of many of the thousands of Miskolc Jews who worshiped in this synagogue, and who were taken away and never returned. Their only crime: they were Jews.

AMERICAN LIBERATORS

All of the American veterans who served in World War II, and especially those who gave their lives, did not just contribute to a better world but actually saved the world. Their sacrifices helped end the tyrannical actions of Adolph Hitler, Benito Mussolini, and the Japanese High Command.

As Hitler and Tojo's actions dehumanized and devalued human life, the deaths of our fallen service members sent the opposite message. As they gave their lives, their actions loudly declared the worth and value of all persons.

Like many other World War II units, my father's 65th INF Division and my father-in-law's 4th INF Division helped liberate Nazi concentration camps and death camps. These liberators saw indescribable, inhuman atrocities. It started with families being wrenched apart and systematically either worked to death, starved to death, or murdered in mass killings.[202]

"NOT, LEST THEY FORGET," BUT "HOW SOON THEY FORGET."

Despite the historical magnitude of World War II, and the great sacrifices of the over 400,000 Americans service members who died, the following illustration points out that for far too many Americans, World War II has receded into oblivion. This demonstrates how easy it is for all of America's wars and warriors to simply become "just a story in the past."

From Stud Terkel's, *The Good War*:

> *In 1982, a woman of thirty, doing just fine in Washington, D.C, let me know how things are in her precinct: "I can't relate to World War II. It's in the*

schoolbook texts, that's all. Battles that were won, battles that were lost. Or costume dramas you see on TV. It's just a story in the past. It's so distant, so abstract I don't get myself up in a bunch about it."[203]

When I hear such things, I'm more committed than ever to the position "these honored dead" need someone to speak for them.

"IF YE BREAK FAITH WITH US WHO DIE WE SHALL NOT SLEEP..."[204]

I want to be a voice for "the fallen," to ask, as John McCrae does in his 1915 poem, "In Flanders Field," "...that they not 'break faith with us who die.'"[205]

As I shared in the Prologue, I was asked to read this poem at a Royal British cemetery in Iraq for a Remembrance Day service in 2006. From that moment, when I shared it over the graves of fallen British Commonwealth soldiers and airmen who were killed and buried on foreign soil, I "heard" it as a soldier's plea to never be forgotten. John McCrae died on foreign soil, and his remains are buried near Flanders Field.[206]

"In Flanders Field"

By Lieutenant John McCrae
November 30, 1872–January 28, 1918

> *We are the Dead. Short days ago, We lived, felt dawn, saw sunset glow*

> *Loved and were loved, and now we lie, In Flanders fields... If ye break*

> *faith with us who die We shall not sleep"*[207]

·················

CHAPTER 13

WORLD WAR II— TOTAL WAR—TOTAL PARTICIPATION

"…One Team—One Fight…"

A S OF THE 1940 CENSUS, THE UNITED STATES POP-ulation stood at 132,164,569.[208] During World War II and by V-J Day on August 15, 1945, over 16,000,000 had served in the nation's military. Almost 1.1 million of these would shed blood for their country by either being non-mortally wounded or killed. The death toll was 407,316.[209]

Much has been recorded, and rightly so, about the millions of US Army, Navy, Army Air Force, Marines, and Coastguard members and their respective units, squadrons, and fleets that served so bravely to win the victory in World War II. The World War II generation is rapidly passing from the scene. I am concerned that as they leave us, the significance of their "saving" the world will fade with them.

I hope this book will contribute to honoring their service, and just as importantly, keep them alive through the retelling of their courageous stories.

Looking at America's history with a wide lens, it is my view that with the exception of the Civil War, no event changed the American cultural landscape more than World War II. I believe this was true as it applied to civil rights and also to the "new" roles that women would assume. According to the National World War II Museum, over 350,000 women volunteers served in the nation's military.[210]

"The Greatest Generation," was also a transformative generation. America would never be the same or look the same after World War II. As World War II unfolded, men and women of all races and from all parts of the country stepped up to ensure America's future, and for it to be a more inclusive one.

Sam Tso, a World War II Navajo code talker related his feeling that America had indeed come closer together through the shared experience and mutual recognition of effort of World War II.

He said: "What I want to do is to thank the whole people of America, the citizens. I learned that they are my people, too. For those that give us recognition through my travel, most of the Anglo people really show appreciation that how we contributed to the Second World War and I really deeply thank them for their recognition."[211]

Later, we will share more of the life story of Colonel Van T. Barfoot, a Choctaw Indian from Mississippi. During World War II, when he was Technical Sergeant Barfoot, he was awarded the Medal Of Honor. After the war, when he returned home to Mississippi, he was questioned by Mississippi Senator Bilbo, a strong segregationist, about Barfoot's perception of the African-American soldiers in the war. Obviously, Senator Bilbo was hoping for some kind of disparaging remarks.

Barfoot responded, "I found out after I did some fighting in this war that the colored boys fight just as good as the white boys...I've changed my idea a lot about colored people since I got into this war and so have a lot of other boys from the South."[212]

For this period in the Deep South, Van Barfoot was pushing back against a lot of negative stereotypes. He expressed a new "enlightened" view when he said, "I've changed my idea a lot about colored people since I got into this war..." In this instance, his use of "colored people" was clearly not intended in a pejorative sense. He chose his words when he said they "fight just as good." World War II for Van Barfoot and "...a lot of other boys from the South" had become a change agent.

"INSURANCE FOR A HOPEFUL FUTURE"

General Colin Powell described our military as a unique asset to the nation, "Our Armed Forces are number one and must remain so. They are our insurance policy for a hopeful future."[213]

Progress has been made, and America is better for it. America is "that city on a hill" in the eyes of multitudes from other lands, but we will always remain a work in progress, striving for that more perfect union.

WOMEN SERVING IN WORLD WAR II

Women from all ethnic groups voluntarily served in the armed services, and a number of these women went into harm's way, such as the Army, Navy Nurse's Corps, and the Women Air Force Service Pilots.

Certain support elements served overseas, such as the 6888th Central Postal Directory Battalion, which was an all-Black female unit who served in Europe. "They provided a vital service—sorting through a mail backlog of millions of letters that were important for maintaining moral."[214]

Many women filled non-traditional roles, such as the 1,100 women who served as Women Air Force Service Pilots(WASP). During the war, the WASP was not considered to be military but civilian volunteers. They finally were granted military status in 1977.[215]

These women flew almost every type of aircraft, including the B-26 and B-29 bombers. Among other things, the duties of these pilots included ferrying new planes, often long distances, from the factories to military bases, testing newly overhauled planes, and towing targets to give ground and air gunners training in firing live ammunition.[216]

Thirty-eight of these female pilots died in the performance of their duty. In December 1944, at the last graduating class of WASP, the commanding general of the U.S. Army Air Forces, General Henry "Hap" Arnold said, "Now in 1944, it is on the record that women can fly as good as men."[217]

WOMEN AIR SERVICE PILOT (WASP): HAZEL YING LEE, WORLD WAR II

The following are portions of an article by Helen Burmeister that touches on the courageous service by women in World War II, and also the commitment of Chinese Americans to the war effort:

> *Hazel Ying Lee, who was born and educated in Oregon, was the first Chinese American woman to fly for the U.S. military, one of two Chinese Americans in the Women Air-force Service Pilots (WASPS)—the other was Margaret "Maggie" Gee from California— and one of thirty-eight WASPs who died in service.*

In the Fall of 1942, she heard about and applied for the Women's Flying Training Detachment (WFTD)— which became the Women's Airforce Service Pilots (WASP) in 1943. She was accepted into the program, and during a six-month training regimen in Texas learned to fly a variety of military planes.

Lee graduated from the program in 1943. Shortly thereafter, the Women's Air Ferrying Service (WAFS) merged with the WFTD and was renamed WASPs. Lee was stationed at the Air Transport Command's 3rd Ferrying Squadron at Romulus Army Air Base in Michigan, where she flew ferrying and administrative flights in Stearman Pt-17s, North American T-6 Texans, and the Boeing C-47, which could transport up to 6,000 pounds of cargo. In 1944, Lee attended Pursuit School in Brownsville, Texas, becoming one of a select group of women qualified to fly high-powered, single-engine, fighter aircraft, including the P-51 Mustang.

Hazel Ying Lee died on November 25, 1944, as a result of injuries sustained in a collision on a runway in Great Falls, Montana. Three days after hearing of her death, her family received a telegram informing them that her brother Victor had been killed in combat in France. The two are buried alongside each other at Riverview Cemetery in Portland.

Lee's service was typical of the over one thousand women who joined the WASPs. On average, they were paid less than men, had to pay for their own room and board and even their own uniforms. They did not receive military benefits; and for those thirty-eight who died in service, the U. S. Air Force did not pay for funeral expenses. In 1977, President Jimmy Carter gave WASPs veteran status.[218]

In July 2009, President Obama signed into law a bill to award the Congressional Gold Medal to the Women Air Force Service Pilots.[219]

U.S. Rep. Ileana Ros-Lehtinen (R-FL), a co-sponsor of the House version of the bill, said the legislation recognizes the women's sacrifice:

"Today, this Congress has recognized their sacrifice and considers them all heroes because these trailblazers and true patriots served our country without question and with no expectations of recognition or praise,… that is what being a true hero is all about…"[220]

I would add, even though belated, it is always a good thing when the country shows appreciation to her veterans.

THE NATION ANSWERS THE CALL

As World War II began, cultural realities in America meant that practically all minorities in America faced racism and prejudice. Yet despite this, some of America's greatest war heroes were African Americans, Native Americans, Japanese Americans, and Chinese Americans. The story of their service was indicative of their love of country, despite America's shortcomings, and also reflected their hope that someday, America would fulfill her promises to "all her children."

From my perspective, because of such committed participation in the war effort from previously marginalized communities,

World War II literally became a change agent, contributing to a "more perfect union."

Discrimination and racism do not end easily or overnight. However, World War II did spur several dramatic events. In 1943, the Chinese Exclusion Act was finally rescinded.[221] In 1948, President Truman signed Executive Order 998,[1] calling for the desegregation of the U.S. military.[222]

In addition, there was an impetus from their war service that stirred many veterans from ethnic minorities to pursue civil rights changes. "Many prominent civil rights activists were ...veterans, including ...Oliver Brown, ...Medgar Evers, and Amaze Moore."[223]

The Pittsburg Courier, the largest Black newspaper in the United States in 1942, at the suggestion of a reader, picked up on the idea of a "Double V for victory" slogan.[224] The Double V Campaign stressed "that victory for democracy abroad required victory for full citizenship rights for African-Americans at home."[225]

This campaign promoted victory, the first "V," over the enemies from without, and the second "V," for victory over the enemies within. This referred to limitations on the civil rights of African Americans in America. This campaign was overwhelmingly received.[226]

"Many historians see the Double V campaign as the opening salvo in the Civil Rights Movement."[227]

As Tom Brokaw concluded, "The Greatest Generation," was indeed a transformative generation. America would never be the same or look the same after World War II. Every ethnic minority group in America saw their sons and daughters voluntarily put their lives on the line and join the fight to defend their country. Patriotism and devotion to country was found in every segment of America.

At a Ceremony in 1997 to award the Medal Of Honor to seven African American World War II heroes, President Clinton said as he concluded his remarks, "They helped America to become more worthy of them and more true to its ideals."[228]

At this point, I think it's important to reflect upon the service of some of these heroes who represented every community from across this wide land. It is an interesting fact—apart from the soldiers from Puerto Rico—all other persons of Hispanic heritage were not recognized according to their ethnicity. There were no restrictions on their service and nothing to distinguish them as Hispanic.

The following stories affirm that every group has earned an "equal place at the table." A mutual appreciation of one another benefits everyone. As you will see, when World War II started in December 1941, there were Americans of certain races and ethnicities who lived in a world of discrimination and blatant racism. Yet, as you will also see, great numbers from each of these groups stepped up to defend their country. And representatives from each of these groups were some of America's greatest war heroes.

As the old adage says, "give credit when credit is due," and we shall!

African Americans in World War II

More than 1,200,000 African Americans served in the US military forces during World War II. By the end of World War II, "…a higher share of African Americans had enlisted than Caucasians…"[229]

Though they were primarily placed in segregated, African-American units, they made tremendous contributions to the war effort. They were difference makers in many situations, examples being: the 6888th Central Postal Directory Battalion, the Red Ball Express, the Tuskegee Airmen, the 92nd Infantry Division, the 93rd Infantry Division, and the 761st Tank Battalion. These were just some of the "famed" units predominately made up of African Americans.

HERO ON DAY ONE: DORIS "DOVIE" MILLER, U.S. NAVY, WORLD WAR II

A true Naval hero who happened to be African American was Doris "Dorie" Miller. On the very first morning of the war, on December 7, 1944, as the Japanese attacked Pearl Harbor, Navy Cook 3rd Class Doris Miller went into action.

He was serving on the Battleship West Virginia and is credited with aiding multiple wounded sailors, including his own seriously wounded Captain Mervin S. Benson. Doris Miller also manned a Browning .50 caliber anti-aircraft machine gun and is credited with shooting down at least two Japanese planes. He was awarded the Navy Cross for his courageous actions, and Admiral Chester Nimitz personally presented it on May 27, 1942.[230]

Doris Miller continued his naval service in World War II until he was killed on November 24, 1943. He was aboard the USS Liscome Bay (CVE-56) when it was torpedoed and sunk with the loss of 646 sailors. On June 39, 1973, USS Miller (FF-2091) a Knox-class frigate, was named in honor of Doris Miller.[231]

THE TUSKEGEE AIRMEN

A legendary combat unit was the Tuskegee Airmen, nicknamed the "Red Tails" because they painted the tails of their P-51

Mustangs red so they could be identified. They were designated as the 332nd Fighter Group, and flew over 15,000 sorties,
escorting the heavy bombers of the 15th Air Force deep into
enemy territory. Their impressive performance earned more
than 150 Distinguished Flying Crosses.[232] The 332nd had "...a
much better success rate than other escort groups of the 15th
Air Force."[233]

Though there are numerous accounts of the bravery of Black
soldiers, sailors, airmen, and Marines, I want to focus on two
soldiers who were awarded the Congressional Medal of Honor.

Following an Army study to correct military records, in
1997, President Bill Clinton presented the Congressional Medal
of Honor to seven World War II Africa-American soldiers, six
of them posthumously.

At the ceremony, President Clinton commented: "In the tradition of African-Americans who have fought for our Nation as
far back as Bunker Hill, they were prepared to sacrifice everything for freedom even though freedom's fullness was denied
to them."[234]

STAFF SERGEANT RUBEN RIVERS, U.S. ARMY, WORLD WAR II

Staff Sergeant Ruben Rivers, of the 761st Tank Battalion,
was posthumously awarded the Medal of Honor for actions
in France during the period of November 16–19, 1944. Staff
Sergeant Rivers was killed in action on the 19th, and was
scheduled to be posthumously awarded the Medal of Honor
on November 20, 1944. However, it was not presented "...until
50 years later due to what was subsequently revealed as racial
discriminatory delays by the U. S. Army bureaucracy."[235]

Just the week before those actions, he was awarded the Silver Star for other acts of bravery. When America entered World War II, Ruben Rivers and two of his brothers left Oklahoma to voluntarily join the armed forces in 1942. Ruben was assigned to the 761st Tank Battalion.[236]

761ST TANK BATTALION

Beginning on November 7, 1944, due to their distinctive reputation as tough fighters, they were continually requested for infantry support, and the 761st served for over 183 consecutive days on the front. Most other tank battalions would typically serve only a week or two at the front before rotating back.[237]

The Battalion's logo was the "Black Panthers," and their motto was "Come out fighting." General Patton requested them, and they were assigned to the 26th Division, and thus part of General Patton's 3rd Army. They fought in four campaigns, including the Battle of the Bulge. During the Battle of the Bulge, they faced off against the13th SS Panzer Division, and by January 1945, the Germans had retreated and abandoned the area.[238]

During the first week of May 1945, the 761st Battalion helped liberate one of the sub-camps of the Mauthausen Concentration Camp. Seventeen-year-old Sonia Schreiber Weitz described the soldier who saved her in a poem she wrote, called "The Black Messiah."[239] My father's regiment was in this area at the same time as the 761st.

The United States Holocaust Memorial Museum and the US Army's Center of Military History have recognized the 761st Battalion as a "liberating" unit.[240]

Eventually, the battalion's soldiers received four campaign ribbons, a Presidential Unit Citation, and almost 400 decorations for heroism. These included: a Medal of Honor, 11 Silver Stars, 69 Bronze Stars, and about 300 Purple Hearts. Out of a battalion of around 700 soldiers, 300 Purple Hearts indicate great bravery and many days in the fight.[241]

Staff Sergeant Ruben Rivers represented the 761st and his country very well. He was a Medal of Honor recipient, a Silver Star recipient, and the recipient of two Purple Hearts.

LIEUTENANT VERNON BAKER, U.S. ARMY, WORLD WAR II

Also, among the seven Medal of Honor awardees, President Clinton presented a Medal of Honor to Lieutenant Vernon Baker. The presentation of his Medal of Honor, like the other six, was also delayed by fifty years due to racial discrimination in the Army bureaucracy. He was the only surviving recipient to receive the Medal of Honor in person.[1] Lieutenant Baker remained on active duty until 1968, becoming one of the first African Americans to command an all-White company.[242]

He was awarded the Medal of Honor for his service with Company C, 270th Regiment of the 92nd Infantry Division. President Clinton, in describing Lieutenant Baker's actions, said he single handedly "...wiped out three enemy machine gun nests, an observer post, and a dugout."[243] "This action was credited with helping breech the Gothic line and drive German forces out of Italy."[244]

Lieutenant Baker's awards included: the Medal of Honor, the Bronze Star Medal, and a Purple Heart.

Vernon Baker was a true American hero, and at his death, Dr. Gordon Mueller, president and CEO of the National World War II Museum in New Orleans, said, "Vernon was an extraordinary soldier and an extraordinary American." He goes on,

"Over the years, he was an integral part of helping our Museum fulfill its mission to bring the history and values of World War II to all generations."[245]

Vernon Baker died on July 13, 2010, and was laid to rest at Arlington National Cemetery on September 24, 2010, attended by three other Medal of Honor recipients, as well as his family.

Despite the indignities he faced, as Dr. Mueller pointed out, Vernon Baker wanted to see the "history and values" of World War II preserved for all subsequent generations.[246] Certainly, Vernon Baker's life and service helped bring about the change in the American fabric that was so badly needed. We honor him as we help fulfill that goal.

CHINESE AMERICANS IN WORLD WAR II

It was mentioned earlier that Hazel Ying Lee died on November 25, 1944, and her brother, Victor Lee, served in a tank battalion and died fighting in France only a few days later. They were children of Chinese immigrants, and were buried beside each other at Riverside Cemetery in Portland, Oregon. Because Hazel Lee and Victor Lee valued America above their own lives, their Chinese-American family paid a very high price in America's defense.

Chinese Americans, like other minorities, experienced mistreatment by their fellow Americans, yet when the war started, they answered the call and risked life and limb for their American homeland. Chinese Americans served selflessly and courageously in World War II.

According to the 1940 census, the total number of persons of Chinese ancestry living in the United States was nearly 80,000.[247]

In the United States, as late as December 7, 1941, there was still tremendous discrimination against any person who was ethnically Chinese. "During the 1840's many Chinese immigrants migrated to the United states, becoming the first Asian group to do so."[248]

Due to many socio-economic factors and a fear that Chinese immigrants were taking labor positions away from the general population, in1882, Congress passed the Chinese Exclusion Act. "Congress passed the exclusion act to placate worker demands and assuage...concerns about maintaining white racial purity. "[249]

The Chinese Exclusion Act did just what its name suggested, it created a ban on Chinese immigration. Through various other Acts and court rulings, Chinese immigrants and their American-born offspring "...remained ineligible for citizenship until 1943 with the passage of the Magnuson Act."[250]

Incredibly, huge numbers of Chinese Americans, despite such treatment, volunteered to put their lives on the line for their country, and 40 percent of them had not yet been allowed to become citizens.[251]

Yet,

Most Chinese Americans, having been born and raised here, celebrating the Fourth of July, joining the Boy Scouts, and learning the history of the United States in school were extremely patriotic. Twenty thousand Chinese Americans enlisted in the American armed forces out of a total Chinese American population of nearly eighty thousand in the entire United States, a far higher percentage (25%) than any other American ethnic community.[252]

The following is from an article written by Russell Low and Ricky Leo talking about Chinese Americans who served in World War II. Each of these men's fathers were both Chinese American World War II heroes:

> *These young men and women were products of decades of struggles by their parents and grandparents to become American. Anti-Chinese sentiments in the U. S. were a constant reminder that Americans saw them as different and excluded them. Some enlisted, and some died, before the Chinese Exclusion Act of 1882 was finally repealed in December 1943.*
>
> *But none of that mattered to these patriotic young men and women.* ***When they saw the Stars and Stripes, they were filled with pride. They viewed it as a symbol of hope and a beacon of freedom to preserve and protect.*** *Maybe they had something to prove: that they were more American than their peers, who took their nationality for granted. Being American was the core of their identity. It showed in their actions and in their numbers. The 20,000 Chinese Americans who served in World War II represented about 25% of the Chinese population in America. That was the highest percentage of service for any American ethnic community in World War II...*[253] (emphasis mine).

Both Russell Low and Ricky Leo's fathers were each awarded the Silver Star. Yet, neither of these humble heroes told about their heroics in their lifetimes. The stories of the gallantry of Sergeant Loren Low, and Sergeant Sonny Leo were revealed after their deaths.

A Congressional Gold Medal ceremony for Chinese American veterans of World War II was held in December 2020. Representative Judy Chou, D-CA, chair of the Congressional Asian Pacific American Caucus, whose father signed up to serve in World War II, said of these Chinese American World War II veterans, "These men and women were proud to serve our country. They deserve our deepest gratitude."[254]

CAPTAIN FRANCIS BROWN WEI, U.S. ARMY, WORLD WAR II

President Bill Clinton awarded the Congressional Medal of Honor to Captain Francis Brown Wai posthumously on June 21, 2000 at the White House. Captain Wai was the first Chinese American to receive the Medal of Honor.[255]

The following article is from the US Department of Veterans Affairs Official Blog:

> *He joined the Army upon the outbreak of World War II. Francis, who received rank as captain, sacrificed his life after assuming command during combat in the Philippines. On Oct. 20, 1944, while pinned down by enemy fire, he exposed himself and was killed while leading an assault to destroy the final Japanese pillbox in the Leyete area.*
>
> *For paying the ultimate sacrifice, Francis received the Distinguished Service Cross, Combat Infantryman Badge, American Campaign Medal, World War II*

*Victory Medal, Asiatic-Pacific Campaign Medal, and
the Philippine Liberation Medal.*

*After the reconsideration of Asian American military
records, Francis was posthumously presented the
Medal of Honor and the Purple Heart.*[256]

JAPANESE AMERICANS IN WORLD WAR II

When the Japanese attacked Pearl Harbor on December 7,
1941, "…about 120,000 persons of Japanese ancestry lived on
the US mainland, mostly along the Pacific Coast."[257]

Due to the surprise attack by the Japanese on Pearl Harbor,
America quickly moved to a state of anger and a desire for ret-
ribution against "all things Japanese." Many in America didn't
think that Japanese-American citizens could be trusted. Two
months after the attack, President Roosevelt issued Executive
Order 9066, which stated, "…residents with 'Foreign Enemy
Ancestry'…could be…relocated by military fiat."[258]

This order focused almost solely upon persons of Japanese
ancestry.[259] And without any due process, over 110,000
Japanese Americans, two-thirds of them citizens, were moved
into ten internment camps, which were not completely closed
until 1946.[260]

Many of these relocated Japanese Americans lost their
homes, businesses, farms, and livelihood. Despite being singled
out for such harsh, prejudicial treatment, more than 33,000
second-generation Japanese Americans (nisei) volunteered to
serve in the US Army during World War II.[261]

"More than 6,000 Japanese Americans served in the Military
Intelligence Service, or MIS during the war."[262] Ironically, a
large number of these came out of the internment camps. Most

of these MIS soldiers served in some fashion in the Pacific Theater. They proved invaluable with translation, interrogation, and gathering intelligence.[263]

The great majority of Japanese Americans who fought during the war served in Europe. For some months, the 100th Infantry Battalion, an all-Nisei combat unit was the only Japanese American combat unit. This battalion made a name for itself in the attacks on Monte Cassino, the breakout from Anzio, and the final Allied push from Rome to the Arno River.[264]

In June 1944, a larger all-Nisei combat force, the 442nd Regimental Combat Team (RCT) was deployed to Europe. The 100th became one of the battalions of the 442nd, and because of their combat reputation, they were allowed to remain the "100th" instead of being designated as 1st Battalion of the Regiment. Over the years, the Regiment would be called the 100th Battalion/442nd Infantry Regiment.[265]

Predominately, the soldiers of the 442nd volunteered from out of the internment camps. Some of them were formerly in the Army, but after Pearl Harbor, had been released from service. Now they had a chance to prove their loyalty and love of their homeland, America. And prove it they did.[266]

TWENTY-ONE MEDALS OF HONOR

An article in <u>army.mil</u> by C. Todd Lopez states:

> *Over 33,000 Japanese-Americans served in World War II. Together, the 100th Infantry Battalion and the 442nd Regimental Combat Team earned seven Presidential Unit Citations, two Meritorious Service Plaques, 36 Army Commendation Medals, and 87 Division Commendations. Individually, Soldiers*

earned 21 Medals of Honor, 29 Distinguished Service Crosses, one Distinguished Service Medal, more than 354 Silver Stars, and more than 4,000 Purple Hearts.[267] (emphasis mine)

The units together are the most decorated units in Army history.[268]

Here are the stories of two of the twenty-one Congressional Medal of Honor recipients from the 100th Battalion/442nd Combat Infantry Team.

PRIVATE FIRST CLASS SADAO S. MUNEMORI, U.S. ARMY, WORLD WAR II

During the war, only one Japanese-American soldier was awarded the Medal of Honor for his bravery, and that was Private First Class Sadao S. Munemori. The others came over fifty years later.[269]

With the formation of the 442nd early in 1943, earlier inductees, such as Munemori, were once again allowed to bear arms, and most were assigned spots in the 442nd. Munemori went to Camp Shelby in January 1944 and became a 100th Infantry Battalion replacement. He went overseas in April of 1944, seeing action in Italy, then in France, where he took part in the rescue of the Lost Battalion.[270]

In 1945, he returned with the 442nd to Italy. In the assault on the Gothic Line on the morning of April 5, he found himself in charge of his squad when his squad leader fell wounded. Trapped with two others in a shell crater by machine gun fire with grenades being hurled at them, Munemori crawled out of the crater and knocked out the enemy machine gun nests with grenades. Scrambling back to the crater, a grenade bounced off his helmet and into the crater. He smothered it with his body and was killed instantly. His two fellow squad members survived.[271]

For his heroic actions, Munemori was posthumously awarded the Congressional Medal of Honor, the only one awarded to a Nisei in the immediate aftermath of the war. His mother received the Medal on March 13, 1946.[272]

CAPTAIN DANIEL INOUYE, U.S. ARMY, WORLD WAR II

After the reconsideration of Asian-American military records, in the 1990s, President Clinton awarded twenty additional Medals of Honor on June 21, 2000, to Japanese-American soldiers for their actions in World War II.[273]

One of the twenty-one Japanese Americans to be awarded the Medal of Honor was Senator Daniel Inouye of Hawaii.[274]

The following is his story, written by Rudi Williams of the American Force Press Service:

> Army Sergeant Inouye "slogged through nearly three bloody months of the Rome-Arno campaign with the U. S. Fifth Army and established himself as an outstanding patrol leader with the 'Go-For-Broke' Regiment."

> Inouye's unit shifted from Italy to the Vosges Mountains in France and "spent two of the bloodiest weeks of the war rescuing 'The Lost Battalion,' the 1st Battalion, 141st Infantry Regiment, of the Texas National Guard, which was surrounded by German forces," according to his biography.

The Japanese American unit sustained more than 800 casualties to rescue 211 Texans. The rescue is listed in the Army annals as one of the most significant military battles of the century.

"Inouye lost 10 pounds, became a platoon leader and earned the Bronze Star Medal and a battlefield commission as a second lieutenant," the bio states.

The regiment went back to Italy, and Inouye was cited for heroism while leading his platoon against the enemy at San Terenzo on April 21, 1945. Though hit in the abdomen by a bullet that came out his back and barely missed his spine, he continued to lead the platoon and advanced alone against a machine gun nest that had pinned down his men.

"He tossed two hand grenades with devastating effect before his right arm was shattered by a German rifle grenade at close range," according to the senatorial bio. "Inouye threw his last grenade with his left hand, attacked with a submachine gun and was finally knocked down the hill by a bullet in the leg."

After 20 months in Army hospitals, Inouye returned home as a captain with a Distinguished Service Cross, the nation's second highest award for military valor, Bronze Star Medal, Purple Heart with oak leaf cluster and 12 other medals and citations. (His Distinguished Service Cross was upgraded to the Medal of Honor in 2000.)

> *He became Hawaii's first congressman in 1959 when*
> *he was elected to the U. S. House of Representatives.*
> *Inouye, a native of Honolulu, was elected to the U. S.*
> *Senate in 1962 and served until his death in 2012.*[275]

NATIVE AMERICANS IN WORLD WAR II

Another minority group of Americans who participated in large numbers in the war effort were Native Americans. Of course, the term, *Native American* refers to persons from numerous different "bands" of indigenous people. The National Congress of American Indians says "there are 574 federally recognized Indian Nations in the United States,…approximately 229 of these …are located in Alaska."[276]

Earlier, we shared the story of Lori Piestewa, a Hopi Indian who left family and the comforts of home, and put herself at the "tip of the spear," in defense of our country. She honored her country, family, and as her brother said, "…all Indian people." She died a brave warrior.

"It is estimated that approximately one million Native Americans lived in what is now known as the United States when Christopher Columbus arrived. Less than 400 years later, the population had dwindled down to around 250,000."[277]

Many became displaced persons, having lost their homelands, plus the consequences of disease, war, and famine took their toll. American Indians have continually faced struggles for fair treatment and equal rights. From the Dawes Severalty Act of 1887 until 1924, 92 percent of Native Americans were not eligible for US citizenship and its benefits.[278]

In 1924, Congress granted citizenship to all Native Americans born in the United States. Until then, they were considered members of their respective separate nations, but not US citizens. Yet, when the wars of World War I, World War II, Korea, and Vietnam broke out, some of the very first volunteers were from the Indian nations.

According to the 1940 Census, the number of Native Americans who lived in the US had grown to around 350,000. Of this number, by the end of World War II, "...over 24,000 reservation Natives, and another 20,000 off-reservation Natives had served," in the military."[279]

American Indians had World War II's "highest rate of voluntary enlistment in the military. In some tribes, 70 percent of the men enlisted. In the Women's Army Corps (WACS), hundreds of American Indian women served."[280] We saw this same high level of Native American patriotism in the Vietnam War.

Another 65,000 American Indian men and women went to work in the wartime defense industry, often relocating from rural reservations to cities, where they formed the first inter-tribal urban Indian communities.[281]

NATIVE AMERICAN CODE TALKERS

"SOMEBODY'S GOT TO GO... SOMEBODY'S GOT TO DEFEND THE FREEDOM."-CPL. CHESTER NEZ, USMC, WORLD WAR II, NAVAJO CODE TALKER[282]

Native American "code talkers" were not new to America's military. In World War I, members of the Choctaw Nation primarily filled this role. At various times, American Indians from over two-dozen American-Indian tribes served as code talkers. During World War II, the best known would be the US Marine Corps Navajo code talkers who served in the Pacific Theater. In Europe, the US Army Commanche code talkers also became well-known, and were credited with saving thousands of lives.

NAVAJO CODE TALKERS

Every World War II combatant appreciated the need for an unbreakable code that would help him or her communicate while protecting his or her operational plans. The US Marines knew where to find one: the Navajo Nation. Marine Corps leadership selected twenty-nine Navajo men, the Navajo Code Talkers, who created a code based on the complex, unwritten Navajo language. The code primarily used word association by assigning a Navajo word to key phrases and military tactics.[283]

Chester Nez, in an interview for the Library of Congress:

> *A lot of Navajo recruits didn't have a good education and didn't speak English well; when he started training at Camp Elliott, the number had been winnowed down to 29 Navajos; near the end of training, the major told them about the nature of their mission and how they would develop a code in their own language; he left them on their own and they spent the rest of the day working out how the code would operate; would use animal, bird, and sea creature names; for example, a whale could stand for a torpedo or a battleship; did not know at the beginning what a big secret this project was.*[284]

The following article from the intelligence.gov website elaborates on this:

> *This system enabled the code talkers to translate three lines of English in 20 seconds, not 30 minutes as was common with existing code-breaking machines. The code talkers participated in every major Marine*

operation in the Pacific theater, giving the Marines a critical advantage throughout the war.

During the nearly month-long battle for Iwo Jima, for example, six Navajo code talker Marines successfully transmitted more than 800 messages without error. Marine leadership noted after the battle that the Code Talkers were critical to the victory at Iwo Jima. At the end of the war, the Navajo Code remained unbroken.[285]

COMMANCHE CODE TALKERS

It is an accepted fact that thousands of lives were saved by the great work of the code talkers who came from the Navajo, Pawnee, Choctaw, and several dozen other tribes. One group of code talkers are directly linked to our family, and we credit them for my father-in-law's survival during the war.

In late 1940, when it seemed war was inevitable, the Army recruited warriors of the Comanche Nation to develop a secret code based on the Comanche language to be used in the Europe Theater of Operations. This group, made up of fourteen warriors, became highly-trained members of the US Army 4th Signal Company, 4th Infantry Division. The code they developed, using their language, allowed secure military inter-unit messages from D-Day, June 6, 1944, until the German surrender on May 8, 1945.[286]

Thousands of American soldiers, particularly those in the 4th Infantry Division, made it back home, thanks to the Commanche code talkers. My father-in-law's life might very well be one of those saved, as he served from D-Day until

VE Day in the same 4th Infantry Division as these American Indian heroes.

Eventually, the Congress of the United States formally recognized the code talkers of World War I and World War II; each American Indian Tribe that provided code talkers was awarded the Congressional Gold Medal, and each individual, a Silver Medal replica.

They were credited with saving the lives of thousands of soldiers, but since their efforts also helped stop Hitler before his development of nuclear weapons, they might also have saved the world. America is blessed that these Native-American warriors fought for their broader American family.

TECHNICAL SERGEANT VAN THOMAS BARFOOT, U.S. ARMY, WORLD WAR II

On the California Indian Education website, it lists five American Indians who were awarded the Congressional Medal of Honor for valiant action in World War II. One of those, interestingly enough, was the well-known Major "Pappy" Boyington, of the Sioux Nation. Another of these American Indian warriors was a Choctaw, Van T. Barfoot.[287]

The story of Van Thomas Barfoot, a Choctaw Indian, begins with his birth at Edinburg, Mississippi on June 15, 1919. He joined the Army in 1940, and by 1944, he was an Army technical sergeant. Before World War II was over, he would become an officer, Second Lieutenant Barfoot. His military career lasted over thirty-three years, and he served in three wars, World War II, Korea, and Vietnam. By the time he retired in 1974, he had attained the rank of colonel.[288]

It was during World War II, on May 23, 1944, when his actions earned him the Congressional Medal of Honor. The following is from the California Indian Education (CALIE) website describing Technical Sergeant Barfoot's actions on that day:

At the age of 25, on May 23, 1944, on a foreign WWII battlefield near Carrion, Italy, Technical Sergeant Barfoot, of L Company, 157th Infantry Regiment, 45th Infantry Division, set out alone on foot to flank German machine gun positions and stop the deadly rain of enemy bullets that were killing his fellow soldiers.

Barfoot advanced through a minefield, took out three enemy machine gun emplacements with hand grenades and expert fire from his Thompson machine gun.

If that wasn't enough for a day's work, young Sergeant Barfoot then picked up a bazooka, took on and destroyed one of the three advancing Mark VI tanks that German commanders ordered in to spearhead their fierce heavy-armored counter attack on Barfoot's platoon position in an unsuccessful effort to retake their lost machine gun positions.

As the tank crew members dismounted their disabled tank, Sergeant Barfoot killed three of the German soldiers outright with his Tommy gun.

Barfoot then continued further into enemy terrain and destroyed a recently abandoned German fieldpiece with a demolition charge placed in the breech.

While returning to his platoon position, Sergeant Barfoot, though greatly fatigued by his Herculean efforts, assisted two of his seriously wounded men 1,700 yards to a position of safety.

Barfoot is credited with capturing and bringing back 17 German prisoners of war (POWs) to his platoon position that day.

But even those heroic efforts probably didn't make much news back home either, given the scope and magnitude of the war, however, they were to earn then Technical Sergeant Barfoot a U. S. Congressional Medal of Honor, and an honorable place in American history.[289]

Colonel Van T. Barfoot was another of America's great patriots. He offered his service to his country for three wars. Colonel Van Barfoot's military awards included: the Medal of Honor, Silver Star Medal, Bronze Star Medal, two Purple Hearts, and eleven Air Medals.[290]

· · · · · · · · · · · · · · · · · ·

WORLD WAR II: HEROES FROM HOME

"Sergeant Don Horne-8th RCT-D-Day-First Wave"

T HROUGHOUT THIS BOOK, THE STORIES OF A LIM-
ited few of our nation's war heroes have been included. I
hope they will be viewed as representative of the millions of
unnamed veterans who have served. One goal of mine was to
bring to life some of these heroes who put country before self,
to show them as "real" persons.

Three World War II war heroes are very dear to me. Two
are family, and one a good friend. All three are now deceased. I
hope to keep their memories alive because I am a better person
and the world is a better place because of them.

SERGEANT JOEL PERRITTE JENKINS SR., U.S. ARMY, WORLD WAR II

My father's middle name, which is my middle name and my
son's middle name, is Perritte. We have that name because it is
to honor my father's mother, Mary Perritt Ellison Jenkins (her
name did not include the "e"). My father was born on May 8,
1926, and his mother, Mary, died giving him birth. An added

tragic irony was that Mother's Day in 1926 was the very next day, the 9th. My dad was the last of his mother's five children.

His father, and my grandfather, Rev. John Henry Jenkins Sr., remarried and had six more children. My father's stepmother, Annie, became "mother" to all eleven, and "granny," to all of us twenty-six grandchildren.

By my father's eighteenth birthday, two older brothers and one sister had already gone off to war. One brother joined the Army, one the Navy, and his oldest sister became a Yeoman 2nd Class in the Navy WAVES.

My father said he planned to follow them as he was "itching" to get off the farm and "out from behind the mule." My grandfather told him he needed him to help work the farm since my father was then the oldest son at home.

But, the local draft board had the last word, and even though my dad's family already had three serving, he received his draft notice in August 1944. He was sent to Camp Blanding, Florida, where he trained for seventeen weeks. By the summer 1944, Camp Blanding was primarily training replacements for units already fighting in Europe.

My father's World War II military occupational specialty was listed as "605," a heavy weapons crew member on the M1917A Browning .30 caliber machine gun. The M1917A was a heavy machine gun that was crew-served, belt-fed, and water-cooled. Not counting the ammunition and water, it weighed over one hundred pounds.

He completed training at Camp Blanding and was assigned as a replacement crew member in a heavy weapons company. He sailed from New York on the Queen Elizabeth, along with about 15,000 other replacements, on January 7, 1945, and arrived in Scotland on January 13. The convoy number for their transport was simply listed as "sailed alone." Earlier in the war, the German U Boat threat would have prohibited such a large troop carrier traveling unescorted. At least, at this time in the war, there was also continual air cover for the entire trip.

Soon, he was in France, trying to catch up with his new unit, D Company, 1st Battalion, 259th Infantry Regiment, 65th Infantry Division. The 65th didn't see combat until March 9, 1945, but then they stayed engaged for fifty-five days in combat until VE Day on May 8, 1945.

Five months before, he was working on the family farm, and now he was manning a powerful weapon of death as a replacement gunner on a machine whose only purpose was to kill and maim. Even though my dad "got to the fight" late, he still saw death, smelled death, and lost friends he'd only known a few weeks.

He was also exposed to ear-piercing noise levels, beginning at Camp Blanding, in his heavy-weapons training, and then during the war, from his own weapon, as was well as from German artillery. The VA rated him with a severe hearing loss disability due to his World War II service.

XX Corps had become operational in France on August 1, 1944, and the 65th became a late addition. As such, the 65th was also part of General George S. Patton's US Third Army, and was written about them, "they acquitted themselves well." They became one of the earlier elements to break through the Siegfried Line, push across the Rhine, and take a number of strategic German towns.[291]

It was in the last weeks of the war that he saw the worst of the human suffering caused by the Nazis. When the 65th helped liberate several concentration camps, he saw the masses of people brutally murdered, starved, or frozen to death.

They were credited with liberating the Plattling Concentration Camp, a sub-camp of the Flossenburg concentration camp on

April 20–21, 1944.[292] The division, including my father, saw the depths of man's inhumanity as they liberated this camp. The United States Holocaust Memorial Museum and the US Army's Center of Military History have recognized the 65th as a "liberating" unit.[293]

I know all the various camps had their unique differences, but in 1991, I visited Auschwitz, the largest, which included the largest death camp. As you walk the grounds, see the exhibits, and hear its history, it seems unfathomable that one group of human beings could do this to another group of human beings.

By May 5, 1944, the 65th had established their headquarters in Linz, Austria. In Linz, my father briefly got to see his older brother Ellison, who was in an artillery battalion of a different division.

The 65th was disbanded by August 1945, and many of the division's soldiers had already been reassigned to other units for European occupation duty. My father, being a late arrival in Europe, was one of those assigned to occupation duty. He was assigned to Rosenheim, Bavaria, Germany, where thousands of displaced persons were housed.

He described, during the summer of 1945, he was a military escort on trains carrying displaced civilians, including some of the concentration camp survivors. He said the soldiers were given adequate rations, but often, there was not much food for the passengers. My dad didn't smoke, so he traded his cigarette ration for candy bars and shared them with as many children as he could. He and other soldiers also shared their meals with their hungry fellow passengers.

In the weeks after VE Day, a massive challenge for the Allies was dealing with the ten to twelve million displaced persons all across Europe. It would actually take years to completely address this crisis.

In December 1945, while in Rosenheim, my father extended his military service and joined the regular Army. He served until his discharge on May 30, 1947. His service totaled two years and eight months. His last year of service was with the 33rd Infantry Regiment in Panama, where he trained for jungle warfare and was an instructor on the M1917A. His service ended with him as a sergeant and a heavy machine gun squad leader.

When he returned home to South Carolina, he had earned: the Combat Infantryman Badge, Bronze Star Medal, Army of Occupation Medal, Good Conduct Medal, World War II Victory Medal, Campaign Ribbons for Rhineland and Central Europe, and recognition of being in a "Liberating Unit."

Many others served longer in combat, and rightfully received recognition for great valor. Yet, for our family, and for me, he was our hero! His country called, he answered, and put himself into harm's way. He never saw himself as a hero, and reminded everyone he didn't see much action. He never lost his desire to serve his country, and for a number of years, he served as chaplain of a Civil Air Patrol squadron in Shelby, North Carolina.

After the war, he became a minister, served churches in North Carolina and South Carolina. At the age of sixty-two, when many persons are thinking of retirement, he and my mother moved to Europe to serve church communities for fourteen years. Their first stop was on the Portuguese Island of Terceira in the Azores. There, for almost two years, they served American military families assigned to the Lajesse Air Force base.

After that, he became an interim pastor to a number of international churches in places, such as Denmark, Switzerland, Italy, Hungary, and Germany. The plan was for him and my mother to serve in a church on a temporary basis, maybe a year or so, until the church found a permanent minister. In some cases, this would require lengthy periods before their replacements arrived.

Among other places they lived and served were the German cities of Dusseldorf and Nuremberg. Once, he arrived as a warrior, later, he arrived as a messenger of love and grace.

Many in their congregations were part of diplomatic missions, including Americans, as well as from other countries. For example, the Ghanian ambassador to Italy attended their congregation in Rome.

After they returned home, at the age of seventy-six, my dad became the chaplain of a retirement home for four years. My mother went into the classroom and was an ESL (English as a second language) teacher in the public schools for five years.

Side note: for two of their years in Europe, My father and mother lived in Copenhagen, Denmark, where my father was the pastor of an English-speaking international church. My wife and I visited my parents there in November 1989. It was an unusually turbulent time in Europe as the fall of the Iron Curtain was imminent.

One event of particular interest for me was the day I attended a Rotary Club meeting in Copenhagen. The guest speaker was the East German ambassador to Denmark. At the end of his speech, someone in the audience asked him about the possible reunification of East and West Germany. I'll never forget his answer; he replied, "That discussion is not even on the table!" Yet, by October 3, 1990, less than a year later, the division ended, and Berlin became the capitol of a reunified Germany.

"The best laid schemes o' Mice an' Men..."- Robert Burns

Sergeant Donald Albert Horne, U.S. Army, World War II

Another personal World War II hero that I will always admire is my late father-in-law, Donald Horne. He was a year older than my father, and he entered the war earlier. He was the only son of Bennie and Tillie Horne of High Point, North Carolina, and at eighteen, was drafted into the Army in August 1943, and left his parents, his sister, Doris, and went off to war.

When I met him in 1969, he was a very successful businessman in the field of real estate, and was president of the High Point Board of Realtors. But far more significantly, I found him to be one of the kindest and caring men that I had ever met. He was a wonderful son to his elderly parents, a loving brother, husband, father, father-in-law, and later, grandfather. Sadly, his heart gave out shortly after reaching his sixty-third birthday.

This "son of High Point" helped liberate people from France, Belgium, Luxembourg, and a concentration camp in Bavaria. He came home with a deep compassion for his fellowman. His resume didn't list country clubs, beach-front property, or expensive toys or hobbies, but instead, his resume focused on service. He was a sought-out leader who found ways to serve practically all segments of his community.

His leadership in his hometown of High Point included serving First United Methodist Church as chairman of the trustees, while also serving the broader community. He cared about the poor and the less fortunate within his city. His concern was turned into action. His service on the boards of a number of helping agencies was impressive. For several years, he was chairman of the board of the Beddington Street Mission, which focused on helping the inner-city poor, especially children. In addition, he served on the boards of the local women's shelter, United Way, and Salvation Army.

Don Horne's civic service also included: past commander of the High Point post of Disabled Americans Veterans, charter member and first president of the Oak Hollow Civitan Club, he served on the board of the Heart Association, and was former president of the High Point Jaycees. In the 1960s, he was presented the Jaycees' Nick Lawrence High Point Young Man of the Year Award, and in the 1980s, he was the High Point Salvation Army's Man of the Year.

He was a huge supporter of his younger son's high school band, and even marched behind them in their one-mile march to the football stadium on Friday nights.

I'm sharing some of the character traits of my father-in-law to show that this eighteen-year-old young man from the middle of North Carolina had no malice toward anyone when he was drafted to go and fight for his country against fascism.

In 1985, he and my mother-in-law, Mary Lou, signed up for a Friendship Force exchange visit to Cologne (Koln in German), Germany. They took their thirteen-year-old granddaughter, Joy (our daughter), with them, and they were genuine ambassadors for goodwill.

He was a very gregarious man with a full face smile. As my father-in-law once put it, the first time he walked into the Cologne Cathedral in March 1945, he "had a rifle slung over his shoulder." The second time, he walked in along with his German hosts, and now, new friends.

Don Horne was five-foot seven-inches tall and weighed 145 pounds when he was inducted on May 14, 1943. After receiving his initial training at Fort Jackson, South Carolina, he was assigned to D Company, 1st Battalion, 8th Regimental Combat

Team, 4th Infantry Division and shipped over to England to prepare for the invasion of France.

His military occupational specialty was designated "605," meaning he was a heavy weapons crew member for a M1917A Browning .30 caliber machine gun. He had the exact MOS as my father. The M1917A was a heavy machine gun that was crew-served, belt-fed, and water-cooled. Not counting the ammunition, it weighed over one hundred pounds. Within less than a year, Private First Class Donald Horne had become Sergeant Donald Horne, and a M1917A squad leader in D Company, the heavy weapons company.

During his time in Europe, my father-in-law saw a tremendous amount of combat and was part of many historical moments. His 8th Regimental Combat Team was part of the "first wave" of the D-Day landings on the beaches of Normandy. The 8th RCT actually earned the distinction of being the first unit among all the invasion forces to touch the coast of Normandy on June 6. Their designated beach was Utah, and due to the different land features, among other things, their casualties were far fewer than those on Omaha.[294]

However, their real struggles came after D-Day. The 8th RCT was part of the 4th Infantry Division, and beginning with their initial landing on the 6th, the 4th ID had 200 straight days of maintaining contact with German forces.[295]

My father-in-law's 4th Infantry Division, along with the French 2nd Armored Division, liberated Paris on August 25, 1944.[296] Actually, the 4th was ready to go in earlier but were told to hold back and let Charles de Gaulle's French 2nd Armor Division be seen as the "first" liberators. My father-in-law also fought in the historic battles of the Hurtgen Forest and the Battle of the Bulge.

The Battle of Hurtgen Forest lasted from September 12, 1944, until February 10, 1945, and resulted in over 33,000 American casualties, killed and wounded. November 7 to December 14, the 4ID fought in the Battle of Hurtgen Forest.[297]

On November 30, 1944, my father-in-law was wounded by shrapnel and sent to a field hospital. Within a few weeks, he was recovered enough to rejoin his D Company of the 8th, in time to fight in the Battle of the Bulge.

The Battle of the Bulge began on December 16, 1944, and ended on January 25, 1945. This battle was a major German offensive to split the Allied lines and retake the Antwerp port. Initially, the Germans broke through and formed a "bulge" in the American lines. When Patton's Third Army arrived the day after Christmas, the tide turned toward the Americans.[298]

"In all, according to the Department of Defense, 1 million-plus Allied troops, including 500,000 Americans, fought in the Battle of the Bulge, with approximately 19,000 soldiers killed in action, 47,500 wounded, and 23,000-plus missing."[299] The total losses for the Germans were around 100,000.[300]

During the Battle of the Bulge, the 4th ID was assigned to hold the line in Luxembourg, which it did. Its tenacity prompted General Patton to announce, "No American division in France has excelled the magnificent record of the 4th Infantry Division."[301]

In January, the Ivy Division crossed the Sauer River and then took one town after another. By V-E Day, it had marched to the Austrian border and was just below Bad Tolz, in southern Bavaria. It had moved fast and had hit hard, but like most other combat divisions, had to pay a heavy price for its gains.[302]

"By V-E Day, the Ivy Division had suffered 21,550 casualties, including over 5,000 killed in action or die from their wounds."[303]

The US Army's Center of Military History and the United States Holocaust Memorial Museum recognized the 4th Infantry Division as a liberating unit in 1992.[304]

During the march into southern Germany in late April 1945, the 4th ID liberated Haunstetten, a Dachau sub-camp. Haunstetten was one of the biggest sub-camps in Nazi Germany.[305]

Don Horne, as most veterans, never saw himself as a hero, though his body would forever wear the scars of shrapnel he received in the Hurtgen Forest. He was very humble about his war service, and only spoke of it if asked about it. Yet, his war experiences and memories of lost friends were never far from his thoughts, and eventually, some thirty years after the war, he walked on the Utah beach again. This time, he walked it with former comrades and his wife, and my mother-in-law, Mary Lou.

Sergeant Donald A. Horne was awarded the Combat Infantry Badge, Bronze Star Medal with Oak Leaf Cluster, Purple Heart, World War II Victory Medal, Good Conduct Medal, European-African-Middle Eastern Campaign Medal, American Defense Medal World War II, Presidential Unit Citation, and four Campaign Ribbons. His Regiment was also awarded the Belgian Fourragere for action in the Belgian Campaign and action in the Ardennes.

Side note: as I write this, I am looking at my father-in-law's World War II "Heart Shield" steel-covered pocket Bible. His parents had given it to him before he left for the war, and the inside inscription says, "Wherever you go and whatever you do my heart goes with you, mother."

Inside the cover, in my father-in-law's hand writing, was listed: Scotland, Wales, England, France, Luxembourg, Belgium, and Germany. My father-in-law's pocket Bible, as a sign of his faith, went with him all over Europe, and returned home with him.

His Bible never stopped a bullet. There are cases, however, where a well-placed pocket Bible, did just that.

Christmas 2006, Staff Sergeant Bennet, my chaplain assistant, and I were visiting patients at the Baghdad ER, and we met a contractor who had been wounded in an IED blast. He stated that each morning before he headed out on a convoy, he read from his Gideon New Testament, said a prayer, and then placed the New Testament in his back cargo pocket.

On this particular day, his vehicle was struck by an IED. Amazingly, his New Testament absorbed the largest piece of shrapnel that struck him. He said the surgeon credited his Bible with saving his life. He showed us his Gideon New Testament that had been sliced completely through. This gentleman did need stitches in a few places, but he didn't suffer the severing of the femoral artery that often happened from such IEDs.

SERGEANT RUSSELL BLOCK, USMC, WORLD WAR II

Russell Block wasn't a relative of mine, but became a friend, and had an amazing World War II experience. He lived to be eighty-seven years old, but his World War II service was never far from his thoughts, rightfully so.

Russell was a Marine sergeant in World War II, whose assigned duty was with the Department of State as a courier. I located a number of US Marine Corps muster rolls from World War II that showed he was assigned to the Marine Corps Barracks in Washington, DC, and ordered to, "Special temporary duty with the Department of State."

Sergeant Block's assignment was to the White House. Though his orders listed his duty as temporary, Russell's assignment to the White House as a personal courier lasted until the war's end. He served President Roosevelt until his death, and then President Truman.

His job required him to meet with the President face to face to receive top-secret military dispatches that were to be hand-delivered. Next, they chained the "diplomatic pouch" to his wrist, and arranged travel to his destination. Russell's mission was not complete until the designated recipient, and only the designated recipient, unlocked the pouch from his wrist.

Russell's courier missions carried him into harm's way often. Courier duty required traveling in all kinds of weather and into hazardous places. Many couriers did not survive the war.

Let me interject something here. Some types of courier duty have been around since the earliest wars. Today, it has become very technological, encrypted, and digitally-driven. The need for a lone individual to "go through the lines" to dispatch a message is in the past. As recent as the War in Vietnam, however, military couriers were still being assigned to go "outside the wire," and deliver messages between commands.

A Virginia friend and hero of mine, Don Webb, was an Army courier in Vietnam. Don was Sergeant Webb at the time, and served in Vietnam during some of the most intense fighting.

In such an environment, especially with a battle raging, it's hard to imagine the courage required for a lone soldier, under cover of darkness, to slip behind the enemy's lines and deliver a commander's intent to his subordinates or to his "higher." Then, this courier reentered the enemies' space on his return trip. Sergeant Don Webb had the "right stuff." It's just a pleasure knowing someone who so highly values freedom and earned the right to enjoy it.

Russell's travels didn't typically necessitate him entering the actual battlefield, but nonetheless, his duty had its own dangers.

Russell's favorite memories were delivering top-secret dispatches to some very important people; for example, Winston Churchill. Churchill was gracious to him. The dispatch was read, and Russell waited for the reply to be written. They would chain Russell to a top-secret pouch from Churchill, and he headed back "across the pond" to deliver it to Roosevelt.

This is an interesting story in itself, but I share it because of something else that Russell Block stated. First, I want to offer some important perspective. During a war, it's hard to imagine the personal toll on those individuals who are responsible for making life-and-death decisions impacting others, such decisions that result in the deaths of those under their command.

Even down to the "four man" team level, this responsibility falls on non-commissioned officers and officers. However, the decisions of a president during wartime can result in the deaths of untold thousands. It's difficult to imagine what went through the mind of someone like President Roosevelt as he received the daily reports of American casualties.

Russell Block's face-to-face encounters with President Roosevelt reveal a great deal about President Roosevelt's genuine concern for those in harm's way. President Roosevelt was not able to have a personal face-to-face moment with all of the sixteen million who served in the Army, Navy, Army Air Corps, Marines, Coast Guard, and Merchant Marines.

Many may not be aware, but all four sons of President Roosevelt and his wife, Eleanor, served in the military during World War II. One was in the Marine Corps, one a pilot with the Army Air Force, and two served in the Navy. All four went into harm's way, and between them, their awards included the Navy Cross, Distinguished Flying Cross, Legion of Merit with Combat V device, two Silver Stars, the Bronze Star Medal, and three Purple Hearts.

Russell told me that every time he met with Roosevelt, before Russell left his presence, the President would stick out his little finger and grab Russell's little finger for a "pinky-promise" moment, and hold it until the President offered a prayer for his safe travels. Russell told me, "You know, those were moments just between the President and me. President Roosevelt was a swell guy, and he made you feel that he really cared about you. He helped put your mind at ease."

I am convinced, the President's one-to-one time with Russell Block was a genuine moment of connection with Russell, but I'm also convinced the sentiments that President Roosevelt expressed to Russell were symbolic of his feelings for all of those millions who served, including his own sons. For President Roosevelt, obviously, the individual mattered to him.

Semper Fi, Russell!

THE D-DAY PRAYER: PRESIDENT FRANKLIN ROOSEVELT

In setting the stage for our next chapter on D-Day, and in light of President Roosevelt's spirit and faith, I am including the "fireside chat," or better said, Roosevelt's "fireside prayer" of June 6, 1944. Russell Block stated that President Roosevelt had the gift of "helping put my mind at ease."

On June 6, 1944, one of the President's own sons, Colonel Elliott Roosevelt, flew with the 12th Air Force, supporting the D-Day invasion.

The following is President Roosevelt's D-Day prayer on June 6, 1944, which "helped put the nation's mind at ease."

My fellow Americans: Last night, when I spoke with you about the fall of Rome, I knew at that moment that troops of the United States and our allies were crossing the Channel in another and greater operation. It has come to pass with success thus far.

And so, in this poignant hour, I ask you to join with me in prayer:

Almighty God: Our sons, pride of our Nation, this day have set upon a mighty endeavor, a struggle to preserve our Republic, our religion, and our civilization, and to set free a suffering humanity.

Lead them straight and true; give strength to their arms, stoutness to their hearts, steadfastness in their faith.

They will need Thy blessings. Their road will be long and hard. For the enemy is strong. He may hurl back our forces. Success may not come with rushing speed, but we shall return again and again; and we know that by Thy grace, and by the righteousness of our cause, our sons will triumph.

They will be sore tried, by night and by day, without rest-until the victory is won. The darkness will be rent by noise and flame. Men's souls will be shaken with the violences of war.

For these men are lately drawn from the ways of peace. They fight not for the lust of conquest. They fight to end conquest. They fight to liberate. They fight to let justice arise, and tolerance and good will among all

Thy people. They yearn but for the end of battle, for their return to the haven of home.

Some will never return. Embrace these, Father, and receive them, Thy heroic servants, into Thy kingdom.

And for us at home—fathers, mothers, children, wives, sisters, and brothers of brave men overseas—whose thoughts and prayers are ever with them—help us, Almighty God, to rededicate ourselves in renewed faith in Thee in this hour of great sacrifice.

Many people have urged that I call the Nation into a single day of special prayer. But because the road is long and the desire is great, I ask that our people devote themselves in a continuance of prayer. As we rise to each new day, and again when each day is spent, let words of prayer be on our lips, invoking Thy help to our efforts.

Give us strength, too—strength in our daily tasks, to redouble the contributions we make in the physical and the material support of our armed forces.

And let our hearts be stout, to wait out the long travail, to bear sorrows that may come, to impart our courage unto our sons wheresoever they may be.

And, O Lord, give us Faith. Give us Faith in Thee; Faith in our sons; Faith in each other; Faith in our united crusade. Let not the keenness of our spirit ever be dulled. Let not the impacts of temporary events, of temporal matters of but fleeting moment let not these deter us in our unconquerable purpose.

With Thy blessing, we shall prevail over the unholy forces of our enemy. Help us to conquer the apostles of greed and racial arrogancies. Lead us to the saving of our country, and with our sister Nations into a world unity that will spell a sure peace, a piece invulnerable to the schemings of unworthy men. And a peace that will let all of men live in freedom, reaping the just rewards of their honest toil.

Thy will be done, Almighty God.

Amen.[306]

CHAPTER 15

· · · · · · · · · · · · · · · · · · ·

D-DAY—116TH INF REGIMENT— COLLEVILLE-SUR-MER

"God was on the beach D-Day; I know He was because I was talking with him." -Chaplain (2nd Lieutenant) John Burkhalter, 18th Infantry Regiment, 1st Infantry Division[307]

ARLIER, I SHARED THAT MY FATHER-IN-LAW'S 8th Infantry Regiment of the 4th ID landed on Utah Beach on D-Day. Incredibly, they incurred less than 200 casualties on the beach.[308] Their greatest fighting came later.

This discussion of D-Day is primarily focused on Omaha Beach, due to my connections with the 116th Infantry Regiment and the terrible losses they incurred. The topics of this chapter are interrelated, and, I might add, personal for me. Though I was not born as of D-Day, I feel forever connected to D-Day, the 116th Infantry Regiment, and the Colleville-sur-Mer American Cemetery. On a number of occasions, as I listened to very intimate memories of those who were on Omaha Beach on June 6, 1944, I realized the "hell" they went through for their fellow Americans.

Pointed out earlier, D-Day, June 6, 1944, holds a tragic record in our American history. On that day, America suffered her greatest US service member losses on a given day, over 2,500.[309] The 116th Infantry Regiment, 29th Infantry Division, incurred the highest number of casualties on D-Day of any other unit. The 116th was in the first wave on Omaha Beach, and over 800 soldiers from this one regiment were killed or wounded on D-Day.[310]

The nation's D-Day National Memorial is located in Bedford, Virginia. There is a reason the National D-Day Memorial was located in the little Virginia town of Bedford. On June 6, 1944, Bedford, then a town of some 3,200 folks, had twenty of her sons (later referred to as the "Bedford Boys") die on the beach at Omaha.[311] Nineteen of these young men were from A Company of the Virginia National Guard's 116th Infantry Regiment.[312]

There are obvious benefits when a National Guard unit from the same community goes to war. Foremost, the soldiers know each other and have trained together for long periods.

There are obvious drawbacks when a unit of National Guard soldiers is from the same community. The major drawback shows up when the unit takes heavy casualties on the same battlefield. That means, of course, that some community has suffered unimaginable losses. That's what happened to the little town of Bedford on D-Day.

Following 9/11, when I received the call to report to the Pentagon, I was serving as the chaplain of this very regiment, the 116th Infantry Regiment (116th Infantry Brigade Combat Team).

This BCT was part of the Virginia Army National Guard and was a famed unit, whose legacy traces its beginnings to November 3, 1741, when the "Augusta County Regiment" of the Virginia Militia was formed. As part of the Virginia Militia, the regiment's soldiers served in the French and Indian War (1754–1763), led by George Washington.[313]

The regiment's soldiers have served in practically all of America's wars, from pre-Revolutionary service until the present, with soldiers serving in such diverse places as the Sinai, Bosnia, Guantanamo Bay, Cuba, Iraq, and Afghanistan.

In August 2004, while chaplain of the 116th, I assisted with "Casualty Notification" for a soldier from 3rd Battalion of the 116th who was killed by an IED in Ghazikel, Afghanistan. Two of us, in class As, made that very difficult notification to the family of Staff Sergeant Craig W. Cherry of Winchester, Virginia. Staff Sergeant Bobby Beasley, of the same unit, was also killed in the incident, and their names were added to that long list of 116th soldiers who died for their country.

As noted, the 116th was part of the 29th Infantry Division. The 29th was called, the "Blue and Gray Division" because it was made up of regiments from Virginia, the 116th, and Maryland, the 115th, whose legacies extended back prior to and through the Revolutionary War and Civil War.[314]

In 1917, the regiment was included into the newly-formed 29th Division and remains part of the 29th Infantry Division today (I had a stint as division chaplain for the 29th Infantry Division). In World War I, the 116th Infantry fought in the infamous Meuse-Argonne Offensive.[315]

On October 8, 1918, "SGT Earl Gregory, single-handedly captured a machine gun and a 7.5-centimeter mountain howitzer along with 22 German soldiers."[316] There are two Virginia National Guard soldiers, both from the 116th, who have been awarded the Medal of Honor, and for his actions, Earl Gregory became the first.[317]

Some twenty-six years later, for his actions on June 8, 1944, at Grandcamp-Maisy, France, Technical Sergeant Frank Peregory, K Company, 116th Infantry Regiment was the second Virginia National Guard soldier awarded the Medal of Honor. Sergeant Peregory single-handedly killed eight Germans, took out a machine gun, and forced more than thirty to surrender. Six days later, he was killed in action.[318]

Frank Peregory was born in Albemarle County, Virginia, in 1931, and was only fifteen years old when he joined K Company, 116th Infantry Regiment, 29th Infantry Division, Virginia Army National Guard. Frank Peregory never returned to the hill country of central Virginia, and his remains rest under the French soil that he helped liberate. Tech. Sergeant Frank Peregory is buried at Colleville-sur-Mer American Cemetery, and I spent some very somber moments beside his grave.[319]

There is a wonderful museum, the 29th Division Museum, that displays historical artifacts and records of the 29th Infantry Division, but also houses extensive historical displays of the 116th Infantry Regiment. This museum is located in Verona, Virginia. I am honored to serve on the 116th Infantry Regiment Foundation, Inc. (116thfoundation.org), which oversees and helps sustain the museum.

This museum sponsors informative tours to the significant battlefields where elements of the 29th Infantry Division and the 116th Infantry Regiment fought. These include tours around America, and overseas tours to World War I and World War II sites. The museum's motto speaks to the issue at hand, "We remember who they were and what they've done: We educate others about them and their accomplishments." I might add, "lest we forget."

"Omaha, Utah, and Colleville-sur-Mer"

In 2014, for the 70th anniversary year of D-Day, a retired Army friend and I visited Normandy. Chaplain (Colonel) Ed Northrop, U.S. Army (Ret.) and I flew "space available" on a C-17 out of Andrews Air Force Base to Ramstein Air Force Base, Germany.

I had previously flown on the flight deck of a C-17 from Doha, Qatar, to Baghdad, Iraq, and nothing compares to the ride. As a matter of fact, the pilot was a young man who went to high school with my nephew.

The trip to Normandy was personal for Ed and me, as both of us had previously served as chaplains in units of the 116th Infantry Regiment. It was also personal for me because my father-in-law was in the "first wave" at Utah Beach.

Over the years, at various "Regimental Musters," we often met survivors from D-Day who stormed Omaha Beach on that infamous 6th of June. These elderly men told vivid stories of that long ago day, yet to them, like it was yesterday. Many of them wore the visible scars of their physical wounds, but all of them wore the emotional scars warriors forever carry.

Ed and I settled in at the Air Force Inn at Ramstein, and for several days, we visited some nearby sites on the Rhine, including a day trip to see a portion of the famed, "Maginot Line." However, our goal was to walk on the beaches of Omaha and Utah.

We traveled from Kaiserslautern "K Town," Germany by "TGV high-speed train" to Paris, crossed town to change train lines, and finally disembarked at Port-en-Bessin-Huppain on Normandy Coast. Our pilgrimage led to a quiet, reflective time on Omaha and Utah Beaches as well as visits to several local D-Day museums.

After Ed and I somberly walked the beaches, we spent an emotional day moving through the American Cemetery at Colleville-sur-Mer, where 9,388 American troops are buried. Many of these died on D-Day. Walking among those markers, denoting young lives cut short, one cannot help but feel that these died for something they would never enjoy, "life, liberty, and the pursuit of happiness."

The Colleville-sur-Mer Cemetery hosts over a million visitors a year and falls under the oversight of the American Battle Monuments Commission.

NATIONAL D-DAY MEMORIAL

"...Delivered us from evil and saved the free world."-President Bush June 6, 2001[320]

In addition to the graves at Colleville-sur-Mer, the sacrifices of those who died on D-Day are memorialized at the National D-Day Memorial in Bedford, Virginia. For me, this memorial's grounds and structures are also "sacred ground," as the names of over 4,500 who died on D-Day are embossed there.

President George W. Bush, in his dedication speech at the D-Day Memorial in Bedford, Virginia, on June 6, 2001, stated: "Fifty-seven years ago, America and the nations of Europe formed a bond that has never been broken. And all of us incurred a debt that can never be repaid. Today, as America dedicates our D-Day Memorial, we pray that our country will always be worthy of the courage that delivered us from evil and saved the free world."[321]

YOUNG SOLDIERS OFF TO WAR

As has often happened through the years, "Company A" of Bedford would once again head off to war. In 2004, sixty years after D-Day, I joined Virginia's governor at the time, Governor Mark Warner, at the D-Day Memorial for a ceremony denoting Company A's deployment to Afghanistan. At the time, I was the 29th Infantry Division chaplain, and was invited to offer an Invocation at the ceremony. I'm sure the anxiety level of this new group of "Bedford Boys" and their families matched that of their predecessors' sixty years prior.

OLD SOLDIER'S FINAL SALUTE

"Chubby" Proffitt was a good friend, and we enjoyed breaking bread together each month at our American Legion Post 74 meetings where I served as Post chaplain.

LIEUTENANT CARL "CHUBBY" PROFFITT, U.S. ARMY, WORLD WAR II

Chubby had long been a local hero in our community, but he was also America's hero. The Distinguished Service Cross is the Army's second-highest military award for "extraordinary heroism in combat." It is second only to the Congressional Medal of Honor. Over 10,000,000 veterans served in the Army during World War II, but the Army awarded only 3,984 Distinguished Service Crosses.[322] Carl "Chubby" Proffitt was one of the 3,984.

He joined the local "K" Company of the 116th Infantry Regiment of the Virginia Army National Guard in the late '30s to make a little extra money. By June 6, 1944, Chubby Profit was fighting for his life on Omaha Beach.[323]

On D-Day, Technical Sergeant Proffitt led his platoon out of a Higgins Boat and onto Omaha Beach. For his actions on D-Day, he was awarded the Distinguished Service Cross. Part of the citation reads: *"In spite of the great number of casualties that were being inflicted on his company, SGT Proffitt on a number of occasions fearlessly exposed himself to this intense fire in order to encourage and lead his troops across the beach."*[324]

A few weeks after D-Day, Sergeant Proffitt, though seriously wounded, was awarded a Silver Star for valor for, as the citation states, *"...making repeated trips into the minefield under decimating enemy machine gun and artillery fire to administer first aid and evacuate the wounded..."*[325]

Though he was a very humble man, he was very proud of his service in the war, and if asked, he would readily talk about his service. By the end of his service in Europe, Chubby Proffitt received a battlefield commission to lieutenant, a Distinguished Service Cross, a Silver Star for valor, two Bronze Stars, and three Purple Hearts.

The day I visited Chubby in his hospital room, though he was ninety-six, there was no indication that within a few hours he would be joining his dear wife, Ollie, who predeceased him. We talked for a while about a number of things, including D-Day.

I actually took a selfie of us during that visit, and the time stamp on the photo shows, "Martha Jefferson Hospital, June 29, 2015, 4:58 p.m." I still have that picture on my phone. I am so grateful I had the opportunity to thank him one last time for his service and the pain and suffering he endured for his country.

The motto for the 116th is "Ever Forward."

"EVER FORWARD Chubby!"

CHAPTER 16

VETERANS AND OLD GLORY

"…time to reflect and honor our flag, to honor those who have fallen before us and to honor the country…" -Senior Airman Taylor Sams[326]

THIS IS AN IMPORTANT TOPIC ABOUT VETERANS and their unique view of the American flag.

If one watches the Civil War documentary, "Remember the Sultana," on Amazon Prime, one cannot help being moved by the events surrounding the explosion and sinking of this Mississippi steamboat. Many may not be aware of it, but the story of the Sultana actually records the worst maritime disaster in American history. Records show that on April 27, 1865, when the Sultana sank, up to 1,700 lives were lost.[327]

Adding to the great sadness of this event is the fact that the Civil War was over, and the Sultana had been engaged to transport recently-liberated Union prisoners of war back into Northern territory and then to their homes and families.

Due to various reasons, including greed and graft, when it left Vicksburg, it was grievously overloaded. It was rated to carry less than 400, and yet on April 27, she transported close to 2,500. Those 1,700 who perished had survived the battle-field and even the southern POW camps of Andersonville and

Cahaba. The South had surrendered; they were on their way home, yet never to make it.[328]

The story of the Sultana is just one more incident where hundreds of young Americans died while in service to their country. These soldiers left home and family and fought for the preservation of the Union and the end of slavery in America. Within the history of the Civil War, the Sultana's victims are mostly overlooked.

As I watched the documentary, I was captivated by an actual quote from one of the recently paroled Union prisoners of war, Lieutenant Joseph Taylor Elliott. As Lieutenant Elliott's prisoner group awaited a ferry to transport them across the Mississippi to their parole camp on the other side, they could actually "…see the Stars and Stripes floating over the parole camp." You can find his full quote in his own memoir, *The Sultana Disaster*, but a portion of it follows:

In his words:

> *It was too far away to see even the stripes, but we knew it was "the old flag," and as it floated out I felt that I loved it as I never had before. Perhaps every American would appreciate it more if he were obliged to live for awhile out from under its protection. "Long may it wave, o'er the land of the free and the home of the brave."[329]*

His sentiments reflect the depth of love that is shared by many veterans for "the old flag."

For most veterans, you cannot separate the symbols of the nation from the veteran. When talking to a group of veterans, from my experience, you will find they associate the flag with a sense of responsibility to the country, a reminder of fallen friends, and a recognition of the many good things about America for which they risked their lives.

When they served, each wore a small flag on their uniforms. Eventually, each veteran's casket is draped by an American flag that will be folded and presented to his or her next of kin from a "grateful nation."

Without a military connection, some may not be able to grasp the depth of attachment that veterans have to this particular national symbol. From your very first day of basic training, you become laser-focused upon a proper rendering of honors to the flag. At a central location on every US military installation, the flag is displayed, and twice a day, honoring the flag and what it means becomes the mission.

A service member's day begins with Reveille, and ends with Retreat/"To the Colors." Both of these bugle calls are of great significance and call everyone to a momentary focus upon the flag. At the beginning of Reveille or Retreat, those outdoors and in uniform come to attention, face the flag or the direction of the music, salute, and hold the salute to the last note.

Even those not in uniform come to attention, face the flag, remove headgear with the right hand, and place right hand over the heart until the last note. A new law passed in 2008 states veterans and military members, not in uniform, may "remain covered," render a hand salute, instead of placing their hand over their heart. If one is driving on a base when either of these begins, military personnel are to safely stop their vehicle until the music ends. Singularly, on Army posts, if possible, you safely stop your vehicle and stand at attention beside it and render the salute.

The memory bank of many veterans includes an inordinate number of memories of the deaths of friends and fellow Americans. For many of these veterans, any action that distracts or breaks from all they have been taught about rendering honors is just "one bridge too far" for them to cross.

Senior Airman Taylor Sams of Joint Base Charleston reflects the view of many in the military. In an interview, she talked about "the honor and tradition" behind these trumpet calls and why they are important. In her words: "Whenever we hear it…it gives us time to reflect and honor our flag, to honor those who have fallen before us and to honor the country…"[330]

Senior Airman Sams' views reflect that veterans, more than most, associate the flag with **the need to honor fallen heroes and honor the country.**

There are numerous reminders to service members of the appropriate responses to the national anthem. Even if you are in civilian clothes on a day off and you go see a movie on base, prior to the movie's showing, everyone stands for the national anthem. It's something engrained.

Many of my generation were children of veterans, and when you went to a ballgame with your dad, as I did, there was no question, you stood, put your popcorn down, put your hand over your heart, and sang with everyone else the nation's anthem.

The Marine Corps has long been known as "The Few, The Proud." One doesn't have to dig deep into their vaunted history to find stories of numerous heroes. Though the smallest of the service branches, 297 Marines have been awarded the Congressional Medal of Honor; the majority of these died in their teens or early twenties.[331]

Many images of Marines in action could have been chosen for the US Marine Corps War Memorial in Washington. What was selected, however, was the depiction of the raising of the American flag on Iwo Jima. The one symbol worthy of the 7,000 Marines who died on Iwo Jima and for all other Marines who would die in other wars was the symbol of the flag planted on Mount Suribachi on February 23, 1945.[332]

One of the six Marines in Joe Rosenthal's iconic photograph portrayed on the Memorial was Private First Class Ira Hayes, a Hopi Indian code talker. Six Marines risked their lives to raise that flag, and several of the six would later be killed on Iwo Jima.[333]

Earlier, we shared comments from the sons of two Chinese-American war heroes. In this discussion of veterans and the American flag, their words are again apropos. They stressed the patriotism of these Chinese-American volunteers:

"When they saw the Stars and Stripes, they were filled with pride. They viewed it as a symbol of hope and a beacon of freedom to preserve and protect. Maybe they had something to prove: that they were more American than their peers, who took their nationality for granted. Being American was the core of their identity. It showed in their actions..."[334] (emphasis mine).

From Chapter 13, in the section on Native Americans in World War II, the story of Colonel Van Barfoot was related. Just as a reminder, his heritage is Choctaw, he joined the Army in 1940, and on May 23, 1944, while a technician sergeant in the Army, he was awarded the Medal of Honor for actions of great valor.[335] He made the military a career and served through the Korean and Vietnam Wars, finally retiring in 1974 as a colonel after thirty-four years of service.[336]

In 2009, at the age of ninety, his patriotism got him into trouble with some of his fellow American neighbors. In 2009, after his wife's death, he moved from his farm in Amelia County, Virginia, into a sub-division in the suburbs of Richmond, Virginia, to be near his daughter.[337]

That's when things got interesting. Colonel Barfoot, as was his custom, put up a flagpole in his yard upon which to fly his American flag, which he raised and saluted every day. Soon, he was notified the flagpole had to come down, that it did not meet the aesthetic requirements of the community HOA (homeowner's association). Even after sharing a bit of his story and his lifetime of honoring "old glory," the HOA insisted his flagpole come down, and they would take him to court if necessary.[338]

Fortunately, enough attention, even nationally, generated great support for Colonel Barfoot, and finally, the HOA relented and let him keep his flagpole.

"All my life, from childhood to now, I have been able to fly the flag," Barfoot told supporters standing outside his house Wednesday. "In the time I have left, I plan to continue to fly the American flag without interference."[339]

He flew the flag and saluted it every day until his death in his ninety-second year. He fell in his yard and hit his head, which led to his death.[340]

Colonel Van Barfoot was awarded the Medal of Honor, Silver Star Medal, Bronze Star Medal, two Purple Hearts, eleven Air Medals, and many other medals and ribbons.[341] I cannot fathom how anyone in America would have the audacity to tell a war hero like Colonel Barfoot to pull down his flagpole that was flying the American flag. Colonel Barfoot's experiences demonstrate many Americans just do not share most veterans' esteem for the "grand old flag."

The following is repeated from the section describing the death of Lieutenant Sal Corma in Afghanistan.

Outside the Corma's home…two dozen America flags ring the shrubbery garden and the tree mounds. The 'Ave Maria' was immediately followed by "The Star-Spangled Banner," [LT] Corma loved the church and the military.

Father Galetto said Corma embodied the spirit of service and good deeds, not for his own sake, but to earn the honor of friends, family and "a grateful nation who gives thanks for men and women like Salvatore Corma."[342]

Look into the eyes of a World War II vet, a Korean War vet, or a Vietnam Vet as they stand for the National Anthem, and you will often see a tear. For these old combat vets, they are not just seeing a brightly-colored cloth, but they are "paying their respects," to the country they dearly love, and honoring the memories of their battle buddies.

During the seventy-fifth anniversary events at Pearl Harbor in 2016, and at the seventy-fifth anniversary events for D-Day in France in 2019, many witnessed the sobbing of very old men as they recalled friends who died long ago.

These days, we veterans from Iraq and Afghanistan now understand the sentimentalism of those older generations of vets, as we express our love of country and shed our tears for our comrades who never came home.

The service of the millions of American veterans, represented by every race, creed, gender, and demographic, gives testimony of their deep love for their country. One thing every honorably-discharged veteran earns is a flag-draped coffin.

Speaking for all of my veteran friends and myself, America's veterans desire national unity. Veterans have a vested interest in America's well-being and future. They have and will listen to the issues and support the hard work required to bring America together. They sincerely, probably more than most, want "justice" for every citizen. They risked their lives for "all" Americans. They remember their combat buddies from different races that, "had their backs," and who didn't come home. Veterans served for every American to enjoy "equal protection" under the law.

Absolutely, we have systemic problems to address, but the issue for many veterans is the manner of the protest that is being used. Most veterans' DNA requires that the only time you kneel in the presence of the flag is when it is presented on bended knee to the next of kin of a fallen hero.

CHAPTER 17

· · · · · · · · · · · · · · · · · · ·

THANKS FOR
THE MEMORIES

*Marcus' Heart Foundation "…mentors youth…in
the crossroads of decision for their future. At the
same time…dedicated to helping our solders…"[343]*

MANY INSTITUTIONS AND ORGANIZATIONS CON-
tribute to the well-being of the nation. A few of them
are of exceptionally high value, such as our educators, farmers,
medical providers, religious leaders, and first responders. Yet,
only the military take the oath to protect us "…against all enemies, foreign and domestic," and fulfills that oath, if required,
on a foreign battlefield and at the cost of their lives. The sun
never sets on all the places where America's military serve,
twenty-four seven, to fulfill their oath. I tried to make the case
that America has a special kind of indebtedness to her military
and veterans.

The title, "Thanks for the Memories," references my rec-
ollections of numerous acts of support shown to our troops. It
is encouraging that many Americans exhibit profound support
for our troops, veterans, and fallen service members. I have
seen firsthand what a grateful nation looks like. At the close
of this chapter, I will include a list of links to those very fine

organizations included in the book that support our military community.

Earlier, we included a section on Marcus Tynes. I mentioned how Marcus's family focused on thanking his fellow paratroopers from the 82nd who came for his funeral. This should have been about them, but they made it about others. His parents, Bruce and Dana Atlas, continued encouraging others. They established the "Marcus' Heart Foundation (marcussheartfoundation.org) in honor of their son.[344] This foundation supports youth with scholarships, mentors youth, and they are dedicated to helping soldiers and veterans.

When our charter flight filled with troops was delivering us to the war zone, we stopped in Shannon, Ireland to refuel. Our flight of over 200 was allowed to disembark and stretch our legs. Soon, one of our senior enlisted came around, informing everyone that an American business man in the airport had just invited every soldier to order a drink and snacks on him. He saw us in uniform, and made this very generous gesture. I'm sure his bill totaled over several thousand dollars. He didn't share his name, as he wanted to do this without recognition, but his actions certainly boosted the morale of a bunch of GIs headed to war.

While in Iraq, it still amazes me to think of it, but in just our one office alone, my assistant and I processed over 5,000 pounds of "care packages" that came from kind Americans from all across the country. These boxes were sent, in care of the chaplain, knowing that we would make sure they were dispersed and enjoyed. One of the gifts that meant the most were the cards made by schoolchildren, "thanking the troops." Many care packages included things, such as snacks, socks, hygiene products, stationary, magazines, books, CDs, and DVDs.

We received far too much "stuff" for just our base, so we began to solicit requests from the troops located at many of the isolated Forward Operating Bases (FOBs). We broke down the packages and repacked them, according to what individual soldiers requested.

Occasionally, we would get a request for something like beef jerky or canned tuna, and we would pass on the request to folks back home. It would soon arrive, and we would send it downrange. By word of mouth, what we were doing got around to some soldiers in Afghanistan, who sent us e-mails, asking if we could send something to them. We took their requests and filled them. It kept us busy between our weekly travels, but we were pleased to be the conduit "passing on the love" from home.

Out of the hundreds, there was one particular care package that will always stand out. In spring 2007, on a Wednesday, Sandy Mawyer, a friend of ours from church, called my wife and asked for my APO address. She made delicious homemade cheese balls, knew how much I enjoyed them, and wanted to send me a care package, including one. By the following Sunday, my wife had received word that Sandy had been killed in a car accident. When I talked to my wife that Sunday evening, she told me about Sandy's request for my APO and her sudden death. We weren't sure if she had mailed the care package before her death.

About a week later, a package arrived with her name on the return address. I'm surprised it didn't read, "Heaven."

It took me a few days to prepare myself to open the package. The day I opened it, I found in her own hand, a very kind note stating her appreciation for what we were doing, and we were in her prayers. She had said to please share "the goodies." One afternoon, I invited those on our office hall to come over for a few minutes. I related our friendship with Sandy and her husband, Wayne, and the story of this special gift package. We paused for a moment of silence in honor of her, and passed around "the cheese and crackers."

For all of us present, and especially for me, her gift was a special blessing and reinforced the truth that within the American family, there were many other "Sandy Mawyers" supporting the country's troops. Her "good deeds" lived on, even after her death; what an important life lesson for all of us.

At the completion of my Iraq tour, the charter flight bringing our group back to America stopped in Bangor, Maine, to refuel. It was after midnight, and as we departed the plane for a brief rest break, someone from Bangor greeted every single soldier. They shook our hands, shared a warm word of welcome, and offered each soldier the use of a cell phone to call family members and tell them we were back on American soil. Those incredible citizens of Bangor also provided us food and refreshments.

I found the website for these greeters, themainetroopgreeters.org, and it states, "And it is our pledge that as long as there are U. S. Armed Forces serving overseas we will be here to greet them."[345] Their website went on to say they "… have greeted over 7,417 flights… more than 1,499,277 service members, 403 military dogs."[346]

I was one of those service members who received that greeting, and I know what it meant to me. It had been a difficult year in Iraq; I lost friends and felt the loss of many others that I did not know. The importance of being welcomed back home to American soil in such a warm way made a powerful impact. Their actions reminded us of the "specialness" of our large American family and why our troops are willing to go into harm's way to preserve it.

These greeters are officially "The Maine Troop Greeters," and have achieved "hero" status within the military family. I would certainly encourage my fellow Americans to visit their website and support their worthy efforts.

During my time as a Rear Detachment chaplain with the 82nd Airborne Division, I traveled often to diverse places to conduct funerals for fallen paratroopers. In over a dozen states, all across America, I was inspired by witnessing community after community honoring their sons and daughters who died fighting in wars far from home.

In literally every case, wherever I traveled to provide chaplain support for a fallen paratrooper, individual communities displayed a sincere appreciation of their "hometown hero" who was killed in action. I saw this in Concord, California, not far from Berkeley, where the marquis on businesses, churches, and other locations posted the name of a local young man who died in Iraq while serving with the 1st BCT of the 82nd Airborne Division. A police motorcycle escort led the motorcade, which escorted his hearse to the cemetery. Along the route, dozens lined the streets, showing their respect.

I saw this type of response repeated in Los Angeles, Chicago, Cleveland, and dozens of smaller towns. There were always escorts provided by police motorcycles, police cars, fire trucks, and rescue vehicles with their lights flashing. Often, a group of Patriot Guard motorcyclists followed, and then the long line of vehicles of family, friends, and strangers who came out to offer support. At times, I saw hundreds of spectators lining the route, from the funeral to the cemetery, paying their respects.

Honoring their own by the military is to be expected. But the support and appreciation rendered by average citizens is a genuine tribute to the soldier, and reflects priorities that speak of a nation's character.

During my service as the 82nd Rear D chaplain, there were numerous accounts of persons and organizations dropping off items for us to forward to our deployed paratroopers. One rather unique offer came from a gentleman named Bobby Jones. This Bobby Jones from Suffolk, Virginia, was a salesman whose territory included eastern North Carolina. Once we became friends, he often dropped by my office and gave me a case of CDs to send downrange. Bobby sang in a Gospel quartet called, "Still Searchin," and they were a talented group. We started getting requests for their CDs.

Another interesting fact about Bobby was the fact he was MLB's Chipper Jones's uncle. I am a lifelong Atlanta Braves fan, and I actually have a Chipper Jones jersey. This was 2010, and at one point, Bobby and I talked about going down to Atlanta for a game, and he would introduce me to Chipper. We were never able to coordinate that trip. We were in such a demanding pace that I didn't take any leave during 2010.

My wife and I live near Charlottesville, Virginia, in Albemarle County. Annually, on Memorial Day, both local VFW posts in our area sponsor a Memorial Day ceremony. On Veterans Day, the local American Legion Post hosts a community Veterans Day service.

In addition to our local veterans groups, there are a number of local organizations whose purpose includes honoring our service members and veterans. One group that honored me for my service was the Thomas Jefferson Chapter of the Sons of the American Revolution. They regularly honor the service of veterans as part of their purpose.

Other local groups that support the military community include, a Blue Star Mothers Chapter and the ParadeRest organization. Our local Blue Star Chapter is very active with many projects to support our active duty military and their families, including sending care packages downrange. ParadeRest supports our local active duty military, veterans, and first responders by arranging free tickets to entertainment venues and sporting events. Other community volunteers sponsor an annual "4 Our Freedom 5K," whose proceeds go to support veterans activities. Our local Civitan International club joins other Civitan clubs across the country to annually honor the "Four Army Chaplains" who died on the USAT Dorchester.

As our city and county are neighbors to the University of Virginia, we benefit from the regular military appreciation days that are part of their athletic schedules. Also at UVA, our local veterans enjoy the camaraderie of an annual "veterans appreciation" dinner that is provided by the UVA Army ROTC.

A number of significant historical sites, as well as the homes of four former presidents, are nearby where my wife and I live. This includes the homes of Thomas Jefferson, James Madison, and James Monroe. About forty-five miles away from Charlottesville, one can visit the birthplace of Woodrow Wilson in Stanton, Virginia.

In relationship to Charlottesville, however, I want to share a more recent and different type of historical site. The very first civic/public memorial in the United States dedicated to those who served and sacrificed their lives in Vietnam is located in Charlottesville. The Dogwood Vietnam Memorial, a project of the Charlottesville Dogwood Festival, Inc., was conceived late in 1965 after news arrived that Army Specialist Champ Jackson Lawson Jr. was killed in Vietnam.

He was the first Albemarle County/Charlottesville area Vietnam War casualty. A group of three men, Bill Gentry, Jim Shisler, and Ken Staples, talking at Staples Barber Shop in the city, came up with the idea of a memorial.

Recently, I spoke again with Jim Shisler, the only survivor of the original three, and he said he knew the father of Champ Lawson Jr. At the time of the original memorial, there was only one young man from this area that had died. Yet, these men, veterans themselves, felt that something needed to be done so that Champ's life and sacrifice would be honored and not forgotten.

Mr. Shisler added, even as early as 1965, there were the beginnings of protests against the war, and they wanted to make sure any local servicemen who died in Vietnam would not be "shamed" or forgotten.

Charlottesville is very proud of being home to many beautiful dogwood trees. There is a local Dogwood Festival board that oversees the annual Dogwood Festival, a festival that incorporates many community activities. Bill Gentry, Jim Shisler, and Ken Staples were Dogwood Festival board members. They presented their vision of a memorial project to the festival board. The project was adopted and named the Charlottesville Dogwood Vietnam Memorial.

This memorial is located in the city at the intersection of the John Warner Parkway and McIntire Road. Its purpose, as stated, is, "The Dogwood Memorial dedicated to the lasting memory of these men and all who served our country in Vietnam."

The Dogwood Vietnam Memorial was dedicated on April 20, 1966, as a part of the annual Charlottesville Dogwood Festival. Since then, every year during the festival, there is a service held at the site, to remember Champ Lawson Jr., and the other 27 Vietnam veterans from our area, who subsequently died in the Vietnam War.

This year marked the 55th year of the memorial's existence. This memorial not only honors the fallen but is also dedicated to the service of the Vietnam War veterans who survived the war. These veterans have given a name to the memorial and its site, the "Hill That Heals."

The city of Charlottesville provided the beautiful location for the memorial, and the community rallied to raise the funds for its construction. Through various stages of development, this memorial is now a place of great beauty, designed as a tribute to young men from different races who left our community to offer their lives in service to their country. These men will never be forgotten. It is operated as partnership between the city and the memorial foundation.

I serve on the Dogwood Vietnam Memorial Foundation Board, and we extend an open invitation to come visit this beautiful memorial and join us in paying respects to these young men. It always feels right to stop long enough to say thanks!

EPILOGUE

"It was too far away to see even the stripes, but we knew **it was 'the old flag,'** and as it floated out I felt that I loved it as I never had before. **Perhaps every American would appreciate it more if he were obliged to live for awhile out from under its protection.** 'Long may it wave, o'er the land of the free and the home of the brave.'"-Lieutenant Joseph Taylor Elliott, U.S. Army, 1865[347] (emphasis mine)

AMERICA: THE CITY ON A HILL

It is ironic that even though America has problems to solve, there are literally tens of thousands who risk their lives each year to try and make it to America. Many Americans don't like to describe our country as exceptional or a special place. Even now, tens of thousands of "would-be" immigrants must see something "exceptional" about America. Maybe we Americans are missing something about our country that others see. Why not remind ourselves of the many freedoms that America affords? After all, we have a Bill of Rights, which includes freedom of speech, freedom of assembly, freedom of religion, freedom of the press, just to name a few.

It may not be fashionable to brag about America, but as recent as October 9, 2016, in a debate with Donald Trump, Hillary Clinton said, "America is already…great…we are great because we are good, and we will respect each other."[348]

I agree with that, but I would sure like to hear that expressed more often.

Since the second half of the 20th century, multiple thousands of so-called "boat people" from diverse places, such as Vietnam, Cuba, and Haiti, risked their lives seeking the shores of the US. Thousands of others fled places, such as Central America, South America, Africa, China, Yemen, Iraq, eastern Europe, and Syria, with the goal of reaching America. They want the life that we have in America.

For these, America is that land of liberty and opportunity. And many have died and will die trying to get here. The great majority of the world's citizens do not have nearly the liberties or opportunities that we have in America.

Certainly, from the long view, America has made strides in facing and overcoming her shortcomings, and most Americans of all races and religious views are good people who care about others. The proof of this is in the willing sacrifices of so many Americans of all races who have not only served in America's military service but who died for their country.

This service by millions of American veterans, represented by every race, creed, gender, and demographic, gives testimony of a deep love for those good things about their country.

It does seem, despite our real problems and shortcomings, we sometimes overlook and even negate the greatness and goodness of America. America's greatness was certainly recognized by the service of all of her veterans, and especially by the deaths of 1.3 million of them.

This is the America who saw over 200,000 African Americans voluntarily join either the Union Army or Navy in the Civil War, with twenty-four Medal of Honor awardees, and over 68,000 killed or missing.[349]

From every American minority group, large numbers have volunteered in all of our wars, from the War of Independence forward.

Lest we forget, in the Civil War, over 360,000 White Union soldiers died to end slavery.[350] This is the America where 117,000 died in World War I, and over 400,000 American military personnel died in World War II to stop the Axis.[351]

Thirty-six US Army Divisions are credited by the National Holocaust Museum with being World War II liberating units who liberated concentration camps and death camps from the Nazis.[352]

In the Korean War, almost 40,000 American service members died, and in Vietnam, another 58,000 died; two-thirds of them were volunteers.[353]

Since 9/11, over 7,000 American service members were killed and more than 50,000 wounded in the Global War on Terror.[354] All were volunteers. Every young man and young woman who joined the military since 9/11 had the reasonable expectation they would head into harm's way to protect their fellow citizens.

I've spoken with a number of our newest immigrants, and more than one has shared bewilderment why America's athletes, especially those who represent the country, and wear the nation's colors, kneel when America's National Anthem is played. It is puzzling that athletes from other countries, even those nations with despicable human rights records, do not choose to kneel before their anthems and flags.

I'm convinced the great majority of Americans share an esteem of the unique values, liberties, and opportunities this country affords. I believe we just need a reminder, from time to time, of how blessed we are to live in such a place, and at the same time, ever striving for "a more perfect union."

Every group of new naturalized citizens that were drawn here by our liberties and opportunities understand far better than many of their native-born counterparts on just how unique America's privileges are. One requirement to become a naturalized citizen is to pass a civics component of the citizenship test, where one must demonstrate a sufficient knowledge and understanding of US history and government.

These newest citizens are taught the essence of this American "experiment" in democracy, is a government "of the people, by the people, and for the people." They've studied and cherish the individual protections that are contained in our founding documents, including the Bill of Rights.

Just for the record, yes, we have work to do in providing equal opportunity for all our citizens. Yet, never in the history of the world has there been a country that has offered as much freedom, has done so much for the people of the less fortunate countries of the world, or has had so many multitudes of people risk their lives to get here.

A HOPEFUL FUTURE

As I close this book, the service of two young Americans, Marcus A. Tynes and Ross A. McGinnis, encourages me that our heroes of the future will be there when we need them.

Many families in America, as the generations before them, are instilling in their sons and daughters a love of country. It's the youth from these homes who can be counted upon to defend our way of life from tomorrow's threats.

Marcus A. Tynes joined the US Army in July 2008, at the age of eighteen, just a few weeks after graduating from high school. He was a paratrooper serving in the 82nd Airborne Division and was killed as his vehicle struck an IED in Zabel,

Afghanistan. When he got out of the military, he planned to serve on the Los Angeles Police Department SWAT team. He wanted to protect and serve his community.[355]

Ross A. McGinnis joined the US Army on June 14, 2004, his seventeenth birthday, on a delayed entry program, and died for his country on December 4, 2006. Without hesitation, he willingly gave his life to save four fellow soldiers.[356]

As long as we have enough young Americans, like this California teenager, who **voluntarily** joined the Army right out of high school, and this Pennsylvania teenager, who, on his seventeenth birthday **voluntarily** joined the Army to serve his country, then America has hopes of a bright future. Just for the record, Marcus was Black, and Ross was White. Each made an equal investment in America's future.

On September 25, and again on September 28, 2001, as we concluded memorial services in the Pentagon auditorium for four fallen Americans, everyone stood and sang Irving Berlin's simple, yet powerful, "God Bless America."

As I conclude **THESE HONORED DEAD**, written as a tribute to all of America's gallant heroes of the past, present, and future, who put country before self, I think it fitting to offer the following prayer:

> "God bless America, land that I love,
> Stand beside her and guide her
> Through the night with a light from above
> From the mountains to the prairies
> To the oceans white with foam
> God bless America, my home sweet home..."

MY HALL OF FAME

Throughout this book, I've mentioned a number of great organizations that I'm personally acquainted with that either promotes remembering veterans, serving veterans, or both. Thankfully, there are many others. I can certainly endorse all of the following. For organizations like these to succeed, they need our support. Let me encourage you to choose one off this list or find a worthy military and veteran's support group of your choice and offer your support:

- **29th Division Museum,**
  https://116thfoundation.org

- **Dogwood Vietnam Memorial Foundation,**
  https://www.cvilledogwood.com/vietnam-memorial

- **Marcus A. Tynes Foundation,**
  https://www.marcussheartfoundation.org

- **Blue Star Mothers Chapter,**
  https://bsfcv.avenue.org

- **ParadeRest,**
  https://www.paraderestva.org

- **The Four Chaplains Memorial Foundation,**
  http://fourchaplains.org

- **The Honor Flight Network,**
  https://www.honorflight.org

- **The Patriot Guard,**
  https://www.patriotguard.org/wp-signup.php?new=patriotguard.org

- **Rolling Thunder Washington, DC, Inc.,**
  https://rollingthunderrun.com

- **National World War II Museum,**
  https://www.nationalww2museum.org237

- **Maine Troop Greeters & Museum of Bangor, Maine,**
  http://themainetroopgreeters.com/

ENDNOTES

1   "Remarks by General Colin Powell Upon Receiving The Sylvanus Thayer Award," September 15, 1998, https://www.westpointaog.org/page.aspx?pid=494

2   "Secretary of Defense," https://www.defense.gov/our-story/meet-the-team/secretary-of-defense/

3   Brad Bennett, "For Love of Country: Black veterans join movement to rid military installations of Confederate names and symbols,"Southern Poverty Law Center, https://www.splcenter.org/news/2020/10/14/love-country-black-veterans-join-movement-rid-military-installations-confederate-names-and

4   Bennett, "For Love of Country."

5   Bennett, "For Love of Country."

6   "America's Founding Documents," https://www.archives.gov/founding-docs/declaration-transcript

7   "Remarks by General Colin Powell."

8   Todd South, "Rising Costs, dwindling recruit numbers, increasing demands may bring back the military draft," *Military Times*, https://www.militarytimes.com/news/your-military/2019/11/19/rising-costs-dwindling-recruit-numbers-increasing-demands-may-bring-back-the-draft/

9   Robert Frost, "The Death of the Hired Man," https://poets.org/poem/death-hired-man

10   "Remarks by General Colin Powell."

11   "Remarks by General Colin Powell."

12   "Give me liberty or give me death!,"Colonial Williamsburg, https://www.colonialwilliamsburg.org/learn/deep-dives/give-me-liberty-or-give-me-death/

13   "Remarks by General Colin Powell."

14   "Remarks by General Colin Powell."

15 "Research & Collections Menu, "The tree of liberty…,"
    Thomas Jefferson Encyclopedia, https://www.monticello.org/site/
    research-and-collections/tree-liberty-quotation
16 "Address by the President of the United States of America, John
    F. Kennedy, Before the Free University Berlin, June 26, 1963,"
    https://www.berlin.de/berlin-im-ueberblick/geschichte/ber-
    lin-nach-1945/john-f-kennedy-in-berlin/rede-an-der-freien-uni-
    versitaet-berlin/artikel.493592.php
17 "America's Wars," Department of Veterans Affairs, https://www.
    va.gov/opa/publications/factsheets/fs_americas_wars.pdf
18 History.com editors, "The Gettysburg Address,"August
    24, 2010, updated November 18, 2019, *History
    Channel,* https://www.google.com/search?client=safa-
    ri&rls=en&q=History.com+editors,+%E2%80%9CThe+Get-
    tysburg+Address,%E2%80%9D+history.
    com.,+August+24,+2010,+updated+Novem-
    ber+18,+2019&ie=UTF-8&oe=UTF-8
19 "Address Broadcast to the Armed Forces, April 17, 1945,"
    Truman Library, https://www.trumanlibrary.gov/library/
    public-papers/5/address-broadcast-armed-forces
20 Lord Alfred Tennyson, "The Charge of the Light Brigade,"Poetry
    Foundation, https://www.poetryfoundation.org/poems/45319/
    the-charge-of-the-light-brigade
21 Ed Vulliamy, "Let's Roll…," "World News," *The Guardian.
    com.,* December 02, 2001, https://www.theguardian.com/
    world/2001/dec/02/september11.terrorism
22 "American Deaths in Terrorist Attacks, 1995–2016," START-
    National Consortium for the Study of Terrorism and Responses
    to Terrorism, https://www.start.umd.edu/pubs/START_
    AmericanTerrorismDeaths_FactSheet_Nov2017.pdf
23 "The Party of God and Its Greatest Satan-The 36-Year
    Confrontation Between Hezbollah and the United
    States,"September 2020, https://hezbollah.org/sites/default/
    files/2020-09/Hezbollah_Report_Updated_CLEAN.pdf
24 Todd S. Purdue, "With Candor, Powell Charms Global MTV
    Audience, *New York Times,* February 15, 2002, "https://www.

nytimes.com/2002/02/15/world/with-candor-powell-charms-global-mtv-audience.html

25 Purdue, "Powell Charms."

26 Dennis Wang, "The Pentagon and 9/11," NIH-National Library of Medicine, https://pubmed.ncbi.nlm.nih.gov/15640678/

27 Michaila Hancock., "Pentagon: The World's Largest Office Building–in Infographics,"*Architects Journal,* August 27, 2015,_https://www.architectsjournal.co.uk/news/pentagon-the-worlds-largest-office-building-in-infographics&ie=UTF-8&oe=UTF-8

28 B. Phillip Bugler,"Pentagon," *Encyclopedia Britannica,* May 21, 2020, https://www.britannica.com/topic/Pentagon

29 History.com editors.,"World Trade Center," *History Channel,* December 3, 2009, updated September 10, 2009, https://www.history.com/topics/landmarks/world-trade-center

30 History.com editors., "9/11: The Pentagon," *History Channel,* December 18, 2009, updated June 10, 2019, https://www.history.com/topics/us-government/pentagon

31 NCC Staff., "When Congress last used its powers to declare war," *Constitution Center,* December 8, 2018, https://constitutioncenter.org/blog/when-congress-once-used-its-powers-to-declare-war

32 "S.J.Res.23-Authorization for use of Military Force," 107th Congress, https://www.google.com/search?client=safari&rls=en&q=S.J.Res.23-+Authorization+for+use+of+Military+Force,%E2%80%9D+107th+Congress,+congress.gov.&ie=UTF-8&oe=UTF-8

33 "MSU Pays Tribute to Alumnus others killed Tuesday," September 9, 2001, https://www.newsarchive.msstate.edu/newsroom/article/2001/09/msu-pays-tribute-alumnus-others-killed-tuesday

34 Hilda Solis, "Profile in Courage Award Acceptance Speech-May 22, 2000," Iowa State University Archives of Women's Political Communication., https://awpc.cattcenter.iastate.edu/directory/hilda-solis/

35 Jennie W. Wenger, "Examination of Recent Deployment Experience Across the Services…", Rand Organization, https://www.rand.org/pubs/research_reports/RR1928.html

36 Kim Parker, et al., "The Veteran Experience and the Post-9/11 Generation," Pew Research, https://www.pewresearch.org/social-trends/2019/09/10/the-american-veteran-experience-and-the-post-9-11-generation/

37 Wenger, Examination."

38 Dannielle Kurtzleben, "CHART: How The U.S. Troop Levels In Afghanistan Have Changed Under Obama," *NPR*, https://www.npr.org/2016/07/06/484979294/chart-how-the-u-s-troop-levels-in-afghanistan-have-changed-under-obama

39 "Chart: U. S. troop levels in Iraq," *CNN*, October 10, 2011, https://www.cnn.com/2011/10/21/world/meast/chart-us-troops-iraq/index.html

40 Editors *Encyclopedia Britannica*, "David Petraeus," https://www.britannica.com/biography/David-Petraeus/additional-info#history

41 Alison Eldridge, *Encyclopedia Britannica*, "Martin Dempsey," https://www.britannica.com/biography/Martin-Dempsey

42 Editors *Encyclopedia Britannica*, "David."

43 Eldridge, "Martin."

44 History.com editors, "The Gettysburg Address."

45 "Remembrance Day – November 11, 2021," *National Today*, https://nationaltoday.com/remembrance-day/

46 "Remembrance Day," *National Today.*

47 "History of Veterans Day," Office of Public and Intergovernmental Affairs, https://www.va.gov/opa/vetsday/vetdayhistory.asp

48 "Rear Detachment Command," *U.S. Army Rear Detachment Commander's Handbook, II.*, https://production-arc-us-gov-west-1-attachments.s3-us-gov-west-1.amazonaws.com/s3fs-public/RDC_HANDBOOK.pdf

49 Henry Cunningham, "Fort Bragg dedicates All American Chapel," *Fayettville Observer*, https://www.fayobserver.com/article/20130115/news/301159853

50 "Fort Bragg Army Base," *Military Bases*, https://militarybases. com/north-carolina/fort-bragg/

51 "82nd Airborne Division," *Army Study Guide*, https://www. armystudyguide.com/content/Unit_history/Division_history/82nd-airborne-division.shtml

52 "82nd Airborne Division," *Army Study Guide.*

53 "82nd Airborne Division," *Army Study Guide.*

54 "Rear Detachment Command."

55 Will Rogers, "We Can't all be heroes...," *Quotes*, The Stands4 Network, https://www.quotes.net/quote/3432

56 "In Praise of Gratitude," *Harvard Health Publishing*, https://www. health.harvard.edu/blog/in-praise-of-gratitude-201211215561

57 "On behalf of a grateful nation," *Grey House Harbor Blog*, http:// greyhouseharbor.com/on-behalf-of-a-grateful-nation/

58 Andrew Glass, "U. S. Military draft ends, Jan. 27, 1973," *Politico*, January, 2020, https://www.politico.com/story/2012/01/us-military-draft-ends-jan-27-1973-072085

59 Danielle Cinone, "Heroes Gone Two 9/11 firefighters dead from Ground Zero-related illnesses on same day," *The Sun News*, February 10, 2020, https://www.the-sun.com/news/382361/fire-fighters-dead-ground-zero-illness-same-day/

60 "9-11-2001 Never Forget," Hauppauge Fire Department, https://www.hauppaugefiredepartment.org/page/show/1656592-9-11-2001-never-forget

61 Tara Law, "9/11 Survivors Are Still Getting Sick," *Time*, March 15, 2019, https://time. com/5540749/9-11-victims-compensation-fund-worries/

62 Ruderman Foundation White Paper on: "Mental Health and Suicide of First Responders," https://dir.nv.gov/uploadedFiles/dirnvgov/content/WCS/TrainingDocs/First%20 Responder%20White%20Paper_Final%20(2).pdf

63 Ruderman Foundation White Paper.

64 Lindsay Lowe, "Powerful JFK Quotes That Still Ring True Today," *Parade*, October 7, 2019, https://parade.com/573677/lindsaylowe/13-powerful-jfk-quotes-that-still-ring-true-today/

65 Gillian Brockell, "'A republic, if you can keep it:' Did Ben Franklin really say Impeachment Day's favorite quote?," *Washington Post*, December 18, 2019, https://www.washingtonpost.com/history/2019/12/18/republic-if-you-can-keep-it-did-ben-franklin-really-say-impeachment-days-favorite-quote/

66 Patricia Kim, "Law Makers Seek Answers on rising military and veterans suicided rates," *Military Times*, December 5, 2019, https://www.militarytimes.com/news/your-military/2019/12/05/lawmakers-seek-answers-on-rising-military-and-veterans-suicide-rates/

67 Kim, "Law Makers Seek."

68 "Martin Luther King Jr. 'content of character' quote inspires debate," The *Associated Press MassLive*, January 21, 2013, https://www.masslive.com/news/2013/01/martin_luther_king_jr_content.html

69 "Remarks by General Colin Powell."

70 "Poetry and Power," *The Atlantic Magazine*, February, 1964, https://www.theatlantic.com/magazine/archive/1964/02/poetry-and-power/306325/

71 Public Papers of the Presidents of the United States: John F. Kennedy, 1962, Kennedy Library, https://www.jfklibrary.org/asset-viewer/archives/JFKPOF

72 "Address Broadcast to Armed Forces," Truman Library, https://www.trumanlibrary.gov/soundrecording-records/sr64-8-address-president-truman-armed-forces-united-states-throughout-world

73 "Gettysburg Casualties (Battle Deaths at Gettysburg)," *HistoryNet*, https://www.historynet.com/gettysburg-casualties

74 David Roos, "How Many Were Killed on D-Day?" *History Channel*, https://www.history.com/news/d-day-casualties-deaths-allies

75 "Teaching and Mapping the Geography of the Meuse Argonne Offensive," American Battle Monuments Commission, https://www.abmc.gov/education/teaching-aid/teaching-and-mapping-geography-meuse-argonne-offensive-introduction

76 History.com editors, "The Gettysburg Address."

77 "Pvt. George Sandoe: Gettysburg's First to Fall," *The Pennsylvania Rambler*, August 4, 2019, https://thepennsylvaniarambler. com/2019/08/04/pvt-george-sandoe-gettysburgs-first-to-fall/

78 "Pvt. George Sandoe."

79 "Pvt. George Sandoe."

80 "Lincoln's Second Inaugural Address," National Park Service, https://www.nps.gov/linc/learn/historyculture/lincoln-second-inaugural.htm

81 Mark Johnson, U. S. Chaplains Corp, "Under Fire: Army Chaplains in Korea, 1950," *Army.mil*, April 10, 2013, https://www.army.mil/article/100572/under_fire_army_chaplains_in_korea_1950

82 John Brinstead, "Chaplains Corps History: The Four Chaplains," *Army.mil*, January 28, 2014, https://www.army.mil/article/34090/chaplain_corps_history_the_four_chaplains

83 Four Chaplains Memorial Foundation, http://fourchaplains.org

84 "Sacred, adjective," *Merriam Webster*, https://www.merriam-webster.com/dictionary/sacred

85 Capt. David Gasperson, "We take care of our own," *Army.mil*, August 19, 2019, https://www.army.mil/article/223200/we_take_care_of_our_own_supporting_families_of_the_fallen

86 "President Kennedy's Commemorative Message On Roosevelt Day," Kennedy Library, https://www.jfklibrary.org/learn/about-jfk/life-of-john-f-kennedy/john-f-kennedy-quotations/commemorative-message-on-roosevelt-day

87 Veterans Affairs National Cemetery Administration, U.S. Department of Veterans Affairs, https://www.cem.va.gov

88 Veterans Affairs National Cemetery Administration.

89 Veterans Affairs National Cemetery Administration.

90 "This Day in History, August 24, 1814," *Weasyl*, https://www.weasyl.com/~simonov/submissions/1674223/this-day-in-history-august-24-1814

91 History.com editors, " Pentagon," *History Channel*, December 18, 2009, Updated June 10, 2019, https://www.history.com/topics/us-government/pentagon

92 "Arlington House, The Robert E. Lee Memorial," https://www.
    arlingtoncemetery.mil/Explore/History-of-Arlington-National-
    Cemetery/Arlington-House

93 "Arlington House."

94 "Address Broadcast to Armed Forces."

95 "Address Broadcast to Armed Forces."

96 "Address Broadcast to Armed Forces."

97 "Robert Todd Lincoln," Arlington National Cemetery,"
    Arlington Cemetery, https://www.arlingtoncemetery.mil/
    Explore/Notable-Graves/Presidents/Robert-Todd-Lincoln

98 Dan Brodt, "Arlington National Cemetery War Comes to Arlington,"
    Army Security Agency, https://www.armysecurityagencyvet-
    erans.net/arlington-national-cemetery-war-comes-to-arlington/

99 "This day In History," March 14, 1963, *History Channel*, https://
    www.history.com/this-day-in-history

100 "President Kennedy's Commemorative Message…"

101 "President Kennedy's Commemorative Message…"

102 Thomas Fleming, "John F. Kennedy's PT-109 Disaster,"
    HistoryNet, https://www.historynet.com/john-f-kennedy

103 "Navy Service," *History Central*, https://www.historycentral.
    com/JFK/bio/Navy.html

104 Peter Chen, contributor, "John Kennedy," *World War II Data
    Base*, https://ww2db.com/person_bio.php?person_id=395

105 Jamie McIntyre, "Another undeserved military honor for
    LBJ," *Washington Examiner*, May 10, 2019, https://www.
    washingtonexaminer.com/policy/defense-national-security/
    another-undeserved-military-honor-for-lbj

106 McIntyre, "Another undeserved."

107 McIntyre, "Another undeserved."

108 McIntyre, "Another undeserved."

109 McIntyre, "Another undeserved."

110 "Remarks At The U. S. Naval Academy, Annapolis, Maryland,"
    Kennedy Library, https://www.google.com/search?client=sa-
    fari&rls=en&q=%E2%80%9CRemarks+At+The+U.+S.+Na-
    val+Academy,+Annapolis,+Maryland,%E2%80%9D++jfkli-
    brary.org.,+August+1,+1963&ie=UTF-8&oe=UTF-8

111 Honor Flight, https://www.honorflight.org
112 Honor Flight.
113 Joseph Lacdan, "After tragedy, former Honor Guard members dedicate docuseries in mentor's memory," *Army.mil*, https://www.army.mil/article/241315/after_tragedy_former_honor_guard_members_dedicate_docuseries_in_mentors_memory
114 Lacdan, "After tragedy."
115 "Medal of Honor, The Story Of SPC Ross A. McGinnis," *Army.mil*, https://www.army.mil/medalofhonor/mcginnis/
116 Robert Poole, "Where the Modern Wars Hit Home," *Politico Magazine*, https://www.politico.com/magazine/story/2014/11/arlington-national-cemetery-section-60-112749/
117 Poole, "Where the Modern Wars."
118 Poole, "Where the Modern Wars."
119 Poole, "Where the Modern Wars."
120 "Medal of Honor."
121 "Medal of Honor."
122 Alex Norton, "Soleimani's Legacy: The gruesome, advanced IED's that haunted U. S. troops in Iraq," *Washington Post*, January 3, 2020, https://www.washingtonpost.com/national-security/2020/01/03/soleimanis-legacy-gruesome-high-tech-ieds-that-haunted-us-troops-iraq/
123 History.com editors, "The Gettysburg Address."
124 "John F. Kennedy: World War II Naval Hero to President," National Park Service, https://www.nps.gov/articles/kennedyww2.htm
125 "3d U.S. Infantry Regiment (The Old Guard)," *Army.mil*, https://oldguard.mdw.army.mil
126 Patti Jo King, "Remembering Lori Ann Piestewa: Hopi Woman Warrior," *Indian Country Today*, https://indiancountrytoday.com/archive/remembering-lori-ann-piestewa-hopi-woman-warrior
127 King, "Remembering Lori Ann Piestewa."
128 King, "Remembering Lori Ann Piestewa."
129 King, "Remembering Lori Ann Piestewa."
130 King, "Remembering Lori Ann Piestewa."

131 Jill Leovy, "Army Private First Class Marcus A. Tynes, 19, Moreno Valley; killed in explosion," *Los Angeles Times*, December 6, 2009, https://www.latimes.com/archives/la-xpm-2009-dec-06-la-me-tynes6-2009dec06-story.html

132 Shruti Mathur Desai, "Army 1st Lieutenant Salvatore S. Corma II," *Military Times*, https://thefallen.militarytimes.com/army-1st-lt-salvatore-s-corma-ii/4609138

133 Parker, "The Veteran Experience."

134 ASA (M&RA), "Army Total Force Policy," *Army.mil*, https://www.army.mil/article/42866/army_total_force_policy

135 Jules Hurst, "No Way To Get To The War," Modern War Institute, October 10, 2020, https://mwi.usma.edu/no-way-to-get-to-the-war-mobilization-problems-and-the-army-reserve/

136 Erin Duffin, "U. S. Military Force Numbers," *Statista*, https://www.statista.com/statistics/232330/us-military-force-numbers-by-service-branch-and-reserve-component/

137 "Reserve Component Personnel Issues: Questions and Answers, Updated June 15, 2020," *Congressional Research Service*, https://fas.org/sgp/crs/natsec/RL30802.pdf

138 "American War and Military Operations Casualties: Lists and Statistics," *Congressional Research Service*, https://fas.org/sgp/crs/natsec/RL32492.pdf

139 Parker, "The Veteran Experience."

140 "American War and Military Operations Casualties."

141 Jeff Desjardins, "U. S. Military Personnel Deployments by Country," *Visual Capitalist*, https://www.visualcapitalist.com/u-s-military-personnel-deployments-country/

142 Mark Cancian, "U. S. Military Forces in FY 2020: Army," *Center For Strategic and International Studies*, https://www.csis.org/analysis/us-military-forces-fy-2020-struggle-align-forces-strategy-0

143 Cancian, "U. S. Military Forces."

144 Mark Thompson, "Here's Why the U. S. Military Is a Family Business," *Time*, March 10, 2016, https://time.com/4254696/military-family-business/

145   "Who Signs Up to Fight," *New York Times*, January 10, 2020, https://www.nytimes.com/2020/01/10/us/military-enlistment.html

146   Thompson, "Here's Why."

147   Poole, "Where the Modern Wars."

148   Lowe, "13 Powerful JFK Quotes."

149   SFC (Ret.) David Hack, "Vietnam War Facts, Stats, and Myths," U S Wings, https://www.uswings.com/about-us-wings/vietnam-war-facts/

150   John T. Cornell, "Origins of the Total Force," *Air Force Magazine*, https://www.airforcemag.com/article/0211force/

151   Steve Walsh, "How the Vietnam War Changed Guard Service," *Weekend Edition NPR,* https://www.npr.org/2015/04/25/402045128/international-guard-how-the-vietnam-war-changed-guard-service

152   Walsh, "How the Vietnam War."

153   "Medal of Honor and Military Heroes," *Home of Heroes*, https://homeofheroes.com

154   Hack, "Vietnam War Facts."

155   Hack, "Vietnam War Facts."

156   National Indian Council on Aging, "American Indian Veterans Have Highest Record of Military Service," https://www.nicoa.org/american-indian-veterans-have-highest-record-of-military-service/

157   National Indian Council on Aging.

158   Hack, "Vietnam War Facts."

159   "Private First Class James Anderson Jr., USMC (Deceased)," Marine Corps University, https://www.usmcu.edu/Research/Marine-Corps-History-Division/Information-for-Units/Medal-of-Honor-Recipients-By-Unit/PFC-James-Anderson-Jr/

160   Dan Doyle, "PFC James Anderson Jr.:First African American US Marine to Receive the Medal of Honor," *The Veterans Site Blog*, https://blog.theveteranssite.greatergood.com/james-anderson-moh/

161   "Private First Class James Anderson, Jr."

162 "Ralph H. Johnson VA Medical Center, Our History." https://www.charleston.va.gov/about/history.asp

163 "Stories of Sacrifice, Ralph H. Johnson," *Congressional Medal of Honor Society*, https://www.cmohs.org/recipients/ralph-h-johnson

164 "Stories of Sacrifice."

165 Senior Airman Jared Trimarchi, "Vietnam War Hero Shares His Story," *U.S. Air Forces Central*, https://www.afcent.af.mil/News/Article/501663/vietnam-war-hero-shares-his-story/

166 "Ralph H. Johnson VA."

167 "DDG 114-USS Ralph Johnson," *Sea Forces Online*, https://www.seaforces.org/usnships/ddg/DDG-114-USS-Ralph-Johnson.htm

168 Jim McCabe, "McCabe:Veteran credits Casper for saving his life," *Golf Week USA Today*, https://golfweek.usatoday.com/2014/04/08/masters-2014-augusta-billy-casper-clebe-mcclary/

169 Editorial Board, "John McCain was a 'maverick' and a patriot," *The Press Enterprise*, https://www.pe.com/2018/08/27/john-mccain-was-maverick-and-a-patriot/

170 Jack Morgenstein, "In Memoriam: John McCain," *The Page*, March 24, 2019, https://chsthepage.com/tag/opinion/

171 Morgenstein, "In Memoriam."

172 "John S. McCain III: A Brief Navy Biography," Naval History and Heritage Command, https://www.history.navy.mil/browse-by-topic/people/profiles-in-duty/profiles-in-duty-vietnam/john-s—mccain-iii/john-s—mccain-iii—a-brief-navy-biography-.html

173 Editorial Board, "John McCain."

174 Editorial Board, "John McCain."

175 Editorial Board, "John McCain."

176 "John S. McCain III: A Brief."

177 Eliza Relman, "John McCain Refused Early Release as a Prisoner in Vietnam," *Business Insider*, August 2018, https://www.businessinsider.com/john-mccain-refused-early-release-as-a-pow-in-vietnam-2018-8

178 "John S. McCain III."

179 Editorial Board, "John McCain."

180 Patriotguard Riders, http://patriotguard.org

181 Rollingthunder, https://rollingthunderrun.com

182 Rollingthunder.

183 Rollingthunder.

184 The editors, "Second Sino-Japanese War," *Encyclopedia Britannica*, https://www.britannica.com/event/Second-Sino-Japanese-War 212

185 The editors, "Allied Powers, International Alliance," *Encyclopedia Britannica*, https://www.britannica.com/topic/Allied-Powers-international-alliance

186 "Casualties of World War II," History of Western Civilization, https://courses.lumenlearning.com/suny-hccc-worldhistory2/chapter/casualties-of-world-war-ii/

187 Anthony Luongo, "Principles or Power: Mussolini's Invasion of Ethiopia," *E International Relations*, March 3, 2019, https://www.e-ir.info/2019/03/26/principles-or-power-mussolinis-invasion-of-ethiopia/

188 R. J Rommel, "Statistics of Japanese Genocide and Mass Murder," https://www.hawaii.edu/powerkills/SOD. CHAP3.HTM

189 history.com editors, "Nanking Massacre," *History Channel*, https://www.history.com/topics/japan/nanjing-massacre

190 "Final Solution: Overview," United States Holocaust Memorial Museum, *Holocaust Encyclopedia*, https://encyclopedia.ushmm.org/content/en/article/final-solution-overview

191 "Casualties of World War II."

192 "About:Life unworthy of life," *DBpedia*, https://dbpedia.org/page/Life_unworthy_of_life

193 "Forgotten Victims: The Nazi Genocide of the Roma and Sinti," copyright:*Wiener Holocaust Library*, https://sg.news.yahoo.com/nazis-murdered-quarter-europes-roma-095912842.html

194 "German Atomic Bomb Project," *Atomic Heritage*, https://www.atomicheritage.org/history/german-atomic-bomb-project

195 Raya Jalabi and Michael Georgy, "Kurdish City gassed by Saddam hopes referendum heralds better days," *Reuters*, September 24, 2017, https://www.reuters.com/article/mideast-crisis-kurds-referendum-halabja-idINL4N1M5053

196 Ian Black, "Iran and Iraq remember war that costs more than a million lives," *The Guardian*, September 23, 2010, https://www.theguardian.com/world/2010/sep/23/iran-iraq-war-anniversary

197 "Releases from the Camp," Auschwitz-Birkenau State Museum, http://auschwitz.org/en/history/life-in-the-camp/releases-from-the-camp/

198 Michael Berenbaum, "Auschwitz," *Encyclopedia Britannica*, https://www.britannica.com/place/Auschwitz

199 Natasha Frost, "Horrors of Auschwitz: The Numbers Behind WW II's Deadliest Concentration Camp," *History Channel*, https://www.history.com/news/auschwitz-concentration-camp-numbers

200 Berenbaum, "Auschwitz."

201 Researchers of ANU Museum of the Jewish People, "The Jewish Community of Miskolc," https://dbs.anumuseum.org.il/skn/en/c6/e120812/Place/Miskolc

202 "Final Solution: Overview."

203 Studs Terkel, *The Good War*, (New York: Pantheon,1984), Introduction, 1

204 Lieutenant John McCrae, "In Flanders Field," https://www.gilderlehrman.org/history-resources/spotlight-primary-source/world-war-i-poems-"-flanders-fields"-and-"-answer"-1918

205 McCrae, "In Flanders Field."

206 "In Flanders Field and John McCrea," *Canadian War Museum*, https://www.warmuseum.ca/firstworldwar/history/after-the-war/remembrance/in-flanders-fields-and-john-mccrae/

207 McCrae, "In Flanders Field."

208 "By Decade," https://www.census.gov/programs-surveys/decennial-census/decade.1940.html

209 "Research Starters: US Military by the Numbers," National World War II Museum, https://www.nationalww2museum. org/students-teachers/student-resources/research-starters/ research-starters-us-military-numbers

210 "It's Your War Too: Women in WW II," National World War II Museum, https://www.nationalww2museum.org/war/articles/ its-your-war-too-women-world-war-ii

211 Edwin Schulman (Muscogee), "Chapter 7, Medals and Praise," National Museum for the American Indian, NMAI, https:// americanindian.si.edu/why-we-serve/topics/world-war-2/

212 Neil R. McMillian, editor, _Remaking Dixie: The Impact of World War II on the American South_, (Jackson, MS: University Press of Mississippi,1997) Preface p. 3

213 "Remarks by General Colin Powell."

214 "It's Your War Too."

215 Susan Stamberg, "Female WW II Pilots: The Original Fly Girls," _NPR_, https://www.npr.org/2010/03/09/123773525/ female-wwii-pilots-the-original-fly-girls

216 Stamberg, "Female WW II Pilots."

217 Stamberg, "Female WW II Pilots."

218 Heather Burmeister, "Hazel Ying Lee (1912-1944)," _Oregon Encyclopedia_, https://www.oregonencyclopedia.org/articles/ lee_hazel_ying/#.YNJLEC9h3nU

219 Kim Stevens, "President Obama Honors Women Who Flew In WW II," _State Aviation Journal_, https://stateaviationjournal.com/index. php/news/president-obama-honors-women-who-flew-wwii

220 Stevens, "President Obama."

221 history.com staff, "Chinese Exclusion Act," _History Channel_, https://www.history.com/topics/immigration/ chinese-exclusion-act-1882

222 Farrell Evans,"Why Harry Truman Ended Segregation in the US Military in 1948," _History Channel_, https://www.history. com/news/harry-truman-executive-order-9981-desegration- military-1948

223 Dr. Kimberly Kutz Elliott, "African American Veterans and the Civil Rights Movement," _Khan Academy_, https://www.

khanacademy.org/humanities/us-history/postwarera/civ-il-rights-movement/a/african-american-veterans-and-the-civil-rights-movement

224 Contributed by Euel A. Nielsen, "The Double V Campaign (1942-1945)," *Black Past*, https://www.blackpast.org/african-american-history/events-african-american-history/the-double-v-campaign-1942-1945/

225 Ronit Y. Stahl, *Enlisting Faith*, (Cambridge: Harvard University Press, 2017) 115

226 Nielsen, "The Double V."

227 Nielsen, "The Double V."

228 "Remarks on Presenting the Congressional Medal of Honor to African American Heroes of WW II," The American Presidency Project, UC Santa Barbara, January 13, 1997, https://www.presidency.ucsb.edu/documents/remarks-presenting-the-con-gressional-medal-honor-african-american-heroes-world-war-ii

229 Nancy Ian and Marco Tabellini, "Discrimination, Disenfranchisement, and African American WW II Military Enlistment," https://storage.googleapis.com/production-sitebuilder-v1-0-1/741/319741/PkwWoHa4/de7644deff3d4265819091840672c000?fileName=QianTab_20200702.pdf

230 "Naval Profiles, Doris Miller," Naval History and Heritage Command, https://www.history.navy.mil/browse-by-topic/diversity/african-americans/miller.html

231 "Naval Profiles, Doris Miller."

232 History.Com editors, "Tuskegee Airmen," *History Channel*, https://www.history.com/topics/world-war-ii/tuskegee-airmen

233 History.Com editors, "Tuskegee Airmen."

234 "Remarks on Presenting the Congressional Medal of Honor."

235 Samuel Momodu, "Reuben Rivers," *Black Past*, https://www.blackpast.org/african-american-history/ruben-rivers-1921-1944/

236 Michael Haskew, "Segregation in the U. S. Military: Reuben Rivers," *War Fare History Network*, https://warfarehistory-

network.com/2016/08/16/segregation-in-the-u-s-military-ruben-rivers/

237 Ryan Mattimore, "The Original Black Panthers Fought in the 761st Tank Battalion During WW II," *History Channel*, https://www.history.com/news/761st-tank-battalion-black-panthers-liberators-battle-of-the-bulge

238 Mattimore, "The Original Black Panthers."

239 Mattimore, "The Original Black Panthers."

240 "Recognition of US Liberating Army Units," United States Holocaust Memorial Museum, https://encyclopedia.ushmm.org/content/en/article/us-army-units

241 Mattimore, "The Original."

242 "Remarks on Presenting the Congressional Medal of Honor."

243 "Remarks on Presenting the Congressional Medal of Honor."

244 Press Release, "National WW II Museum salutes Vernon J. Baker," National World War II Museum, https://www.nationalww2museum.org/media/press-releases/national-wwii-museum-salutes-vernon-j-baker

245 Press Release, "National WW II Museum."

246 Press Release, "National WW II Museum."

247 U.S. Census by Decade, https://www.census.gov/programs-surveys/decennial-census/decade.1940.html

248 Jared Horoski, "American Ethnics and World War II," https://sites.udel.edu/hist268-030-f15/author/jhoroski/

249 history.com staff, "Chinese Exclusion Act."

250 history.com staff, "Chinese Exclusion Act."

251 Cynthia Silva, "Chinese American WW II veterans honored with Congressional Gold Medal," *NBC News*, https://www.nbcnews.com/news/asian-america/chinese-american-wwii-veterans-honored-congressional-gold-medal-n1250767

252 Staff, "Chinese Americans in World War II," *Chinese American Heroes*, http://www.chineseamericanheroes.org/history/Chinese%20Americans%20in%20World%20War%20II.pdf

253 "Brothers in Arms-Chinese American soldiers fought heroically," *Association of the United States Army*, https://www.ausa.org/

articles/brothers-arms-chinese-american-soldiers-fought-hero-ically-wwii

254 Silva, "Chinese American WW II."

255 "The Hall of Valor: Francis B. Wai," The Hall of Valor Project, *Military Times*, https://valor.militarytimes.com/hero/867

256 Mei-Mei Chun-Moy, "Veteran of the Day Francis Brown Wai," October 6, 2017, https://blogs.va.gov/VAntage/42051/veteranoftheday-francis-brown-wai/

257 "Japanese American Incarceration," National World War II Museum, https://www.nationalww2museum.org/war/articles/japanese-american-incarceration-education-resources

258 Barbara Maranzani, "Unlikely World War II Soldiers Awarded Nation's Highest Honor," *History Channel*, https://www.history.com/news/unlikely-world-war-ii-soldiers-awarded-nations-highest-honor

259 Maranzani, "Unlikely World War II."

260 "Japanese-American Internment," *US History*, https://www.ushistory.org/us/51e.asp

261 "American Heroes: Japanese Americans WW II Nisei Soldiers and the Congressional Gold Medal," Smithsonian Institution Traveling Exhibition Service, https://www.sites.si.edu/s/archived-exhibit?topicId=0TO36000000Tz8yGAC

262 Maranzani, "Unlikely World War II."

263 Maranzani, "Unlikely World War II."

264 Maranzani, "Unlikely World War II."

265 "442nd Regimental Combat Team." *Go For Broke Blog*, https://www.goforbroke.org/learn/history/military_units/442nd.php

266 Rob McIlvain, "442nd legacy takes Soldiers from 'enemy aliens' to heroes," *Army.mil*, https://www.army.mil/article/68392/442nd_legacy_takes_soldiers_from_enemy_aliens_to_heroes

267 C. Todd Lopez, "Japanese-American vets earn nation's highest civilian honor," *Army.mil*, https://www.army.mil/article/68563/japanese_american_vets_earn_nations_highest_civilian_honor

268 "40 Bronze Stars awarded to Japanese American vets," *Army.mil*, https://www.army.mil/

article/68471/40_bronze_stars_awarded_to_japanese_amer-ican_vets

269 Brian Niiya, Densho, "Sadao Munemori," *Densho Encyclopedia*, https://encyclopedia.densho.org/Sadao_Munemori/

270 Katherine Baishiki/Yaeko Munemori, "Private First Class Sadao Munemori," 100th Battalion, December 2, 2001, updated September 19, 2003, https://www.100thbattalion.org/wp-content/uploads/Munemori-Sadao.pdf

271 Baishiki, "Private First Class Sadao."

272 Niiya, "Sadao Munemori."

273 Niiya, "Sadao Munemori."

274 Rudi Williams, "21 Asian American World War II Vets To Get Medal of Honor," *Digital History*, https://www.digitalhistory.uh.edu/active_learning/explorations/japanese_internment/medal_of_honor.cfm

275 Williams, "21 Asian American."

276 "Tribal Nations and the United States-An Introduction," *National Congress of American Indians*, https://www.ncai.org/about-tribes

277 "The Role of Native American's During World War II," Armed Forces History Museum, December 17, 2013, https://www.lhschools.org/Downloads/Native%20Americans%20in%20WWII.pdf

278 "Indian Citizenship Act, June 2, 1924, Library of Congress, https://www.loc.gov/item/today-in-history/june-02/

279 "Native Americans in the Military-WW II," Val Nihau's, Forest County Potawatomi, https://www.fcpotawatomi.com/news/native-americans-in-the-military-world-war-ii/

280 "1941-1945: American Indian war effort in WW II is remark-able," *Timeline, US National Library of Medicine*, https://www.nlm.nih.gov/nativevoices/timeline/461.html

281 "1941-1945: American Indian war effort in WW II is remark-able," *Timeline, US National Library of Medicine*, https://www.nlm.nih.gov/nativevoices/timeline/461.html

282 "Experiencing War: Chester Nez," Veterans History Project, American Folklife Center, Library of Congress, https://memory. loc.gov/diglib/vhp-stories/loc.natlib.afc2001001.54891/

283 Shondiin Silversmith, "1942: Navajo Code Talkers, Inventors of the Unbreakable Code," Barrior Breakers in History, *Arizona Central, July 11, 2018*, https://www. azcentral.com/story/news/local/arizona/2018/07/11/ navajo-code-talker-facts-unbreakable-code/460262002/

284 "Experiencing War: Chester Nez."

285 Silversmith, "1942: Navajo Code Talkers."

286 "Comanche Code Talkers," https://www.okhistory.org/publi-cations/enc/entry.php?entry=CO013

287 Edited by CALIE, "Van T. Barfoot," https://www.californiain-dianeducation.org/native_american_veterans/van_t_barfoot/

288 Edited by CALIE, "Van T. Barfoot."

289 Edited by CALIE, "Van T. Barfoot."

290 Edited by CALIE, "Van T. Barfoot."

291 "Patton and his Third Army-65th Infantry Division," http:// www.pattonthirdarmy.com/history/army-history-65infdiv.html

292 "Remembering: Plattling Concentration Camp," *65th Infantry Division Association*, https://65thdiv.com/remembering

293 United States Holocaust Memorial Museum, "Recognition of U.S. Liberating Army Units," *Holocaust Encyclopedi*a, https:// encyclopedia.ushmm.org/content/en/article/us-army-units

294 "History of the 4th Infantry Division in WW II," *The Furious Fourth*, http://furiousfourth.weebly.com/

295 "History of the 4th Infantry."

296 history.com editors, This Day in History, "Paris is liberated after four years of Nazi occupation August 25, 1944," *History Channel*, https://www.history.com/this-day-in-history/paris-liberated

297 Master Sgt. Craig Zentkovich (4th ID)," 4ID and the Battle of Huertgen Forest," *Army.mil*, https://www.army.mil/ article/145660/4id_and_the_battle_of_huertgen_forest

298 history.com editors, "Battle of the Bulge," updated July 27, 2020, *History Channel*, https://www.history.com/topics/world-war-ii/ battle-of-the-bulge

299 history.com editors, "Battle of the Bulge."
300 history.com editors, "Battle of the Bulge."
301 "History of the 4th Infantry."
302 "History of the 4th Infantry."
303 "History of the 4th Infantry."
304 "The 4TH Infantry DIV During World War II," United States Holocaust Memorial Museum, https://encyclopedia.ushmm.org/content/en/article/the-4th-infantry-division
305 "The 4TH Infantry DIV."
306 "Franklin D. Roosevelt's D-Day Prayer," Roosevelt Library, https://www.fdrlibrary.org/d-day
307 Provided by Joseph Glove, III, "D-Day Story: John G. Burkhalter," https://www.military.com/history/d-day-story-john-g-burkhalter.html
308 Boyd Childress, contributor, "National D-Day Memorial," *Encyclopedia Virginia*, https://encyclopediavirginia.org/entries/national-d-day-memorial/
309 David Roos, "How Many Were Killed on D-Day?" *History Channel*, https://www.history.com/news/d-day-casualties-deaths-allies
310 "Brief History 116th Infantry Regiment," https://116thfoundation.org/museum/history/
311 Shelley Seale, "A Virginia town remembers the Bedford Boys, who gave their lives on D-Day," *Los Angeles Times*, https://www.latimes.com/travel/deals/la-trb-d-day-virginia-town-bedford-20150604-story.html
312 Seale, "A Virginia town."
313 "29th Infantry Division," Virginia National Guard, https://va.ng.mil/Army-Guard/29th-ID/
314 Daniel Davis, "The 116th Infantry Regiment," *American Battlefield Trust*, https://www.battlefields.org/learn/articles/116th-infantry-regiment
315 Davis, "The 116th Infantry."
316 Davis, "The 116th Infantry."
317 Davis, "The 116th Infantry."
318 "Virginia National Guard's Medal of Honor Recipients," Virginia Guard, https://vaguard.dodlive.mil/vng_moh/

319 "Virginia National Guard's."

320 "Remarks by the President at Dedication of the National D-Day Memorial Bedford City, Virginia," *White House Archives*, https://georgewbush-whitehouse.archives.gov/news/releases/2001/06/20010606-2.html

321 "Remarks by the President at Dedication of the National D-Day."

322 "Distinguished Service Cross–World War II," *Home of Heroes*, https://homeofheroes.com/distinguished-service-cross/service-cross-world-war-ii/distinguished-service-cross-world-war-ii/

323 SFC Terra C. Gatti, "Virginia Guard D-Day veteran laid to rest in Charlottesville," Virginia Guard, https://vaguard.dodlive.mil/2015/07/12/7739/

324 *Daily Progress* Staff, "Chubby Proffitt, local veteran who stormed Omaha Beach on D-Day, dies at 96," *Daily Progress*, https://dailyprogress.com/news/local/chubby-proffitt-local-veteran-who-stormed-omaha-beach-on-d/article_96b1eb2a-1f69-11e5-8994-53fb802befa9.html

325 *Daily Progress* Staff, "Chubby Proffitt."

326 Brendan Clark,"Good Question: Why Can I hear 'taps' being played every night in North Charleston?," *Count On News 2*, https://www.counton2.com/news/good-question-why-can-i-hear-taps-being-played-every-night-in-north-charleston/

327 "The Sultana Disaster, April 27, 1865," *American Battlefield Trust*, https://www.battlefields.org/learn/articles/sultana-disaster

328 Alan Huffman, articles319, "Surviving the Worst the Wreck of the Sultana," *Mississippi History Now*, http://www.mshistorynow.mdah.ms.gov/articles/319/surviving-the-worst-the-wreck-of-the-sultana

329 Joseph Taylor Elliott, *The Sultana Disaster*, (Indianapolis: E J Hecker Printer, 1913)

330 Clark,"Good Question."

331 "Marine Corps Medal of Honor Recipients," Marine Corps University, https://www.usmcu.edu/Research/Marine-Corps-History-Division/People/Marine-Corps-Medal-of-Honor-Recipients/

332 Bernard C. Nalty and Danny J. Crawford, "The United States Marines on Iwo Jima/The Battle and the Flag Raising," History and Museums Division Headquarters U.S. Marine Corps, Washington, DC, https://www.marines.mil/Portals/1/Publications/The%20United%20States%20Marines%20On%20Iwo%20Jima_The%20Battle%20and%20the%20Flag%20Raisings%20%20PCN%2019000316600.pdf

333 Nalty, "The United States Marines."

334 Low, "Brothers In Arms…"

335 Edited by CALIE, "Van T. Barfoot."

336 Edited by CALIE, "Van T. Barfoot."

337 Blake Stilwell, "Why this Medal of Honor recipient fought his home owners association," https://www.wearethemighty.com/mighty-trending/veteran-fights-hoa-for-flag/

338 Stilwell, "Why this Medal."

339 Stilwell, "Why this Medal."

340 By Richard Goldstein, "Van Barfoot, Medal of Honor Recipient, Dies at 92," New York Times, March 5, 2012, https://www.nytimes.com/2012/03/05/us/van-barfoot-medal-of-honor-recipient-dies-at-92.html

341 Edited by CALIE, "Van T. Barfoot."

342 Desai, "Army 1st Lt."

343 Marcus' Heart Foundation, https://www.marcussheartfoundation.org/

344 Marcus' Heart Foundation.

345 "Maine Troop Greeters & Museum of Bangor, Maine," http://themainetroopgreeters.com/

346 "Maine Troop Greeters."

347 Elliott, *The Sultana Disaster.*

348 Dan Mangan, "Clinton Blasts Trump: We are great because we are good," CNBC, October 10, 2016, https://www.cnbc.com/2016/10/09/clinton-blasts-trump-we-are-great-because-we-are-good.html

349 Steven Mintz, "Historical Context: Black Soldiers in the Civil War," The Gilder Lehrman Institute of American

History, https://www.gilderlehrman.org/history-resources/
teaching-resource/historical-context-black-soldiers-civil-war

350 HistoryNet editors, "Civil War Soldiers," https://www.histo-
rynet.com/civil-war-soldiers

351 "America's Wars," Department of Veterans Affairs, https://
www.va.gov/opa/publications/factsheets/fs_americas_
wars.pdf

352 "Recognition of US Liberating Army Units," *Holocaust
Encyclopedia,* https://encyclopedia.ushmm.org/content/en/
article/us-army-units

353 "America's Wars," Department.

354 "Casualty Status," US Department of Defense, https://www.
defense.gov/casualty.pdf

355 Leovy, "Army Private First Class Marcus A. Tynes."

356 "Medal of Honor, The Story Of SPC Ross A. McGinnis,"
Army.mil, https://www.army.mil/medalofhonor/mcginnis/